GLOBAL TREASURY MANAGEMENT

GLOBAL TREASURY MANAGEMENT

Key Strategies for Bottom-Line Results in
Today's Global Financial Markets

Bill Millar

Director, Treasury Services
Business International Corporation

HarperBusiness
A Division of HarperCollins*Publishers*

International Standard Book Number: 0–88730–469–9

Library of Congress Catalog Card Number: 91–12645

Printed in the United States of America

Library of Congress Cataloging-in-Publication Data

Global treasury management : key strategies for bottom-line results in todays global financial markets / edited by Bill Millar.
    p. cm.
  Includes index.
  1. International business enterprises—Finance—Management. 2. Cash Management. 3. Investments, Foreign. 4. International business enterprises—Finance—Management—Data processing. 5. International finance. I.Millar, Bill, 1958- . II. Title: Treasury management.
HG4027.5.G56 1991
658.15′99—dc20   91-12645
                                                                          CIP

91 92 93 94 CC/CW 9 8 7 6 5 4 3 2 1

Table of Contents

Preface

International treasury management is undergoing a radical transformation. Increasingly, companies are looking to their global treasury departments to actively manage currency, interest rate, and other business-related risks. In the most extreme cases, treasury is even being called upon to contribute directly to the bottom line.

At the same time, dramatic trends are reshaping the financial environment. Treasurers must now manage in a world of intensely competitive regional trading blocs; deregulated, globalized, and volatile financial markets; rapidly evolving financial instruments, including swaps, options, and other engineered products; and software and hardware system breakthroughs.

To help international treasurers meet new expectations in a complex operating environment, the following checklists offer thousands of tips from leading treasury management practitioners. These checklists have been culled from various Business International publications, including research reports like *Financial Innovations* and *Global Cash Management* and weeklies such as *Business International Money Report* and *Business Asia*.

The checklist format has been chosen to provide a highly efficient tool for decision making, management, and training. The checklists are designed for use both by those who are new to international finance and by knowledgeable managers who are encountering new terrain. Even the most experienced treasury hands will find this reference a solid and thought-provoking resource.

This collection represents the most current thinking in treasury management today. The checklists were compiled by BI Senior Analysts Brad Asher, John Geanuracos, Bill Millar, and Michael Williams. The book itself was edited by Bill Millar under the direction of Vice President and Worldwide Financial Services Director Barry Rutizer. Of course, special thanks are directed to all those financial executives who took the time to share their views and experiences with BI. Without their kind and patient assistance, this work—and many others like it—would not have been possible.

GLOBAL TREASURY MANAGEMENT

Chapter 1
Organizing for Active Treasury Management

Managing treasury in the 1990s involves coping with an increasingly complex and volatile financial environment. In today's climate more than ever, multinational corporations (MNCs) that wish to remain competitive need proactive management and maximum efficiency from their corporate treasury function.

Treasury managers must ensure that their departments are operating at peak efficiency. Without the proper organizational structure and policies in place, companies may miss opportunities or—even worse—commit costly errors because of cumbersome internal bureaucracy, poor communications, or lack of specific guidelines.

The checklists in this first chapter will help treasury managers accomplish two goals. First, they help managers focus on and define an appropriate mission for their treasury management. Second, they help managers pinpoint the most effective means of building an organization capable of delivering these stated objectives.

1. Peter Drucker: Seven Observations on Corporate Treasury Management

In his keynote address at a recent BI Chief Financial Officers' Conference, the well-known management expert Peter Drucker of the Claremont Graduate School offered numerous critical insights into the practice of international treasury management. The following highlights are drawn from his speech.

(1) Exchange rates are inherently unstable and will remain so. Many people believe it is written in the first chapter of Genesis that "the Lord created fixed exchange rates." However, rates are an act of government. Governments can postpone dealing with unpleasant realities by debasing the currency—until the next election, anyway (though we are not so easily fooled as in the past). Once the tiger tastes blood, it does not become a vegetarian. And governments have tasted blood.

(2) Predicting currency rates is a foolish game. A currency cannot be talked down? Wrong. Inflows into the United States continued and increased during the dollar's mid-eighties decline even as ministers of finance talked down the dollar by 40 percent. Imponderables such as this make it dangerous to engage in rate-dependent financial maneuvers. Your first duty is to protect your company—in other words, you had better hedge.

(3) Not to hedge is to speculate. Exchange rates are a factor of production that financial executives must manage. In 1850, the *Economist* said textile producers who did not hedge cotton were speculating. In the same spirit, an MNC with 60 percent foreign sales had better sell forward this year's expected earnings.

(4) MNCs must take advantage of global markets. Most MNCs still finance largely in one country. This is an increasingly dubious luxury. Managers should protect earnings by financing capital in the same currency.

(5) MNC finances must be managed centrally and for the entire group. The chief financial officer (CFO) must be totally divorced from any single operation and must manage on a worldwide basis. Earnings, cash, and investment streams must be companywide, not national. We will see a restructuring of MNCs along these lines over the next three to five years.

(6) Finance managers cannot blame corporate losses on market volatility. The company's business is not finance but making widgets. However, in today's environment, business is disrupted by short-term financial movements. In the next violent currency fluctuation—this will begin during the business life of everyone working today—many managers will find that corporate profits are down, say, 40 percent owing to foreign exchange (FX). This will not be accepted and the company will say, "You are paid to protect us from that."

(7) You must give your up-and-coming staff true international experience. The best training ground is not in business school but in the treasury function. Multinational banks have done an excellent job of training people for international finance. Most important, do not wait until managers are at very high levels before you move them around. When they are still quite mobile, expose them to the realities of multinational business. Only a few banks and Japanese trading companies do that now.

2. What the CEO Expects from Senior Financial Executives

In recent years, the growing importance of finance has raised the corporate profile of both the treasury and finance functions to new heights. To gain insight into the ways financial officers may meet the increasing expectations of senior management, BI invited John M. Pietruski, formerly Chairman and CEO of Sterling Drug, to address the Tenth Annual CFO Conference. The following checklist, drawn from Pietruski's presentation, outlines his views on the skills essential to today's CFO—and his support staff—and on the proper scope of the treasury and finance departments in an age of volatility.

"As a key member of the Sterling Drug management team," says Pietruski, "my CFO must have all the characteristics I would look for in any other manager." Three of these qualities are critical for success in any field: intelligence, motivation, and sensitivity to both people and situations. However, the following additional attributes are particularly essential:

- **Technical competence.** A good CFO does not need to be an expert in high finance, but he must have a reasonably thorough knowledge of the financial activities carried out within his department, from budgeting to taxes. If he does not know the specifics, he must know how and where to get that information—fast.

- **Objectivity and outspokenness.** The CFO must be an impartial arbiter, open and candid in his evaluation of each situation. A CEO is going to have a tough time if his CFO sits tight and waits to see which way the breeze is blowing. He wants the CFO to call it as he sees it.

- **An ability to spot trouble in advance.** The CFO must be able to anticipate problems—to be proactive rather than reactive. The CFO and the finance department must be able to spot trouble brewing early enough to allow the CEO to take action while the problem is still manageable. This applies to every aspect of a company.

- **A "watchdog" attitude.** The word has a bad connotation, but no company can function without watchdogs alert for errors and overruns. Says Pietruski, "At Sterling our internal audit function, under the leadership of our CFO, is both strong and effective. It not only ensures that policies and procedures are being followed but also makes constructive and cost-saving suggestions about operations."

● **A talent for playing devil's advocate.** A CFO must not be afraid to challenge expense and capital-funding requests. He is the steward of the company's assets, and he must guard them jealously.

● **A vision of the "big picture."** The financial function inherently involves an immense amount of detailed information, data reports, and paper. But the CFO must never be blinded by all this detail. He must coordinate the data to present an accurate picture of the overall financial state of the company. In this way, he plays an important part in keeping everyone focused on improving the bottom line.

● **An understanding of the profit and loss (P&L) conse-** quences of operating decisions. The CFO must be a predictor, not a record keeper. He must be on top of budgets, major projects, and proposed changes in systems and procedures so that he can estimate their impact on P&L. He must contribute to the decision-making and planning processes. At Sterling, says Pietruski, "My CFO and his VP of budgets and financial control attend every long-range operating planning meeting that I hold. I look to their counsel on matters in all areas of operations so that I am sensitive to the P&L and balance-sheet impact of each proposed course of action."

● **The ability to train and develop people.** A strong CFO must take the lead in counseling so that key managers in all areas of the business become more comfortable with financial information and can use it to increase their effectiveness. A strong CFO must also develop a cadre of successors. He must make sure that a good financial training program is in place and that opportunities exist for people within his department to be exposed to all its disciplines.

---

3. What the CEO Expects from His Treasury and Finance Departments

The opening of communist bloc markets in Eastern Europe, the Persian Gulf Crisis, and the savings and loan (S&L) debacle are just a few of the reminders that the financial markets today are subject to great volatility. What does this increasing risk mean in terms of the CEO's demands on the treasury and corporate finance departments? John M. Pietruski presents his views on the changing role of treasury and financial management.

● **Financial planners and treasury managers must use the best available techniques for forecasting.** The volatility factor has increased the need for accurate forward projections. "At Sterling," points out Pietruski, "we have a five-year forecast that is the quantification of our long-range plan; a detailed budget that is the quantification of a one-year operating plan; and a monthly estimate that represents the flash update—our 'early warning system,' if you will." The creation of these reports begins with the finance managers in all of Sterling's operating units and forms a vital part of the management process at every level of the organization, up to and including the CEO.

Pietruski emphasizes that he does not expect his finance officers to predict the future. "What I do require from them is their application of the best available techniques for forecasting, budgeting, and estimation; their production of output reports that are timely and to the point; and their help in deciding what questions need to be raised and what actions implemented."

● **Finance staff must actively coordinate with local operations.** The CEO must also count on the finance division to work with manufacturing management to develop tight standards and emphasize cost reduction and efficiency. These cost reductions must then be built into budgeted standards and into detailed reporting to provide timely feedback on every element of product cost. A similar alliance between finance managers and the marketing sector can yield equally impressive results.

Another area of cost containment is administrative costs, including the cost of the finance function itself. Sterling has found that a number of steps can be taken to reduce the administrative burden, including rigorous analysis, simplification, consolidation, and automation of administrative procedures.

● **Treasury and financial managers must become involved in global tax management.** Finance executives must lead the effort to optimize the corporate tax situation and achieve a lower effective tax rate. This is easier said than done, since tax issues usually involve two or more national tax authorities, almost always with differing objectives. But today's CEO must look to the finance function more than any other for recommendations on structural changes to the tax entity, worldwide material-sourcing programs, dividend policies, and regulatory agencies.

● **Financial managers should cultivate an active link with the investing community.** In the present financial climate, firms must maintain an ongoing dialogue with the financial community. Through regular meetings with financial analysts and improved written communications, they can enhance their credibility with investors and analysts. As Sterling has discovered, these efforts can have a positive effect on share prices.

4. Staffing the Finance Function

The growing sophistication of global financial markets poses serious personnel problems for MNCs. On the one hand, finance departments need highly skilled managers who can analyze complex proposals and devise creative financing strategies. On the other, firms risk treading on investment bankers' territory, and that can mean costly competition for professionals with significant corporate experience. "Some say they can't afford to pay for these experts," says one Fortune 100 treasurer. "In many cases, they can't afford not to pay."

As banks expand their services, corporate finance staffs offer an enticing hunting ground. "If you're good at what you do, you get calls," states the director of FX and interest rate risk management at Union Carbide. "And it's a tough decision, because there's good money out there in the financial arena."

While corporations have a clear need to retain staff well versed in the intricacies of modern finance, many have not established battle plans for warding off executive search raiders. BI interviews indicate that companies are taking six different approaches to the staffing dilemma.

(1) Do nothing. Some say, in light of the numerous mergers and acquisitions that have taken place in recent years, that there is no shortage of financial expertise. The treasurer of one company comments: "There's been a tremendous compression in the number of treasury jobs in corporations. I think there's probably more demand than supply." The cutbacks (and, in many cases, complete trashing) in banks' treasury consulting groups have added to the available pool of talent.

Corporations, as opposed to financial institutions, are getting more interest from new MBA recipients. "Since the crash, we've seen a lot of quality resumes, from [Amos] Tuck, Harvard," says one New York area treasurer. This situation has made many firms question high salaries.

However, there are regions of the world where financial expertise remains in short supply. "There's a shortage of good people in our market," notes the VP of finance of a major Swedish corporation. "We try to use all the tricks we can to hold on to staff. But, in the end, we have to be prepared to lose a number of people regularly, because we can't pay the salaries they demand. It's just a fact of life."

(2) Confer responsibility. Some firms simply cannot afford to pay a wage commensurate with expertise. The treasuries of many companies are still viewed as service or cost centers and are thus handed a shoestring budget.

In these cases, a key component of compensation must be constant challenge. BI interviews indicate that what really keeps talented people from jumping ship is the feeling of accountability. "I try to give everyone responsibility for something," notes one deputy treasurer, "rather than just putting the wheel nuts on the car." He adds, "I find that giving people just enough rope keeps them interested, keeps the entrepreneurial juices flowing. And that makes people grow."

(3) Encourage creativity. Nothing frustrates a talented professional more than having his ideas ignored. "You need to create an environment that tolerates, even encourages, creativity," says the deputy treasurer. "This goes a long way toward keeping the individual satisfied."

(4) Stress quality of life. One of the easiest ways to avoid investment banker salaries is to recruit those averse to that particular lifestyle. "Bankers are more service and sales oriented," says one MNC's treasury manager. "They have highly mobile lifestyles, taking big risks and changing jobs when they lose. They're big gamblers."

What should a firm look for? Union Carbide's FX director explains that the people hired for treasury should have a true love of corporate finance and aspire to a corporate career—not a banking path. He says, "You have to ask yourself: 'Do I want to be a financial manager of a major manufacturing company?'" Says the director of U.S. borrowings for General Motors Acceptance Corporation, "The staff who work for GMAC in Detroit are a different type of person. They don't want to live in New York."

(5) Fight fire with fire . . . Some corporations feel compelled to offer higher salaries to their financial professionals. Explains R. J. Reynolds' treasurer, "Most major companies are competitive with all but the highest salaries in the banking community." Salaries have also increased as MNCs have grown to recognize the critical importance of the finance function. No longer is the treasurer "a guy who keeps a little tin box in the back room and pays the bills," in the words of one finance director.

Profit center treasuries are especially keen to offer the highest salaries. BP, for example, hired experts from the banking community when it established its credit corporation. Salaries were necessarily in line with those offered by U.K. merchant banks. Declares the group treasurer: "In both London and our regional finance centers, we have had to recruit specialists from the banking community—and pay the salaries these specialists command." BP has sometimes sent newer employees to investment banks for training in the basic skills required for dealing in the new international financial environment.

(6) . . . but be aware of the career path. When it comes to pay raises, the sky is not always the limit. Eventually the financial manager may be asked to move into another management area. An executive groomed for a senior management position should not be paid so much that he is reluctant to move into other areas of the company. "It's always a delicate balance between paying people sufficiently to be competitive with the market and yet ensuring that they aren't put off from moving into other parts of the organization," says a treasury manager at one MNC.

5. Why Centralize Treasury Operations?

As Peter Drucker noted in the opening checklist, centralizing treasury management should be a key goal for MNCs. Indeed, a BI survey of over 100 MNC treasury managers shows that nearly 45 percent plan greater centralization at parent headquarters over the next few years—the highest figure recorded since BI began asking the question in 1980.

Another 11.8 percent are at least consolidating treasury operations into regional headquarters. By contrast, only 8.8 percent are moving toward decentralization. As the spokesman for a major U.S. natural resources firm explains, "These days, you just can't afford the luxury of subsidiary autonomy—it's too expensive."

Senior managers still considering centralization should consider the following points gathered from dozens of interviews. Specifically, the trend toward centralization is the result of three corporate objectives:

(1) To obtain cost savings. Centralized companies can lower their borrowing and FX trading costs through financial innovation much more easily than decentralized firms. The assistant treasurer of a U.K. natural resources company echoes the views of many others when he states, "You need to centralize because the group can raise money far more cheaply than any local operation. When you look at a subsidiary that is borrowing at well above group rates (or conducting FX transactions at suboptimal levels), you realize that a lot of money is being lost unnecessarily."

(2) To concentrate financial expertise. Although decentralized companies may try to build up their local managers' financial acumen, this is a redundant and ultimately expensive proposition, as a manager with higher skills will require a commensurately higher salary.

In any case, with the level of skills required to manage in an era of currency and interest rate swaps, puts, calls, collars, and futures—to name just a few new instruments—the wisdom of trying to maintain a financial expert in every location is clearly questionable.

(3) To improve control and reduce risk. The key weakness of a decentralized treasury function is that it becomes difficult to manage myriad locations' transactions. Decentralized treasury operations increase the likelihood that redundant hedges may be entered; that an FX, loan, or investment business with a particular bank will exceed prescribed limits; or that local traders will violate company policies against speculation.

6. Building Treasury Controls: The High Stakes After Volkswagen

A centralized treasury is not necessarily a secure one. The discovery of fraudulent currency transactions involving some Dm480 million at the German auto maker Volkswagen had far-reaching repercussions on how MNCs manage currency exposure and treasury operations in general. Commenting on the way finance and treasury departments handle FX operations, a senior currency manager says, "For financial managers around the world, one question goes begging: Are there FX time bombs ticking away at other major MNCs?"

Volkswagen's crisis raises questions about the adequacy of in-house controls at a time of heightened currency and interest rate volatility, rapid financial innovation, and the evolution of some corporate treasuries into profit-center operations. One U.S. treasurer argues, "No company in the world can ever have sufficient controls to absolutely ensure that no one will commit fraud."

Rather, as an assistant treasurer for a consumer goods company suggests, the degree of supervision should be viewed as a trade-off between the need to avoid unauthorized FX trading (and fraud) and the need to give treasury enough leeway to exploit market opportunities to the company's greatest advantage. This tension will be most apparent at highly aggressive firms, especially those operating the treasury as a profit center. While it is clear that no system is infallible, the following checklist presents the bare essentials of FX control.

● FX contracts must be signed and countersigned by authorized individuals within the department;

● Contract confirmations should be on serial forms, with copies immediately delivered to at least two control functions (for example, accounting and internal auditing);

● Banks should have permission and should be encouraged to routinely record phone calls they receive from the treasury;

● Banks should be informed that the firm will be routinely monitoring and recording calls received from the bank trading rooms;

● Contract documentation should be circulated in hard copy to corroborate the electronic data base;

● Internal guidelines for treasury's FX operations should be thoroughly reevaluated once a year; and

● All treasury staff members should be required to take their vacations regularly.

7. Treasury Performance: How to Evaluate a For-Profit Treasury

Though still a minority, a growing number of MNCs are handling their treasury function as a profit center. The following checklist shows how one pioneer of this approach tracks and quantifies treasury profit.

The firm has attempted to define its profit by identifying specific sources of treasury earnings. Says a spokesman, "We're trying to concentrate on those areas in which we appear to be making the most profits and to eliminate areas in which we're making only marginal profits or slight losses."

The company breaks profits into five categories.

● **Organization profit** is that portion of total profit that accrues naturally from centralization—greater efficiencies, economies of scale, trading at better prices due to greater volume, etc. According to recent estimates, centralization currently accounts for 30 percent of total profit.

● **Investment profit** arises from treasury's ability to earn higher interest on pooled excess cash. Because internal business units are required to deposit funds at the centralized treasury location, treasury is fully responsible for realizing the highest earnings possible. This activity accounts for 20 percent of total profit.

● **Market-making profit** stems from the banklike structure and activities of the treasury unit. The spokesman explains, "For example, if we have a long deutsche mark position and somebody wants to buy marks from us, we trade off our own position rather than going to the market."

● **Position-taking profit** is derived from maintaining intraday positions within clearly defined parameters, including daily trading limits and outright position limits.

● **Arbitrage profit** is earned by opening and closing a position simultaneously in order to create a (relatively) risk-free profit. Categories three, four, and five together account for approximately 50 percent of treasury's total profit.

8. Defensive Surveillance: One Firm's For-Profit FX Management

In this final checklist of the first chapter, the incentives and controls of one firm's for-profit treasury are highlighted. This large U.S. exporter has a natural short dollar position and a long foreign currency position. To keep its traders active in managing this chronic situation, it has implemented the following system.

● **The full-time FX staff is responsible for P&L.** Each professional is accountable for decisions on the timing and amount of hedges. Each decision results in a profit or loss that is tracked and recorded.

● **Hedging is conducted through several small transactions rather than a few big deals.** This keeps traders constantly involved in the market and minimizes the effects of wrong decisions. With an average transaction size of $2 million, the company can reverse hedges easily if the market changes.

● **Position limits have been established to cut risk.** To prevent big FX losses, the following rules apply: Trading cannot exceed the natural short dollar position, and the firm can only sell forward the amount of its long currency position—generally 90 days' receivables on the books—plus an extra month's worth of current sales. If traders want to exceed the four-month limit, they must apply to a committee composed of representatives from FX, pricing, accounting, and treasury.

● **Trading responsibilities have been separated to allow a cross-check of positions.** Since three of the firm's main exposures move independently of the dollar-deutsche mark rate, the FX team has one individual assigned to each of the currencies. This setup increases the chance of being right about the dollar.

● **The firm rewards banks that provide good market information.** Because the firm is located far from the major FX markets, it has to rely on banks for good market information. Price is an important consideration, but even more important is the need to get consistently accurate and fast quotes.

● **Compensation for the lack of 24-hour trading.** Overnight developments can turn a profitable hedge at 4 P.M. into an unprofitable one by morning. Therefore, the head trader has been provided with a Reuters screen at home so that, each night, he can check the Tokyo opening and the early morning exchange rates. Traders abroad have been instructed on how to deal with dramatic rate changes.

● **Close monitoring and evaluation of hedging performance.** Each day, as exposures are created, a computer record is generated of the prevailing exchange and forward rates in order to get an average booking rate and an average forward rate. Three months later, a new average spot rate can then be established that can be compared with the average forward rate at which the company could have hedged three months earlier.

Chapter 2
Automating the Treasury Function

In preparing treasury management and operations for the 1990s, companies find computers an indispensable ally. Says the treasury manager at a large U.S. MNC, "You couldn't run a globalized finance unit without automation." The treasurer of a huge electronics firm concurs: "Part of being a worldwide treasury function is the ability to raise capital and manage currency risks according to economies of scale. To do this you need a systems orientation."

The following checklists will help managers identify the key areas where automation could play a principal role in their own treasury functions. The chapter will present specific features of leading firms' spreadsheets and systems, and will assist managers in making their own hardware and software decisions.

9. Why Treasurers Love Automation

Fascination with automated treasury systems began in the late 1970s and early 1980s, when the deteriorating economy and high interest rates propelled many corporate treasury departments into the computer age. For many firms, treasury remains an ideal area to automate. Research reveals six reasons for this.

(1) **Pressure on profits.** Many firms have turned to improved treasury operations to shore up sagging profits. For example, a U.S. electronics firm set up an automated in-house factoring company in Geneva. In a single year, the center showed profits of $600,000. It also saved the corporate group $750,000 in reduced FX losses, $150,000 in fund transfer costs, and $333,000 in lower borrowing expenses. The combination of profits and cost efficiencies thus totaled nearly $2 million.

(2) **Thin treasury staffs.** Computers ensure that treasury departments stay lean as they confront a greater volume of information and a higher degree of complexity in the financial markets. For example, the treasurer of a rapidly growing $2 billion U.S. high-tech manufacturer estimated that he would need a 14-member rather than a 9-member staff without computers. Because of its automated system, a Swedish auto giant needs only a minimal staff to record 25,000 FX transactions per year, worth Skr35 billion, and to generate bank confirmation letters.

(3) **Voracious information needs.** At the heart of efficient treasury management lies the gathering and management of accurate, reliable information. Companies need information on currency exposures before they can hedge. They cannot develop investing and borrowing strategies unless they have timely data at all stages of the cash cycle. "Treasury management is entirely dependent on information," says a treasury consultant at a money center bank, "and that is why computers can play such a dramatic role."

(4) **A more complex environment.** Computers and electronic services help treasurers keep pace with the growing sophistication and complexity of global financial markets and intracorporate cash flows. One U.S.-based international finance manager summed up his use of computers this way: "There are a lot more problems and a lot more ways to solve them than have existed in the past. All these new markets have opened up—the options markets, interest rate futures, stock and currency swaps. Pushing a pencil on the back of an envelope is becoming a less sophisticated way of doing it—and a less accurate way."

(5) **A lower degree of existing automation.** Since accounting and control typically receive first priority in financial automation, there is more room in treasury management for computers to streamline operations. "Treasury has remained an untapped area for automation," declared a bank consultant. "It therefore has the greatest opportunity for putting automated systems in place. Since treasury was not as automated in the past as other functions, it is now going through a rapid growth period. It's catching up with where a lot of the other parts of the institution already are."

(6) **Widespread publicity of automated systems.** Intense marketing efforts by banks and the media focused on financial software applications have spread the gospel of treasury computerization among companies all over the world. As the treasurer of a U.S. capital goods manufacturer put it, "It's the buzzword these days. Treasury management systems seem to be the thing. Once the word gets around, it's just like designer clothes or anything else."

10. Step One: Selecting the Right Bank for Automated Balance Reporting

One of the first phases of treasury automation is often a bank balance reporting system. Automated bank balance reporting systems must be chosen very carefully. Not only can the unprepared executive end up with a service that does not meet his cash management requirements, but the decision can have a strong impact on both subsidiary and parent banking relations. Companies will want to go first to the banks with which they have a large volume of account business to avoid upsetting present relationships. After weighing these concerns, cash managers can use the following checklist to do some comparative shopping.

● **Emphasize system dependability.** Banks try to impress customers with the bells and whistles of their electronic system. As a result, companies sometimes forget to find out how dependable a system is. This can be a crippling mistake, as the following example demonstrates.

A U.K. firm found that the bank system it employed was out of commission on average 4 of every 22 working days. Said the cash manager, "I had dozens of clerks and supervisors sitting out there with nothing to do each day." The manager estimates that this cost over $9,000 a month in wasted work time.

The best way to avoid such problems is to talk to present users. A good way to start is to speak to bank-provided references. However, treasury managers should also use whatever network is available to find users not in the bank's marketing brochures. These users will give a more independent view of the system's merits.

● **Ask for test runs.** Before buying a system, companies should insist on having the bank demonstrate the system in house. These test runs should demonstrate the different screen and printout formats that are available with the reporting system. Some banks will even put in actual company information for the test and will make alterations to accommodate a company's needs.

Firms should also learn the sign-on procedure for accessing the data. This is particularly important for companies that use electronic reporting systems from a number of banks, since systems that have lengthy sign-on requirements can be unnecessarily time-consuming.

● **Insist on close ties to bank support staff.** Make sure the bank will give you direct and ongoing access to its own operations staff. If the system is down, for example, a staff member should be able to identify the problem and tell the user when the system will be running again. Data can also show up on the screen or printer in a garbled state. A staffer should be able to identify the problem, correct it, and let the user know when the data can be accessed.

● **Select appropriate data frequency.** It is a rare firm that needs real-time interactive data. Understanding that costs rise in tandem with the frequency of data transmission will help a treasury manager determine just how soon he needs balance information.

● **Consider using a smart terminal.** Most consultants would agree with the banker who said, "The delivery vehicle of the future is a microstation, not a dumb terminal." Indeed, confronted with the choice of receiving electronic data over a dumb or a smart terminal, a growing number of cash managers are opting for the latter. Smart terminals, or micros, can be better integrated with internal automated systems to halve clerical time and cut cost. In the words of a U.K. finance manager, "It was very time-consuming to wait for a full printout on our dumb terminal just to get one piece of information from the end of the report. With a smart terminal, I can go right to the information I need."

The assistant treasurer of a large U.S. chemicals concern agrees: "We can save a few hours out of a person's day by using smart terminals. First of all, the smart terminals can call up each of the individual bank reporting systems. This way, we don't need someone watching over a dumb terminal waiting for one bank report to finish so he can call up the next bank report. Second, the smart terminal can be programmed to automatically manipulate the data into the formats that we need. This adds up to a tremendous time saving."

---

11. Do You Need a Treasury Workstation?

Often, a bank balance reporting system is not enough. The success of treasury management depends on the financial staff's ability not only to obtain but also to interpret data. This is the concept behind one of the most widely publicized products for corporate treasury: the treasury workstation.

According to a BI survey, the number of treasury workstations currently in operation will double in the next two years, from 23 percent to 47 percent of companies. The principal value of such a system is that it gives firms on-line balance reporting and allows electronic transaction initiation, all in one place. In addition, the systems can be used to perform all kinds of cash flow analysis.

But for firms that still need persuading, the following checklist details the added benefits such a system can provide.

(1) Automated cash worksheets. These allow treasurers to access and manipulate not only bank data but also information from other areas of the company. Firms can use their workstations to enter these data directly into an electronic spreadsheet and so generate a cash forecast. As one Canadian treasurer put it, "It keeps a rolling record of real and anticipated receipts in both U.S. and Canadian dollars."

A number of companies, however, believe such automated worksheets are better built in house than brought in from the banks. Some managers consider bank systems too inflexible. More important perhaps, many firms are trying to move functions in house to avoid bank charges. As one New York cash manager explained, "Why pay for it when we can do it ourselves?"

(2) Debt and investment. Using these modules, treasurers can more effectively track and manage outstanding investments and borrowings and choose the best available debt and investment instruments. The Belgian regional headquarters of a major U.S. chemicals firm recently installed such a package on its treasury management system. The program analyzes the firm's domestic and foreign investment portfolios in terms of yields, terms, and volumes. The software also searches out the best investment instruments, which, in the words of the regional assistant treasurer, "is particularly useful in countries where the money markets are more developed." The computer also generates reports on the borrowing positions of European subsidiaries and indicates the least expensive credit arrangements available to the firm.

But larger firms may find these simple personal computer (PC)-based modules inadequate. The treasurer of a large U.S. oil company, with total investments of more than $2 billion, has found that his requirements overwhelm even the most advanced treasury workstations. For this reason, the company recently decided to move the entire treasury management system to the corporate mainframe.

(3) Bank relations management. MNCs are increasingly using workstations to facilitate the tracking and monitoring of bank activities and fees. For example, the U.K. subsidiary of a U.S. auto maker recently bought a module to automate its system for analyzing bank risk with respect to investments and FX dealings.

The company is currently trying to integrate its bank relations management system with the corporatewide data base. A spokesman says, "If our limit is $100 million worldwide with one bank and I invest $50 million, I need to know where else in the world anyone else is investing with that bank so that we don't run the risk as a corporation of going beyond our limit. What I'd like to have is the limit constantly updated worldwide in real time. Unfortunately, no one offers that system now."

The bank relationship module in use at a large U.S. oil company offers another benefit. "It generates correspondence to the banks, like a word processing program, but with the valid signatures for a given account," says a spokesman. "It's the least critical of the modules we use on the workstation, but it is convenient."

(4) Financial models. Some workstations enable firms to perform "what-if" analysis. A major chemicals concern, for example, purchased a bank's software to track receivables and payables patterns at various times during the year. The firm uses this information with modeling software to adjust its forecasts for seasonal trends. In addition, the company inputs various currency and interest rate forecasts for "what-if" analysis. According to the treasurer, this enables the firm "to play with the data and see what would happen if conditions change by such an amount. It's a very useful tool."

12. How to Select a Treasury Workstation: The Corporate Experience

The choice of a treasury workstation is a complex decision, demanding careful analysis and deliberation. A U.S. foods manufacturer recently purchased a treasury workstation following a rigorous analysis of the options available on the market. Lacking sufficient internal expertise, the firm hired a software consultant who worked with a special in-house committee composed of treasury, credit, and electronic data processing (EDP) staff. The entire review process took several months, but the company was very confident of the end results.

The committee's first step in the purchasing process was to compile a formal list of the features the company needed. Based on this list, it composed a questionnaire with detailed feature matrices to be sent to selected vendors. Each vendor received a copy of the questionnaire; a detailed description of the firm's needs, existing systems, and treasury organization; and a request for copies of annual reports and promotional literature.

After a close review of the questionnaire responses, the committee used an intricate scoring system to narrow the field to three vendors, which were invited to make on-site presentations. The vendors were informed that the company was particularly concerned with training, data storage, and several other issues, and that the presentation format should include an hour of discussion and two to three hours of software demonstration. The demonstrations covered all major areas of cash management for which the package would be used. They were scheduled several days apart to enable the staff to absorb and debate the experience.

To ensure an objective evaluation, the demonstrations were attended by staff from different areas, enabling them to ask the vendors questions, especially relating to technical difficulties. Finally, using a checklist format, the staff evaluated the presentations and graded each vendor in a variety of categories. After checking references, the firm chose the package deemed most appropriate for the firm's treasury needs.

Companies can use the following checklist to make certain that they do not overlook any important steps or issues in their search for the best package.

Software Features

● Is the workstation fully compatible with your hardware? Every PC is different, and software must be designed specifically to operate on particular models.

● Are you paying for modules and capabilities that you do not need? Are there too many bells and whistles? Is it possible to buy only the modules you need?

● Are any essential modules missing? The key functions include a daily bank activity report, a cash position worksheet, debt and investment portfolios, bank relations management, transaction initiation, and data storage. Are there any unique additional modules such as a spreadsheet interface, graphics, word processing, report writer, communications, "what-if" analysis capability, or accounts reconciliation?

● Is the system user-friendly? Can you switch easily from menu to menu? Are the menu codes easy to remember and interpret?

● How large is the data storage base? Is it too small or too big (and therefore an unnecessary expense)? Does each module provide sufficient detail? Keep in mind that companies often underestimate the data storage capacity they need, especially for a few years hence.

● Are security safeguards adequate to control access to sensitive information? Are there backup facilities to protect the user in the event of computer failure or natural disaster?

● Are there links with the general ledger or other data bases (e.g., an exchange rate data base)? Can you upload and download?

● How many banks and accounts can be accessed for balance and transaction information? How much does it cost for additions?

● How quickly is data processed? Can more than one operation be performed at a time?

● Does the system alert you to target balances and maturing investments and debts?

Service and Support Features

● Is the vendor vulnerable to an industry shakeout so that it might become unavailable to service its software?

Has another institution (e.g., a bank) made arrangements to take over servicing commitments if the vendor collapses? Who has the source code? Does the vendor have full rights to the package or is it a licensee?

● How extensive is your support agreement? Could future servicing run into a lot of money? How expensive is regular maintenance, and are monthly fees mandatory or optional?

● Does the vendor's support staff appear knowledgeable, helpful, and committed?

● Is customer service available when you need it, either over the phone or through on-site visits? Does the vendor have a strong commitment to future service and the resources to back it up?

● As a client, are you eligible to receive future enhancements and modifications for free or at a minimal cost? New modules and features are constantly being added and improved.

● Will the vendor customize the package if necessary? How much will this cost and how long will it take?

● Is there an active user group you can join to trade ideas and solve common problems?

● Is the user manual complete, detailed, and up to date without being overly voluminous and obscurely written?

● Are there software installation and training charges? How many days of training are offered? What arrangements for future training of new personnel are provided by the vendor?

The Selection Process

● Have you looked at enough packages? As a rule, companies should look at 5 to 10 different models before making a decision to buy.

● What was the quality of the vendor's proposal and presentation? Was it sufficiently detailed? Did you receive satisfactory answers to hard questions that went beyond the buzzwords (e.g., what does "flexible" really mean)? Did you advise the vendor of your particular needs and provide company-specific data to use in the demonstration?

● Can special pricing arrangements be made, such as a discount or payment through balances (if the vendor is a bank)?

● What is the payback time for the system? (First, calculate the costs of hardware and software, monthly fees, and other anticipated service charges; then determine the savings from reduced time-sharing and dumb-terminal costs, improved interest and investment earnings, and lowered labor costs.)

● Did you get input from all appropriate parties before making the purchasing decision? Relevant staff includes treasury, cash management, EDP, accounting, and credit.

● Should you use an outside consultant to help you with your purchasing decision?

● Did you construct comparative charts or checklists to track the differences between packages and record the responses of staff and consultants to the vendors' presentations?

● How well did the vendors' references check out?

13. Automating Cash Management: One Firm's Blueprint

The following case example shows how automation—in the form of a treasury workstation—can be used to improve cash management. After conducting a thorough audit of its cash management activities (see Chapter 8 for more on auditing cash management), one firm's subsidiary discovered significant delays during the collection process—that its banks were not living up to value-dating agreements, and that it was consistently in overdraft in one bank while piling up surplus funds (at a low interest rate of 0.5 percent p.a.) at another. A report on the review concluded that "an effective information system that can plan rather than react to problems will improve both the decision-making process and the profitability of the company."

The firm called in a team of consultants from a U.S. bank that recommended installing a computerized daily cash management reporting system, supported by sales and customer account ledgers and by direct coordination with the firm's banks. The goals set in establishing its automated system are worthwhile considerations for a company with similar problems. The steps are outlined below.

Banking

● Monitor the collection and mobilization of customer receipts by banks to ensure that negotiated value-dating standards are being applied.

● Ensure that collected funds have been credited to overdraft positions on a timely basis.

● Determine the gross and available balance of cash and overdraft positions to develop either investment or borrowing strategies.

Internal

● Provide a rationale for determining the amount and timing of intercompany transactions to balance cash, debt, and FX exposure strategies.

● Revise daily customer aging schedules based upon established terms of trade and clearing arrangements.

The computerized reporting system developed by the company to meet these objectives is illustrated in Figure 1, which shows the type of information the firm stores in its

Figure 1
Financial Information Reporting System
Input Data Flows

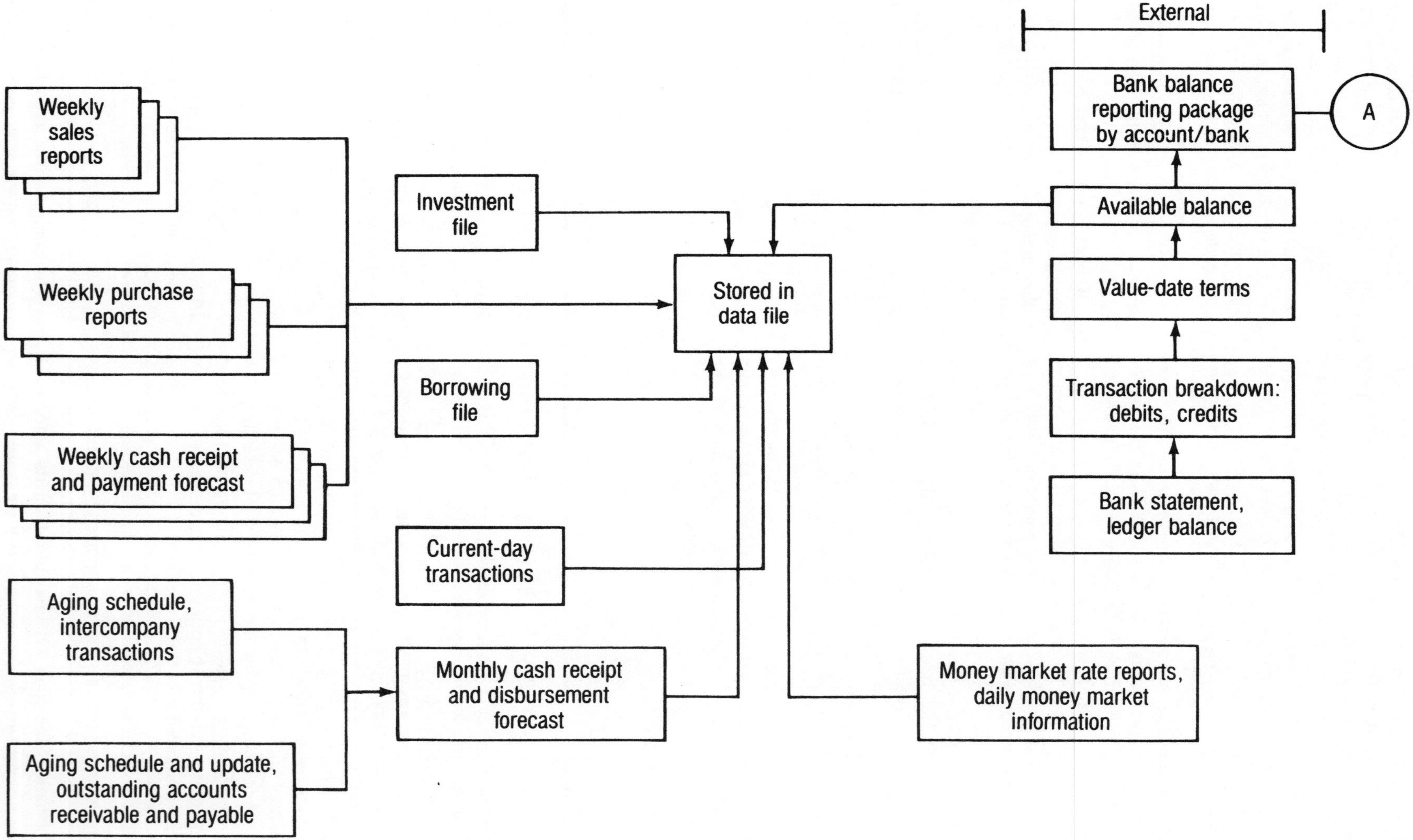

A

External

Bank balance reporting package by account/bank

Available balance

Value-date terms

Transaction breakdown: debits, credits

Bank statement, ledger balance

Money market rate reports, daily money market information

Stored in data file

Investment file

Borrowing file

Current-day transactions

Monthly cash receipt and disbursement forecast

Weekly sales reports

Weekly purchase reports

Weekly cash receipt and payment forecast

Aging schedule, intercompany transactions

Aging schedule and update, outstanding accounts receivable and payable

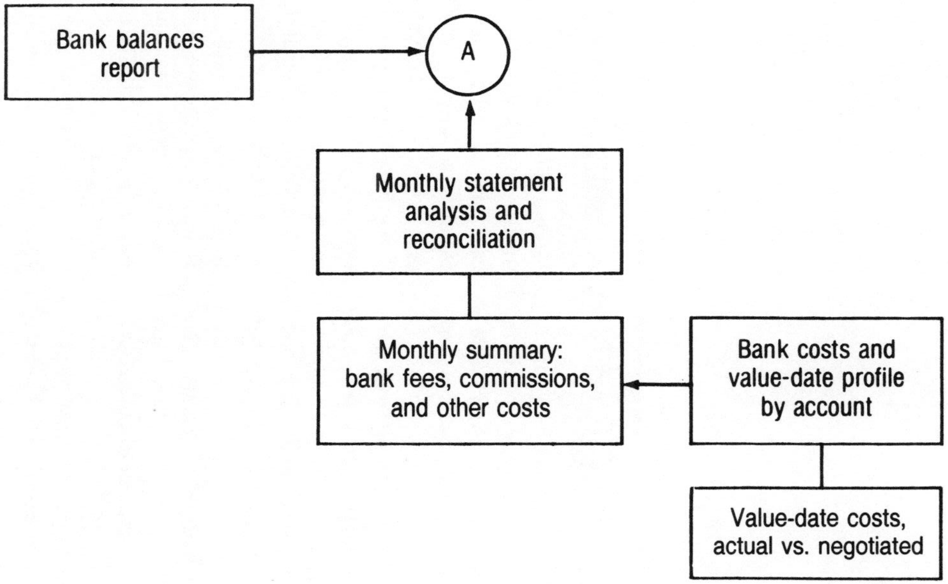

Figure 3
Financial Information Reporting System Output Reports

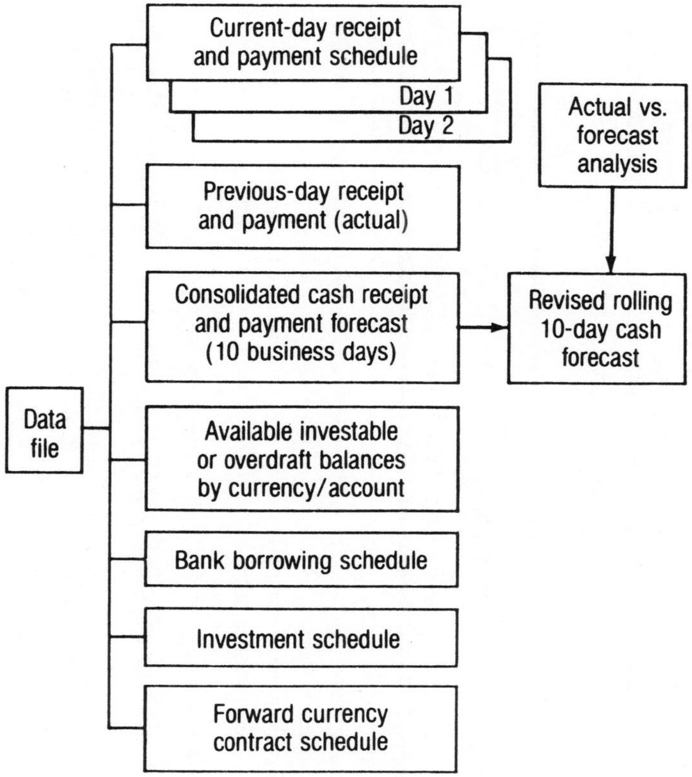

Current-day receipt and payment schedule
Day 1
Day 2

Actual vs. forecast analysis

Revised rolling 10-day cash forecast

Previous-day receipt and payment (actual)

Consolidated cash receipt and payment forecast (10 business days)

Available investable or overdraft balances by currency/account

Bank borrowing schedule

Investment schedule

Forward currency contract schedule

Data file

Figure 2
Account Activity Reports

Bank balances report

A

Monthly statement analysis and reconciliation

Monthly summary: bank fees, commissions, and other costs

Bank costs and value-date profile by account

Value-date costs, actual vs. negotiated

computerized data base, including internal sales and purchasing reports, cash forecasts, aging of receivables and payables, and borrowings and investments. The company also obtains money market information from external sources and balance and transaction data from its banks. By tapping this comprehensive data base, the company's computer can generate the cash management reports shown in Figures 2 and 3.

14. Building a DSS System: Choosing Software and Hardware

The most sophisticated firms are moving beyond mere operational automation and into decision support systems (DSS). These systems allow financial and treasury analysts to collect, manipulate, and analyze data with remarkable efficiency. A BI survey identified four basic types of DSS applications: retrieving data from a central data base; ratio and regression analysis; sensitivity analysis and financial modeling; and input from external data bases.

Firms considering the purchase of a DSS must consider the broad array of hardware and software options available on today's market. The tables below show the systems currently on the market that can service these applications, along with user and hardware information.

Most Popular Mainframe/Mini DSS Systems

Vendor	Package	No. of customers
Execucom Systems	IFPS	1,500
Thorn EMI Comp. Software	FCS	1,400
Compro Financial Systems	Foresight	550
Comshare	System W	275
Computer Associates	CA-Fin. Planner	250
Applied Data Research	Empire	200
Simplan Systems	Simplan	130
Lloyd Bush & Co.	Model	125
Information Resources Inc.	Express	120
Integrated Planning	Strategem	65
Boeing Computer Services	EIS	41
Interactive Data	XSIM	20
Other		600

Source: International Data Corp., *Software News,* September 1986.

Decision Support Package Systems

Package	Development language	Mainframe	Mini	Micro
IFPS	Fortran	X	X	X
FCS-EPS	Assembler	X	X	X
Foresight	Fortran	X	X	X
System W	Pascal	X	X	X
Ca-Fin. Planner	Assembler, SPF	X		
Empire	Fortran	X		Planned
Simplan	PL/1, Assembler	X	X	X
Model	Fortran	X	X	X
Express	AED	X	X	X
Strategem	C	X	X	Planned
EIS	Fortran	X		X
XSIM	AED	X	X	X

Source: Real Decisions Corp., *Software News,* September 1986.

15. Dividend Planning: One Firm's Automated Worksheet

Never assume that any aspect of operation is too simple to warrant some degree of automation. Compared with other areas of treasury and financial planning, the calculation of dividend payout ratios is relatively simple and is thus rarely automated.

However, companies may want to tap into internal and external data bases to retrieve information on short- and long-range cash flow forecasts, dividend payout ratios of other firms in the same industry, historical dividend ratios, interest rate histories, and market yields of capital market securities.

The most demanding exercise in dividend planning is the determination of an optimal remittance. In this area, firms find that remittance decisions can be significantly improved by the use of technology.

To formulate the best strategy, companies must predict interest, FX, and tax rates in the parent country and in each foreign subsidiary. For example, a major U.S. MNC has to make remittance decisions for 60 subsidiaries in the Americas, Europe, Africa, and the Asia/Pacific region. The complexity of keeping track of that volume of data was described by the firm's financial planner: "In 60 countries everything is going up, down, and sideways every minute of every day. You've got to have some way to organize that information and set your priorities."

The firm has developed a PC-based spreadsheet with a global funds matrix that enables the planner to decide when to remit by forecasting the future dollar value of local funds. It tells him how much he should be willing to pay to bring local currency home (in terms of a discount on local currency, a withholding tax, or any other cost involved in bringing the funds out of the country).

The spreadsheet incorporates assumptions on interest rates, tax rates, and currency trends in each country from which a remittance is due. These are used to compute an "attrition rate"—a number that indicates how local investments will perform over a six-month period in dollar terms.

Decisions based on the spreadsheet are only as good as the underlying assumptions. Nevertheless, the matrix does enable the manager to set time priorities and evaluate the cost of remittance alternatives.

The matrix is based on a simple remit/do not remit decision rule. Funds are remitted if the dollar after-tax return on six-month bank deposits is greater than the local-currency after-tax return, adjusted for expected devaluation. Funds are not remitted if the dollar after-tax return on six-month bank deposits is less than the local-currency after-tax return, adjusted for expected devaluation. In other words, if $i(1T)$ (in dollars) is greater than $i(1T)d$ (in local currency), remit; if $i(1T)$ (in dollars) is less than $i(1T)d$ (in local currency), don't remit (i = interest rate; T = tax rate; d = devaluation rate). The spreadsheet contains the following columns:

- **List of countries.**
- **Six-month nominal investment rate.** A six-month term was chosen because it represented the average maturity of the company's global excess cash investments.
- **Tax rate.** This is the tax rate applicable to interest income in the countries listed.
- **After-tax investment rate.** This is the six-month local-currency yield adjusted for taxes.
- **1 + D.** The calculation begins with a $1 local-currency

equivalent. This column shows the yield on $1 after six months, before adjusting for devaluation.

- **Last six months' devaluation rate.** While not part of the calculations, these numbers do provide a quick check on the currency forecast. If the projections for devaluation in the next six months are dramatically different from actual devaluation in the last six months, the manager should be prepared to justify the difference.
- **Next six months' devaluation rate.** These numbers are taken from various external sources.
- **(H) 1 − G.** This shows how many cents are left from each dollar after six months, before interest and taxes.
- **Composite effect.** This adjusts the after-tax return on a six-month investment for devaluation. It shows what $1 deposited locally would be worth in six months.
- **Ratio of local-currency value to U.S. value.** This is the "slope" of the remittance curve. A number greater than 1 indicates an uphill slope from the subsidiary to the parent—in other words, a remittance that should be left in local currency. A number less than 1 shows a downhill slope: Excess liquidity should be pulled from the subsidiary. The lower the number, the more the corporation is losing on local funds and the more important it is to bring funds home.
- **Six-month attrition rate.** A negative number indicates a positive return. The number to beat is the U.S. attrition rate. The larger the positive number, the greater the loss to the company in local-currency funds.

---

16. Automating Exposure Management: The Modules on Offer

The final checklist of this chapter will help firms decide what they need from an exposure management software package. These systems are normally available in a number of modules, specific functions from which MNCs can choose. Exposure packages are also a key option for most treasury workstations. The following checklist describes one firm's exposure management software and gives pointers that should help other companies in their choice of system. (See Checklist 24 for a description of an options management package.)

(1) Exposure reporting and forecasting. Most vendors provide a package to help firms build an exposure report. Normally, for a fee, this will include consulting to help determine actual exposure, as well as custom tailoring of the existing software to meet a firm's specific needs.

"The reports are basically the balance sheet broken down into the various currencies," explained a consultant who helped develop the model used by the firm. "Each sub also submits a three-month forecast for each currency. These are entered into the system at the parent, and the system consolidates all the currencies and produces reports that show the currencies by asset and liability field. It also produces a summary report for each subsidiary, so you get a full,

detailed background on your exposure in German marks, for example."

(2) Forward contract monitoring . . . Once exposure is defined, most software is very effective in helping firms manage the position. This firm's system requires that a manager input the amount of the contract, the currency, the dollar equivalent, the maturity date, the traders' names, the names of the bank representatives, and, if desired, an interim date at which the status of the contract should be reviewed. (Other vendors' systems include a data base of current rates that can be downloaded daily or as needed, thus avoiding many of the above steps.)

(3) . . . and management. Armed with this information, the system can produce several useful reports. "It can produce information on contracts by currency, contracts by bank, contracts by bank within currency, contracts by date done, contracts by maturity date—there's a whole slew of different contract reports the FX department can get," stated the consultant. The system also updates the exposure report to reflect the hedging actions taken.

(4) Bank confirmations. "Once the computer files have been updated," the consultant commented, "the system will generate a letter of confirmation for the bank that the contract was made with, which is the formal document that solidifies the contract." This is a standard feature of vendor packages.

(5) Bank performance evaluation. One useful feature common to several packages examined by BI is a review of bank's FX pricing. With this firm's system, FX traders routinely call three banks and input their bid/offer spreads on each deal. The system then tracks each relationship, keeping the firm current on which bank has been providing the best overall service. In addition, users may be able to detect certain currency-specific trends. One bank may have a particular strength relative to other players.

(6) Bank exposure monitoring. "The company wants to limit its exposure with any given bank," declared the consultant. "The system automatically logs the amount of the contract and keeps the company aware of how close it is to the established exposure limits. There are two sets of bank limits the system monitors." The first is a volume limit. For example, the company decides that it will have a $100 million limit on the number of contracts it has with a New York bank in a net posture. The second is called a "three-day limit." In this case, the company sets a restriction of so many dollars on contracts that are in the process of being confirmed and contracts that are in transit between the time the deal is made and the formalization of the deal. If the bank goes under in those three days, the company is vulnerable.

(7) Tax analysis. By inputting various tax rates on FX gains and losses from the countries in which the firm operates, the company can keep track of the tax implications of hedging in those markets. "They have to sit down and understand the tax situation in each of the given countries and determine what the gain or loss posture may be as a result of contracting in that country's currency. Since the contracts can be for billions of dollars, there can be substantive tax effects," said the consultant.

For example, suppose the firm had $100 million in net assets in deutsche marks representing all the subsidiaries that deal in the German currency. "If I know that three of the countries represented in that combined exposure are going to take some of those assets in taxes, I don't want to protect that proportion of the assets," explained the consultant.

(8) Accounting reports. The FX manager at the firm wanted to lighten the burden of his reporting responsibilities to the accounting department. Explained the consultant, "The system automatically goes through the process of amortizing the cost of exchange protection on each contract on a monthly basis. It then automatically distributes the cost of exchange protection across the divisions that are involved in a specific contract. The company may have seven or eight divisions that the contract is protecting against exposure, and the cost of that protection is allocated to those companies according to a predetermined allocation formula. At month's end, the system presents the required journal entries for entry to the general ledger."

(9) Cash vouchers. The company's cash disbursement department must also be aware of the FX manager's actions so that the money is available to cover the cost of a maturing contract. Said the consultant, "Fourteen days before the contract is due, it appears on a daily listing of upcoming cash requirements. The FX manager then decides whether to roll the contract over or settle it. If he settles it, he needs a cash voucher for the cash disbursement people. He keys in that the contract is to be settled, and the voucher is produced automatically."

(10) Exchange rate tracking. At the company, the closing spot rate is keyed into the system on a certain workday near the end of the month for internal accounting purposes. "It's an ITR—internal translation rate," said the consultant, "for translating balance sheets and P&L."

Chapter 3
Managing Financial Risks and Costs with Options

With the strategic issues of organization and automation discussed, Chapters 3 and 4 of this guide deal with a key treasury endeavor: FX and interest rate risk management. Chapter 3 outlines the use of options; Chapter 4 highlights interest rate and currency swap techniques.

Options have become one of the most widely publicized of the new breed of innovative financial instruments. Even so, they have failed to gain widespread acceptance among corporate treasurers for numerous reasons.

In this era of volatile currencies and interest rates, however, a growing number of treasury managers feel the time has passed when MNCs can afford the luxury of ignoring any tool that can contribute to their financial well-being. As one treasurer put it, "Volatility is a fact of life, and so is financial innovation. Any treasurer worth his salary owes it to his company to keep up on hedging developments—and that means understanding options."

This chapter is designed to give companies a grounding in the ABCs of options. It provides answers to the basic questions about options: what they are, where they are purchased, and how to get the best price. It also addresses the more complicated issues, such as how to establish and manage an options position. Finally, it shows how companies are using options structures to solve currency and interest risk management problems in the most cost-effective manner.

17. Why Use Options?

The growth of currency and interest rate options is one of the most exciting new developments in the financial markets. But only a minority of companies have actually developed an active options portfolio. For companies that are still reluctant to move beyond traditional exposure management techniques, the following three option benefits should be considered.

(1) Options allow management of uncertain exposures. In the words of a U.S. FX manager who uses options to hedge anticipated sales, "Forwards are a very crude hedging instrument because they have a straight risk/reward curve; contract gains or losses are exactly offset by losses or gains on the underlying exposure. That's fine if the situation you're facing is black or white. But if your exposure is uncertain, then you need options."

(2) Options allow enhanced flexibility. Options allow firms to adjust hedging positions quickly in response to a change in exposure, exchange spot rates, or timing of the underlying commitment. Declares the treasurer of a well-known U.S. chemicals company, "Options aren't like forwards; options enable you to act responsively to a position."

(3) Options eliminate risk but allow the opportunity for cash gains. A fundamental difference between forwards and options is that forwards lock into a rate whether it is good or bad. Options, on the other hand, limit potential losses but create opportunities for unlimited gain.

This is an especially attractive feature for those firms with a profit-center approach, but it is applicable to all treasuries. Says one currency manager, "We want to eliminate the downside risk, and we are willing to pay to do that. But unlike forwards, options give us the opportunity to hit a home run."

18. How Options Are Priced: An Introduction

Companies frequently cite price as the major stumbling block to their use of options. The reasoning is simple: Option prices appear high, particularly since they take the form of highly visible up-front premiums.

However, it is critical for companies to understand that all financial transactions have a cost, whether in cash or opportunity terms, implicit or overt. The obvious response to a manager who says options are too expensive is: Then why aren't you selling options?

In order to determine whether options are too expensive, firms need to begin an examination of just how their value is derived. While option pricing is quite complex, hedgers can use the following short checklist to focus attention on the key variables.

- **Volatility.** Volatility, rather than the actual direction of exchange rate movement, is the critical measure of an interest rate's or currency's potential for change. For example, as a currency begins to fluctuate, its volatility increases. When volatility is high, the premium for either a put or a call option will be higher than when volatility is low.

Volatility measures the size of changes in currency rates. It is usually calculated as the standard deviation of the log of day-to-day returns (today's rate divided by yesterday's), expressed in annualized percentage terms. A volatility of 15 percent suggests that there is only a one-in-three chance over the coming year of the spot price moving more than 15 percent—one standard deviation on either side—from the current forward price.

Options traders consider two different types of volatility for pricing. Historical volatility is based on the past frequency of day-to-day price moves of various sizes. Implied volatility is determined from option prices dealt in the market. A standard pricing model is used to find what figure assumed for volatility would give the observed market price of the option. It therefore reflects market expectations of future volatility.

- **Time value: the length of time until expiration.** In general, the greater the amount of time until expiration, the more expensive the option. The reason for this is that the price of the underlying commodity (an interest rate or currency in this context) has a higher probability of changing as the length of time considered increases.

Hedgers should note that the time value of a given option will decay exponentially, not linearly. This means that value is lost at an accelerating rate as the option approaches its expiration date. It also means that a six-month option with a strike price identical to that of a three-month option will cost less than twice as much. This exponential decay is a key focus in managing any options position.

- **Economic value: the difference between the *strike* and *cash* prices.** An option's strike price is a key component of its cost. For example, a call option on a currency with a strike price below that currency's present market value will have an economic value. That value will be determined by the difference in the strike and spot prices multiplied by the size of the contract. By adjusting the strike price, an option can become more or less expensive as it moves in or out of "the money."

- **Relative interest rates.** Like simple forward contracts, option premiums are influenced by interest rate differentials. This means a call option on a nondollar currency will become more expensive as dollar interest rates increase and the interest rates in the target currency decline. A put option will become more expensive as dollar interest rates decline and the interest rates in the nondollar currency rise.

- **Market fluctuations.** The variables discussed above

summarize options pricing theory. Corporate managers can use this theory to gain insights into and to profit from market dynamics.

For example, because volatility also reflects an "uncertainty premium" that increases with time, longer options normally have higher volatilities. But when the spot market is active and options traders think it will calm down later, the implied volatility curve can be inverted. Any aberration from normal option pricing patterns might lead corporations to wait for better volatility levels or to consider options strategies other than a standard option purchase, such as purchasing a flexible forward.

19. Nine Steps for Testing Options

Learning to use options is like learning how to swim: It is best to start in the shallow end of the pool. To find out the best way to get started, BI asked option users from major U.S. firms to outline their first steps. The checklist below details how these firms developed commonsense procedures for testing and implementing an options program.

(1) Follow the options markets. Before entering the options field, the FX department at Eastman Kodak kept in touch with option traders and corporate users and monitored the latest developments. In this way, the company could measure its own ideas and plans against those of other market participants. It was also a no-risk way to learn from the successes and errors of others.

(2) Investigate all options strategies. Firms must know the basic options strategies and understand the kind of cover they produce. "I don't think you want to get involved in any kind of market without knowing about it yourself and knowing what the strategies are," warned one FX specialist. "You can't look at the options market from a one-sided perspective and say you will only buy calls or sell puts; you have to look at it as a whole."

(3) Simulate options cover on your exposures. One FX department chose a past period and simulated options cover to see how an options hedge compared with the company's actual hedging procedures. The results of the simulation helped the firm decide which options strategies would be best suited for each type of exposure, since different strategies yield different results.

Explains one FX manager, "You have to set some guidelines appropriate to your situation—such as hedging 100 percent of that exposure with options, or half with options and half with forwards. If you plan to trade options, you should take that into account. Then look again at the loss that you would have realized."

(4) Educate senior management. As one FX manager explains, senior management needs to be nudged, not bludgeoned, into understanding a new technique. "You just can't go cold to the treasurer or CFO and say, 'I want to start doing FX options next week,'" he warns. "You have to educate them—go slow—make it very clear." The manager believes that the conclusion should be made obvious to the ultimate decision makers. A strong case should sell itself.

For currency options, the FX manager began educating senior management at an early stage. He wrote what he termed a "white paper," a detailed explanation of what a foreign currency option was, how it worked, what the risks were, and how it might be used.

At least one currency manager feels the internal selling job is not as tough as it appears. "People overemphasize the difficulty of getting top-level approval for options. There has been a lot of talk that options shouldn't be done because they're too risky. I don't think most managers have that view anymore. Senior managers are a lot more open-minded than some people think."

(5) Develop a formal set of trading procedures. Once you have determined that options can help you manage exposures and improve performance, the FX department should plan exactly how it proposes to use them. As Kodak's spokesperson put it, "You have to develop a concrete plan of what exactly your trading procedures will be, what limits will be set on the operation, and which currencies or types of exposure will be hedged with options."

(6) Try it out on a small scale. Firsthand experience is invaluable, but it pays to go slowly at the start. At one firm, the initial three option deals were quite small—just $10,000. "Getting a bank to sell you $10,000 of call options is a big favor," the manager reveals. "But they knew if we got it to work, they could count on a good chunk of my option business."

(7) Identify other uses. One firm's evaluation found that buying options did not fit the company's currency management profile. "Monitoring the market on a 24-hour basis like we do—you don't need options as an insurance policy," a manager argues. "Just to buy an option and say, 'Okay, I've hedged myself,' is lazy." Instead, the manager began exploring the instrument for other uses.

He eventually found a more aggressive use of options. While most companies simply buy options, the FX manager found it made sense for his firm to write options. He thought the firm could begin writing options against certain defined dividend and royalty streams. "This way, we earn the premium," he says. "Obviously, we do it only when it's favorable to us from a market view—depending on whether the dollar is rising or falling."

(8) Clear tax and accounting hurdles. Obstacles to options use can include tax and accounting aspects. It has to be determined, for example, whether options will have any negative accounting effects. Therefore, managers should provide the tax and accounting departments with literature on the implications of options and ask them to render an opinion on the matter.

(9) Modify your system to accommodate options. Most corporate FX management systems are not equipped to handle currency options. Said one treasurer, "Our present system, which we developed in house, handles both FX management and FX accounting. As the system was first set up, it could not handle options. We decided to make the changes in house, which meant a commitment of time and resources on our part."

One firm that followed the above steps has been actively writing options for some time. Notes the FX manager, "We know it's working well. We're definitely beyond the experimental stage."

20. Eleven Applications for Currency Options

Once a firm is confident in the options arena, its treasury personnel can begin to identify more and more cases where options can be deployed. The following checklist serves as a survey of the many ways corporate treasuries can benefit from options.

(1) Hedging contingent exposures from bid-to-award situations. Most MNCs use options to cover contingent exposures resulting from a bid on a foreign contract quoted in a foreign currency. If foreign currency cash flows are covered with forwards and the contract is not awarded, unnecessary exposures are created. If no forward cover is taken, currency movements may eat into the profit margin before the contract is awarded. Options are frequently the instrument of choice in such bid-to-award situations.

(2) Covering anticipated receivables. The manager for one firm explains that he hedges forecasted sales because the company lacks pricing flexibility. "Conventional exposure management says that you wait until your sales are booked before hedging," he says. "In our business, the local-currency-denominated price doesn't necessarily adjust right away to changes in the dollar. Until the price adjusts, we may lose money." The firm looks at the option premium as a cost of doing business. "Forwards are an imperfect tool," says the manager. "We use options to hedge that potential loss."

(3) Hedging anticipated payables. Cadbury Schweppes uses options to supplement forward cover for its anticipated payables. According to the company's treasurer, the price of its key product input, cocoa, is quoted in sterling, but it is really a dollar-based product. The objective of the company's FX strategy is to eliminate the currency element in the decision to purchase the commodity, thus leaving the company's buyers free to concentrate on fundamentals. Because the company's projection of future purchases is highly uncertain, however, this task is complicated.

As a result, Cadbury Schweppes has turned to currency options. After netting the group's total exposure, the company covers with forward contracts a base number of exposed, known payables. It covers the remaining—uncertain—portion with options. "The options act as an insurance policy. Our headquarters has informed me that since we began using options, our costs for purchasing this commodity have declined significantly."

(4) Hedging translation exposure. Many firms dismiss out of hand the possibility of hedging translation exposure because they know the pitfalls of hedging with forward contracts: A noncash translation gain could be offset by a large cash loss. Some FX managers argue, however, that when a translation exposure must be hedged, options cover can be much cheaper and more effective than forward cover.

A Geneva-based treasurer explains the danger of forward cover for translation exposure: "If you were afraid the Belgian franc would decline, you could hedge that with the offsetting forward contract. That's valid because the expected loss on the asset would be offset by the gain on the contract. But if you are wrong and the Belgian franc strengthens, your assets would have a paper write-up of, say, C$5 million, and your forward would lose C$5 million in cash." With options, "if you are dead wrong in your forecast, you lose the premium, but the cash impact is nowhere near as severe."

(5) Turning paper gains into cash. Some firms are using options to extract value from more conventional balance-sheet hedges. For example, one medium-sized U.S. company has used put options to cash in on translation gains resulting from existing foreign currency debt.

During the period of high U.S. interest rates and a strong dollar, the firm turned to unhedged Swiss franc borrowings to fund equipment purchases. As the franc weakened, the firm enjoyed paper gains from both the appreciating dollar and the low Swiss franc interest rate.

To turn these paper gains into cash, the company's president decided to write a six-month in-the-money Swiss franc put option that expired close to the maturity date of the note. If the franc appreciated beyond the strike price, the contract would not be exercised, and the firm could use the option premium to partially offset the higher dollar amount of the Swiss franc interest payments. If the franc depreciated to a level weaker than the strike price, the option would be exercised. Notes the president, "This is tantamount to buying the currency forward at the strike price versus the spot rate." In this case, the loss would be partially offset by the premium earned up front. And the company would still register a profit on its repayment of the Swiss franc note.

(6) Converting foreign currency issues. "When you do a foreign currency borrowing," suggests one treasurer, "it usually takes two to four weeks to receive your proceeds. If you don't execute cover as soon as you make the decision to launch, or you have to negotiate swap documentation before you get things locked up, you have currency exposure." To cover, the treasurer buys a put at an out-of-the-money strike price. The expiration date is set after the time he would get the proceeds, ensuring that the option still has time value when the proceeds arrive.

The treasurer prefers options over forwards to cover this exposure for two reasons: "With an option you can sell it and take the profit or keep it and just let it expire. And it has no cash flow impact, except the amount that you pay for the premium." He also likes the accounting treatment of an option. "You can make the case from an accounting perspective that the cost of the premium is part of the issue. Therefore, you can amortize the cost of the option over the life of the bond."

(7) Hedging equity injections. Westinghouse used a sterling option to hedge an anticipated equity injection into its U.K. subsidiary. Notes the company's FX manager, "We were fairly certain the injection would be made, but there was no board approval yet, so we couldn't go ahead and cover with a forward contract."

Treasury purchased the option in order to take advantage of the favorable exchange rate that existed at the time. According to the FX manager, however, "Sterling dropped, so we were able to make the injection at an advantageous rate, even taking into account the cost of the option."

(8) Protecting profit margins from currency fluctuations. Hewlett-Packard, a U.S.-based computer firm that sells dollar-costed products in Europe, found options to be more flexible than forwards in protecting its profit margins. The firm needs to be able to lower local-currency-denominated prices if the dollar weakens and to hold prices steady for about three months if the dollar strengthens. Says the firm's European director of finance, "Options help us delay price increases when the dollar strengthens."

The director explains how options coverage best meshes with pricing strategy: "If we buy dollars forward at Dm3:$1, and two months later the dollar weakens to Dm2.5:$1, we're under tremendous competitive pressure to drop our deutsche mark-denominated prices. With forwards, we've locked in a big contract loss. If we cover with options, we would let them expire, and we would only lose the premium." He feels strongly that options coverage is worth the price. "We average about 1.5 percent premiums for our coverage. That's very little compared to the risk to our business if the dollar moves 15 percent against us and we have to raise prices in two months."

(9) Hedging exposure to a competitor's currency. Corporations competing for export markets with firms from other countries may find their products at a price disadvantage if their competitor's currency weakens, allowing price reductions in the export market. Thus, the company may feel it is exposed in a competitor's currency even if it has no sales whatsoever in that currency.

One Canadian firm found itself competing with a European MNC to dominate the U.S. import market. The European firm's currency declined substantially against the U.S. dollar, permitting it to underprice its competitor. Even though the Canadian company had no direct investment in the other firm's country, "We came to the conclusion that we had competitive exposure to that European currency," says the treasurer. "To cover that risk, we hedged with options. Depending on how one assesses the risk, one could sell out-of-the-money options and pad the profit margin or buy out-of-the-money options for a relatively small cost and sell them for a profit if they moved into the money, thus compensating to some degree for the lost competitiveness."

(10) Earning premium income. The majority of firms purchase options as a way to cap FX losses and allow potential for unlimited gain. But some firms take a more speculative approach: writing options based on underlying commitments in order to earn premium income. These corporations are betting that the options they write will never be exercised. If they are, the writer must deliver currency at the strike price regardless of current market rates. Option writers, therefore, face a limited gain (the premium) and the potential for unlimited loss. At one firm that uses this strategy, speculative outstanding contracts represent 5 percent of total annual FX conversions.

(11) Locking in profits on forwards. One options expert argues that using options combined with a forward is an attractive way to lock in a minimum gain while preserving the opportunity of further profit on the underlying exposure if the exchange rate turns the other way.

For example, the firm took out a forward contract at Sfr1.9:$1 on a Swiss franc payable. After three months, the forward contract was in the money for a net gain of 19 centimes. The expert liked the profit, but with one month to go on the payable he felt some uncertainty: "If the dollar strengthened, it would be favorable for the underlying exposure, since we could buy the Swiss francs more cheaply. But a dollar correction would erase the nice contract gain we had up to that point." The solution was to buy a put option at the strike of Sfr1.65:$1. At a premium of 3 centimes, the cost still left a nice net profit for treasury.

---

21. Establishing and Managing the Optimal Options Position

Once firms decide to hedge a particular exposure with options, they have several basic choices to make in setting up the best position: the strike price, the maturity, whether to buy or sell options, and whether to hedge with one option or use a spread strategy (a simultaneous put and call). Choosing the best position is critical, because it will affect the cost and performance of the hedge. Companies must answer the following seven key questions before establishing an options position.

● **What do you want the hedge to accomplish?** The answer will be management's risk/reward profile for a particular exposure. Said the FX manager for a giant U.S. firm,

"Different options positions will result in different risk/reward curves. You have to ask yourself how much risk you are willing to take under certain conditions. Or you have to determine how much money you would spend in order not to have a certain risk." Many firms use options as "disaster insurance": They set the strike price at the rate beyond which losses on an exposure would be intolerable.

● **Do you want a profit from your hedge?** Companies with profit-center treasuries are willing to spend a lot of cash in return for potential profit. Buying an at-the-money or in-the-money option is costly but can yield a big profit if exchange rates move substantially. Selling options can produce income but opens the firm to unlimited losses should the exchange rate move against the position.

● **Do you want to just cover your hedging cost?** Firms that want to use options but do not necessarily want to make a big profit (or open themselves to big losses) will be willing to take a moderate risk for a moderate reward. In this case, many FX managers recommend "spread" strategies.

Spread strategies are achieved by buying a desired call and subsidizing the purchase by writing (analogous to selling) a corresponding put (or vice versa). By adjusting the strike prices on the put and call, a firm can achieve a degree of upside potential slightly higher than the downside potential for virtually no cost.

● **What is your currency view?** The FX manager's view of currency direction will aid in choosing an options position. If the hedger has no view of currency direction, he might be satisfied with a spread strategy. Currency outlook will also determine whether a company purchases or sells an option.

● **What is your underlying commitment?** The characteristics of the underlying exposure are critical in selecting an options strategy. Said the FX manager of a U.S. high-tech company, "When we hedge on behalf of our operating units, we ask them to assess the degree of uncertainty with the exposure." The greater the uncertainty, the more flexibility the hedger would want to build into the position.

One FX manager at a U.S. MNC told BI, "If we expect a dividend payment in three months but anticipate some delay from a sub, we would buy a six- or nine-month option. For some added cash up front, we get extra protection. Then if the payment comes in on schedule, we trade in the option and recover a large portion of the premium."

● **How volatile is the market?** A highly volatile market means more expensive premiums. Some FX managers purchase options when currency markets are in a lull period, such as the summer or Christmas holidays. Said one experienced options user, "The market was pretty dead in August, so we bought a lot of options then."

● **What maturity do you want?** Since options lose more time value at the end of maturity than at the beginning, some firms prefer to lengthen the maturity of options in certain situations. For example, one U.S. MNC was bidding on a German contract and would learn of the decision in three months. Upon award of the contract, there would be a further delay of nine months before the first payment. Management had to decide between buying a one-year option or buying a three-month option and rehedging if they won the contract.

The FX manager saw that the long-dated option was not much more expensive than the short-dated instrument. The three-month deutsche mark put option cost $0.0189/Dm1 (or 3.87 percent), and the one-year put cost $0.0212/Dm1 (or 4.34 percent). The company decided to take out the one-year option. The rationale was that if the contract did not materialize, the company could sell the option back and recoup a considerable portion of the premium paid out. If the contract did come through, the deal would be fully hedged for the period of exposure.

22. How to Reduce the Cost of Options

Corporate managers often complain that currency options cost too much. But there are several easy ways to remove this obstacle to using options.

● **Shop the over-the-counter (OTC) and listed markets.** Although the price differential between the OTC and listed markets has narrowed dramatically in recent years, shopping the OTC market should not be ignored when looking for the best price. Says one corporate hedger, "It's definitely worth shopping around the banks. If your option happens to fit someone's book, they could give you a great price. In a way, with the exchanges you'll always get the average price. But with an OTC option, you'll either get a horrible or a great price." (See Checklist 23 for more on listed and OTC options.)

● **Take advantage of the time value of options.** Because most of the time value is lost during the last several weeks before expiration, a firm can recover a significant portion of the premium it paid by trading in a six-month option one month before maturity. This also means that options with longer maturities are a better deal than options with shorter maturities. For example, the price of a six-month option is substantially less than twice the price of a three-month option for the same strike price.

● **Consider spread strategies.** By sacrificing some of the potential gain on an option, a company can also significantly reduce the cost. To do so, the firm might employ a spread strategy—combining calls and puts for the same maturity at different strike prices.

One FX manager from a dollar-based MNC used such an approach to hedge a foreign currency receivable. At the time, the spot rate was $1.4842:£1, and the manager expected the dollar to fall. He sold a call at a strike of $1.5:£1, earning a premium of $0.027. He bought a put at a strike of $1.4:£1, paying a premium of $0.014. In this way, if the dollar weakened, the manager would have limited his profit on the call (which is exercised on him) because of the cost of the put (which expires worthless). On the other hand, if his dollar prediction was incorrect, he would limit his loss by the premium earned on the call, which the purchaser would allow to expire. This factor would partially compensate for the cost of buying the put, which the manager would then exercise or sell.

23. How to Choose Between Listed and OTC Options

Several years ago, corporate treasurers generally preferred listed or exchange-traded options to OTC options on the basis of price: The OTC options sold by banks at that time were regarded as generally more expensive. However, because arbitrage between these markets—mostly carried out by banks hedging their own OTC offerings on the exchanges—has brought OTC prices way down, it is now worthwhile to play both fields.

Each of the two instruments has its own appealing features. For firms trying to decide which way to move in their approach to option purchases, the following checklist cites the advantages offered by both exchange-traded and OTC options.

The Advantages of OTC Options

● **Shopping the OTCs yields an occasional bargain.** Active corporate users of options note that while prices on the listed exchanges are generally consistent, OTC options prices often vary widely. "I'm always surprised at the range," explains one firm's FX manager. "From three or four banks you might see a 20 percent variation in price."

According to the manager, this price variation can provide as many opportunities as it does pitfalls. "That oddball price might be for or against you." Therefore, managers who want to get the finest options pricing will shop around to find OTC bargains.

● **The OTC market can handle larger deals.** While the size of deals done on the exchanges has increased over the past several years (as wholesaler participants have discovered the market), the most attractive listed option deals are generally limited to the $5–25 million range. "If you are doing deals of any sizable amount, you can do them more effectively in the OTC market," observes one chemical company's FX manager. Experienced banks will easily handle deals larger than $25 million, sometimes undertaking an options hedge on a managed basis—laying off the risk in smaller segments when they can.

● **OTC options are custom-tailored.** For novice players, this can be an attractive feature. Further, custom tailoring can be a simpler means toward special-purpose tactics like spread strategies.

● **OTC options have no margin requirements.** Perhaps the most attractive feature of OTC options is that no margin is required. "Maintaining the daily margin requirements with listed options is an administrative hassle," explains one FX manager.

That is not to say, however, that firms will be able to manage an OTC position without cash on deposit. "You are typically dealing with a relationship bank," explains another manager.

The Advantages of Listed Options

● **Listed options' prices are more visible.** One FX manager advises that newcomers use listed options simply because their pricing is more visible than the OTC variety. "It's good to start out with exchange options because you can see the prices every morning. You don't need to buy expensive software to price these options."

This is particularly important for managers who may have met a degree of internal resistance for the new options program. "If the CFO or your manager calls you and asks how your option is doing, you immediately know with listed options; it gives you a feeling of control," explains the FX manager. "With OTC options, you wouldn't know until you called your bank."

Treasurers will find exchange-traded options more convenient for managing an active hedging position, since it is easy to call up listed options prices on a trading screen and market prices can be monitored consistently. "Exchange-traded options give you a good liquid market where you can always be certain of offsetting your positions," says a manager at GAF. "You also have a way of knowing what your position is worth daily."

● **Listed options can be used to emulate the OTC version.** By using listed options, managers are not necessarily losing out on a custom fit. The most obvious difference between OTC and listed options is that an OTC option contract can be tailored to fit exactly the strike price, maturity, expiration date, and currency amount specified by the FX manager. By contrast, listed options have preset strike prices, which vary by currency; standard maturities (1, 3, 6, 9, and sometimes 12 months); fixed expiration dates (March, June, September, and December); and established lot sizes.

Active options users know that the standardization of listed options contracts is not really a drawback, despite the view put forward by bankers. "If corporate treasurers don't do their homework, they can fall prey to some of the banks' marketing ploys," explains one treasurer. "The bankers' contention is that only the OTC market can furnish coverage for odd-dated expirations."

The treasurer points out that this is simply not the case. He argues that for an exposure expiring on February 2, an FX manager should purchase a listed option expiring on March 15—and sell it February 2. "Lo and behold, there's your coverage until February 2. Bankers conveniently skip over this kind of reasoning." The manager recovers the extra time value he has paid for when he sells back the option.

Further, sophisticated option players would rarely buy an option with an expiration equal to the underlying exposure's maturity. Because time value decays faster as the option moves closer to expiration, most players buy longer-dated options than are actually required.

● **Listed options are more tradable.** Corporate option users unanimously agree that listed options are more tradable than OTC options. This is of critical importance because this flexibility allows the FX manager to adjust his options position to fit changes in the underlying exposure.

Holders of OTC options may have trouble trading out of a position, particularly if there is a large exchange rate movement. For example, one FX manager relates what happened the day after the G-5 announcement in September 1985: "When the dollar dropped from Dm2.84:$1 to Dm2.7:$1 [over the G-5 weekend] and we called to sell some of our OTC options, there were banks that wouldn't return our calls. Why? Because they were in a lot of trouble, too; they had more important things to worry about than me wanting to sell $10 million worth of options."

Her experience has made the manager appreciative of listed options' liquidity. "The good thing about listed options is that if you want to sell them—because the market goes against you—it's a phone call away."

● **The exchanges can offer more sophisticated advice.** Treasurers who want to use the most sophisticated strategies should rely on the greater experience of exchange brokers. "Options are still a new venture for the banks, and they lack depth and breadth of experience in dealing with them," says one experienced user. "The sophisticated strategies that must be used to obtain the maximum potential from options still lie in the hands of the brokers."

Using Both Options

The most sophisticated corporate hedgers use both varieties of options to obtain the best pricing. Comparing prices of listed and OTC options, however, is easier said than done. Although prices of the standard listed options are publicly quoted by the exchanges, OTC option prices are not. Moreover, since OTC options do not have the same contract specifications—strike prices, expiration dates, and maturities—as the listed variety, FX managers cannot explicitly compare the premiums of options.

The solution is to compare the options' implied volatilities, which are calculated by options pricing models available from banks and the software companies. Implied volatility is derived from the change in an option's premium price and the underlying spot rate over time. For most FX managers and banks, implied volatility is the benchmark of comparison. Firms getting seriously involved in the options market should buy a software package for calculating implied volatilities.

---

24. Packaged Options: The Pros and Cons of Second-Generation Forwards

At an ever-quickening pace, bankers are marketing new instruments for hedging currency risk to their corporate customers. Most of these products, including range, participating, and break forwards, can be viewed as combinations of options designed to create a specific hedge. Based on dozens of corporate interviews, the following checklist highlights the reasons why some treasurers are experimenting with these new tools while others continue to hold back.

The Pros . . .

● **Second-generation forwards are not options.** Although derived from a combination of options, second-generation forwards are not themselves options. Says one finance executive, "All these second-generation forward contracts have one great thing going for them: the name. The 'forward contract' has been the most widely used weapon in the armory of currency risk management products. It seems okay to use a forward, while the 'option' still has connotations of speculative activity."

● **They are administratively convenient.** Even at firms where senior management accepts options, treasurers still face the inconvenience of getting checks cut each time op-

tions are purchased. "It must be reviewed, so it lacks flexibility and causes delays," explains an executive. "By entering into contracts where the fee is not paid up front, we are in a position to take advantage of favorable market opportunities as they become available."

● **Performance-evaluation practices encourage their use.** Some treasurers are attracted to range forwards and other new hedging products because of their firms' policies of measuring hedging performance against the current spot rate rather than the corresponding forward rate. Explains one such treasurer, "When hedging export receivables in a currency selling at a premium in the forward market, I like to have a floor at or very close to the spot rate. By doing so, I ensure that there are no FX losses on these transactions. There could, of course, be gains. Range forwards permit betting on a currency without incurring a loss."

This outlook, however, can be misleading. When the yardstick for comparison is a forward contract instead of spot, hedging with a range forward could result in either a gain or a loss. Unfortunately, many firms persist in making a comparison with the current spot rate because of administrative simplicity, past habits, existing information systems, and so forth.

• **They are easy to use.** To produce the same effect as, say, a range forward, treasurers can construct their own hedge by writing and buying options (a spread strategy). But this do-it-yourself alternative is too cumbersome for some. It involves too many transactions and counterparties and too much effort to monitor trades, maintain variation margins, and keep records on an exponentially growing number of hedge contracts. Says one treasurer, "The beauty of the synthetic contract is its administrative simplicity, customization, flexibility, and novelty. It arouses the intellectual curiosity of my treasury staff and sharpens their analytical skills."

. . . and Cons

• **There are marketing problems.** Like any new product, the new forwards have encountered some initial market resistance. Some managers are frustrated by the terminology of the new products. Others are troubled by what they view as a "used-car salesman" approach by some banks. "In buying any new product, you need a fair amount of advisory support," complains a manager. "I hesitate to trust people who just want a quick deal."

• **The new instruments lack liquidity.** If managers want to unwind contracts before maturity, they will run into a problem with the market's lack of liquidity. Says one manager, "Because these products are customized, I need to go back to the institutions from which I bought them." This "captive market" nature of second-generation forwards means that any unwinding tends to be done at unfavorable off-market prices.

• **Companies' internal systems and procedures are inadequate.** When the European Currency Unit (ECU) first arrived on the scene, managers had to decide whether their internal reports should show a new, separate exposure or whether the new currency's component parts should be unbundled. Similarly, explains one manager, "If we use range forwards, should we have a separate report for that product or should we break it down into constituent puts and calls and include them in the summaries of those puts and calls?"

The lack of liquidity in the new instruments also creates reporting problems. "We periodically mark to market all our hedge contracts for accounting, internal monitoring, and decision-making purposes. The problem with these new contracts is that we don't have readily available on-screen quotations, the way we do for standard products."

• **There are accounting and tax uncertainties.** Sums up one executive, "Accounting and tax professionals are playing 'catchup' with these developing financial products. Our own accounting and tax people are determining the approach we need to take; we don't want to face any uncertainty on these issues."

• **Treasurers fear the unknown.** Are there hidden risks in the new products? Says one manager, "We are worried about the potential control problems stemming from the newness and complexity of these products. If the financial institutions and people at the forefront of product development are having the problems you read about in the press, imagine what could happen in corporate treasuries."

• **Treasurers prefer the do-it-yourself approach.** For some treasurers, the cost savings, and perhaps the excitement of packaging their own hedging solutions, are preferable to buying products off the shelf. "I can create, by combining the basic building blocks, any hedging product to suit my company's risk-return preference," says one treasurer. "By creating these products from basic ingredients, we become less dependent on the outside institutions that sell them, we retain greater flexibility to package them the way we want, and we cut some costs. Basic building blocks have greater standardization and liquidity, and are easier for top management to understand. And the accounting, tax, and systems personnel are familiar with the procedures."

25. How Automation Helps Bacardi Manage Its Option Positions

Bacardi is a leading beverage manufacturer heavily involved in the options markets. The firm's capital director of foreign exchange told BI that he has turned to computers to manage his substantial portfolio of several thousand outstanding options. "Because the number and volume of options contracts have grown so much in the past few years, we scrapped our manual system and purchased software," he said. "The computer allows a much higher level of sophistication in structuring and adjusting our options positions."

Bacardi purchased an options software system developed and marketed by Devon Systems AG. The software runs on IBM or IBM-compatible micros or mainframes or on a DEC VAX mainframe. The company uses the system for a number of activities.

• **To determine the optimal level of hedging.** Unlike a forward contract, the change in the value of an options premium does not always precisely mirror the change in the spot rate. Instead, the change in the value of the premium is always less than or equal to the change in the spot rate. For this reason, an FX manager who wants to cover 100 percent of a foreign currency receivable always buys at least as many put options as the number of underlying receivables.

After taking his initial position, the director adjusts it daily depending on the hedge ratio, a number between 0 and 1 that tells how much the premium changes for a given change in the spot rate. This ratio tells him the "equivalent delaying positions," or how many contracts he should sell or buy given the day's spot rate movement.

Suppose, for example, he wants to cover a £10 million receivable by buying puts. If the hedge ratio is 0.4, his equivalent dealing position is £25 million (10 million divided by 0.4). Dividing 25 million by the lot size of 12,500 yields 2,000—the number of puts he should purchase in order to protect his £10 million position. If the hedge ratio goes to 0.5 the next day, the manager needs only 1,600 contracts (£10 million divided by 0.5 divided by 12,500), so he sells 400. When the option goes into the money, the hedge ratio goes to 1, and he reduces his position to 800 put contracts. "The hedge ratio is a valuable tool we use every day," he said. "It gives us an idea of how effectively we are hedging our underlying currency position."

● **To simulate effects of FX movement.** The system's "what if" function shows how specific currency movements would affect both the FX manager's equivalent dealing position and the profit or loss if he trades in his options. The spokesman explained, "The system gives me an upside and a downside for my positions and a profitability band. If I'm considering a particular trade, I can run it and see how profitable a choice it is."

In a recent position analysis, the director had two outstanding deutsche mark options: He bought a put due to expire in August and sold a put due to expire in March. He wanted to see how a range of deutsche mark movements would affect his equivalent position and the trade-in price of the contracts. To do this, he specified the change in spot movement, a time period, and a volatility factor. He could choose his own volatility factor or use a calculation based on data already in the system (premium, strike price, and maturity of outstanding contracts).

The system told the spokesman that if the deutsche mark depreciated by 0.97 percent overnight, his equivalent position would be a positive Dm23,073. To offset that equivalent position, he should buy Dm23,073 worth of put options.

The system also calculates how spot movements affect option premiums. In the example, if the deutsche mark appreciates 1.97 percent, the system informs the manager that he will make a profit of $896.53 by trading in his contracts. (The system converts deutsche marks to dollars using the forecast spot rate.) That is, he will sell back the put he bought and buy back the put he sold.

● **To account for FX gains and losses.** After a clerk keys in spot exchange rates, the system automatically marks to market each contract for general ledger purposes. "Each morning, after the daily updates are made, I can pull up my positions on the screen and know exactly where I stand."

● **To monitor exposures.** The system tracks exposures across multiple markets and currencies. The director specifies the types of exposure reports he wants to see: total positions by counterparty, currency, or accounting area. Although designed for options, the system also handles the company's forward and futures contracts.

Chapter 4
Using Swaps and Futures to Manage the Balance Sheet

In a few short years, swaps have revolutionized financial management. Built on a simple arbitrage, swaps lower borrowing costs, minimize interest rate risk, and protect against transaction and translation exposure, just to name a few benefits. In short, interest rate and currency swaps are among the most notable innovations in financial market history. Says one experienced treasurer, "If you don't respond to that kind of innovation, you've missed the boat."

This chapter will help to ensure that your company is tapping the enormous potential of the swap markets. It covers everything from the steps necessary to enter the markets and the basics of managing a swap position to the availability of swap-emulating interest rate futures. Finally, the chapter discusses a company's options when the time comes to unwind a swap position.

26. Preparing to Enter the Swap Markets

Whether a manager seeks to reduce financing costs through an interest rate swap or to hedge balance-sheet exposure through a currency swap, the first step is to know the rules of the marketplace. To help firms find a cost-effective swap-market strategy, the following checklist shows the key steps necessary before entering the market.

(1) Define your objectives. Swaps are a powerful tool with profound balance-sheet and cash flow effects. Before entering any swap, a firm must know precisely what it is trying to accomplish and be aware of any risks embedded in the strategy. Bank strategists are a valuable source of advice regarding swap decisions, but firms must insist that the advantages as well as the risks be clearly defined. A suitable swap strategy can then be implemented in accord with the firm's own risk appetite.

(2) Organize your documentation. Documenting a swap is time-consuming; a firm poorly prepared for this step may miss out on more than a few good deals. Before a firm puts itself on the market, it should obtain copies of standard agreements (banks are normally more than happy to provide relevant documents).

Swap contracts typically take two forms: the International Swap Dealers' Association (ISDA) and the British Bankers' Association Interest Rate Swap (BBAIRS) versions. Many firms have gone to the trouble of writing their own contracts, but it speeds the negotiation process to simply use ISDA or BBAIRS documents.

The contracts (approximately five pages each) define the specific workings of the swap, including calculation and settlement of interest payments. For example, the contracts specify that if fixed- and variable-rate payment dates coincide, the payments can be netted. Other clauses cover late payments, withholding taxes, representations and warranties, provisions for termination, and remedies in the event of default or supervening of legality. No filings are necessary, and usually no covenants are required.

The next step is to get together with corporate counsel and carefully determine which clauses are acceptable and, more important, which are not. Once your firm is familiar with the standard documentation, it can proceed rapidly with swap negotiation.

(3) Carefully select who will see your deals. The swap market has become so competitive that companies are tempted to show their deals to a group of banks or even a swap broker to facilitate bidding. While this can be an effective strategy in certain instances, it is best to weigh market conditions prior to making such a move.

Before deciding how aggressively a deal should be shown, a firm must examine the market's relative appetite for fixed- and floating-rate debt. If the market is currently over-booked with takers of the same structure you are seeking, you will need a bank with which you have close relations to achieve a competitive price; stick with one or two line banks. But if you want to swap into debt that has few takers on the market, your position is highly valued; in this case, competitive bidding can often result in savings of several basis points (see Checklist 27 for how to benefit from using a broker).

(4) Be aware that not all deals are made as principal. Dealing with banks that are brokering a deal can often result in on-again, off-again deals—deals in which the ultimate counterparty is not totally committed. While being open to all transactions can often result in cost savings, not all firms feel the added potential hassle is cost-effective.

(5) Get your timing right . . . When swap timing is not critical, it is often advantageous to wait for market windows. For example, companies can ask their line bankers to keep them in mind when a large multiparty swap is about to close. A firm that is ready to act quickly (having documentation in order is critical here) can often take advantage of the counterparties' eagerness to close.

As one swap veteran put it, "You can have a situation where someone has a $100 million bond issue and they have $80 million in counterparties lined up. The $20 million that closes the deal will probably do better than the $80 million."

(6) . . . and be flexible. The best way to get a good deal is to provide the market with what it needs—not exactly with what you need. For example, a firm may be looking to swap $20 million fixed into three-year floating. However, to close the dollar interest rate portion of a currency swap, a bank may be looking for $18.3 million for two years, nine months. By accepting the bank's less than standard structure, a firm can often glean three or four basis points or more in pricing advantage.

Insisting on a specific amount or maturity can also set a firm up to suffer the fate experienced by a major U.S. MNC. The firm entered the market insistent on swapping into a targeted fixed rate or not swapping at all. Eventually, the company was forced to fold into a higher rate three months and a few near-deals later. As a consequence, the firm lost thousands of dollars in opportunity costs as its floating-rate funding costs rose relative to those of the earlier available swap rate.

Firms need to evaluate their portfolio to determine just how aggressive they should be. For example, a firm with a high ratio of floating-1 to fixed-rate debt is more vulnerable to interest rate swings. In a volatile market, this firm probably cannot afford to be as aggressive as a firm with a smaller floating-rate exposure.

27. Weighing the Cost of Using a Broker

Using brokers to execute off-balance-sheet transactions such as swaps offers a number of advantages. At the same time, brokers introduce a number of added costs and complications. Managers should consider the following points when deciding whether or not to use a broker.

● **Brokers can identify the most aggressive pricing in the market.** Top brokers are in touch with upward of 100 banks daily. This enables them to identify quickly which banks are offering the most aggressive pricing across the spectrum.

● **Managers can use broker bids as leverage.** While brokers can obtain excellent pricing, some firms prefer to use them only as a source of leverage. A firm can find the best bid from among its line banks and then show the bid to a broker. If the broker can top the price, the firm will show the broker's bid to its banks—which are then inclined to match it. Only if the bank does not come back with a sweeter offer will the firm use the broker.

● **Brokers can be useful for market information.** Most brokers are only too happy to offer treasurers a "run" of current market prices, which they can then use any way they choose.

● **There is an up-front fee.** The advantages of using a broker must be weighed against the costs. First of all, brokers charge an up-front commission on swap deals. While this is not an excessive cost, it does create a problem in terms of selling the deal to management. Some are "fundamentally opposed to paying an up-front premium on a swap," says one U.S. fast-food company treasurer. "That's something for which we need board approval." Others care less. "I will do the deal with whoever gives me the lowest all-in cost at an acceptable risk," says a Canadian treasury manager. "If that means an up-front payment, so what?"

● **See where your all-in cost lands.** A single basis point can, in some cases, reduce a brokered deal's pricing advantage in comparison with that of a bank. Therefore, it is necessary that a brokered deal be below competing bids by at least two basis points.

28. How to Devise an Overall Swap Management Strategy

Companies that have made strong forays into the swap markets have often been pleased with the results of individual transactions. But having a significant portfolio of swaps on the books requires the development of a specialized set of techniques for management. Some of the following swap management strategies are drawn from the experience of the treasury management team of Sallie Mae (Student Loan Marketing Association), one of the leaders in utilizing innovative capital market instruments. They should help managers tailor a strategy to their own needs.

● **Analyze the risk of each swap individually.** Each swap added to a portfolio has unique risks associated with the transaction. Rating agencies can be strongly relied on to provide reports useful in analyzing a swap. But it is also important to conduct an internal review, looking at financial ratios and company statements going back five years. Although a laundry list of requirements is not necessary, a general assessment of the impact a particular swap transaction would have on the potential counterparty's business and balance sheet is important. In some cases, collateral should be requested to offset a less than sufficient credit rating.

● **Diversify portfolio risk.** Portfolio risk cannot be ignored, and managers should carefully diversify their swap portfolios as much as possible in order to minimize counterparty risk. Sallie Mae's treasury team manages over 200 separate counterparty contracts in its portfolio. "If we had a $300 million financing to hedge, instead of taking all the counterparty risk in one swap we would look to divide it up in pieces," explains the capital markets manager. "We might have pieces of $20 million, $30 million, or even $100 million. That would spread our risk among various counterparties, so we wouldn't be exposed to just one institution."

To cut down on the risk of difficulties affecting the financial soundness of a particular sector, a portfolio can be diversified by industry as well. "You wouldn't want to have all of your swaps with one type of counterparty—like savings and loans, for example," says the manager. "You would be more diversified by doing part of a swap with an S&L, part with a bank, and part with an insurance company or some other corporate issuer."

● **Apply tougher standards to currency swaps than to interest rate swaps.** Because currency swaps add foreign exchange risk to interest rate risk, a higher credit rating from currency swap counterparties should be standard policy. This is especially true for companies that do not have a natural need for a particular currency included in the swap. In these cases, a company has no ready access to foreign exchange with which to cover itself if problems with the swap arise.

● **Monitor swap values at all times.** Even after a swap contract is signed, counterparties should be monitored regularly for any financial problems that might appear. "Once we have done a swap with somebody, we don't just forget about it," says the manager. "We continue to watch it to see if there are any problems we can head off at the pass, so to speak."

● **If problems do occur, ask for collateral.** For Sallie Mae, "heading them off at the pass" can involve demanding collateral somewhere down the road. In some cases, a clause in the contract can be invoked forcing the counterparty to provide collateral if its net worth falls below a certain level. Other options include buying down the obligation from the counterparty or reassigning the swap, though these solutions may be costly and difficult to arrange.

● **Be careful about relying on protective clauses in your swap contract.** Companies must exercise a great deal of caution in relying on legal clauses in swap contracts, such as early termination provisions. If they are faced with a potential breach of a swap contract by their counterparty, such provisions may provide only minimal protection. Only a few cases have come before the courts, and those have not completely clarified pertinent laws. In the near future, some of the uncertainties under U.S. law may be resolved by the courts or removed by legislation. But now the risks must be analyzed with care both when a contract is drafted and if a counterparty bankruptcy occurs. This will help a company avoid invoking clauses that a court may refuse to enforce and thus incurring potentially significant and unrecoverable costs.

29. The Exposure Benefits of Currency Swaps

One of the most effective ways for MNCs to benefit from the swap market is by creating an efficient hedge of balance-sheet exposure. According to one treasurer, swaps offer "an effective strategy for reducing our translation exposure at little cash cost."

In the past, MNCs tried to hedge balance-sheet exposure with foreign currency borrowings. However, interviews with MNC managers and bank swap dealers indicate five reasons to favor currency swaps.

(1) Swaps are easier. Once an MNC becomes comfortable with a swaps program, additional swaps are no big deal. According to one New York bank's swaps dealer, "The way Euromarket deals are run requires much more in the way of approvals. We can do a swap with a phone call."

One major U.S. MNC's policy is to run most swap deals as needed, up to the authorized borrowing level. The treasury manager need only inform the CFO and treasurer of his intention; rarely are the deals questioned.

Moreover, the firm's board of directors is also familiar with the company's swaps program and is informed of deals only on an after-the-fact basis.

(2) Swaps give firms more room for price maneuvering. Swaps, being less involved, give firms more flexibility in timing. Since deals can be done the same day over the phone, firms are able to choose from among the best rates. Says the assistant treasurer for a major U.S. foods conglomerate, "We can choose the day, we can choose the price. If the market isn't going our way, we can come back some other time." In the Euromarkets, however, "We are far less likely to be afforded the luxury of saying, 'let's back off the deal.' "

The treasury manager at another MNC says his firm swap shops as well. The firm often calls its bankers asking for a quote. If the manager likes the rate, he does the deal. More often, the manager has found that the banks have given in and come back to him with a better price.

An effective price strategy for many MNCs is to use a swaps broker. This will help firms attain the lowest pricing available in the market at any given time. "Treasurers normally call two or three banks to get a price," explains a New York-based swaps broker. But each morning, the broker is in touch with over 200 banks. "That means that with a phone call, you can see exactly where the market is; we are the market."

Firms may still be able to get a better deal from banks with which they have a relationship. But as the assistant treasurer explains, "We can sometimes use the brokers to give [our banks] a little nudge."

(3) Swaps have less detailed documentation. Euroissues, with their more involved approval process, require more documentation. Not only does this slow the process, but it significantly increases documentation costs. According to a New York investment bank's swap dealer, for smaller deals, "swaps are definitely less involved, and clearly less expensive in terms of documentation."

But that is not to say that there are no difficulties. The New York swap broker explains, "There is no set documentation standard." The lack of standardization limits the fungibility of swaps—and therefore their flexibility—but "this is something that will work itself out."

(4) Swaps have more appeal—courtesy of U.S. tax reform. In cases where the parent is better known than the subsidiary needing a hedge, Euromarket borrowings are normally run from the parent's books to pare basis points. However, under the U.S. tax regulations, such borrowings have the effect of lowering foreign-sourced income in countries where such an effect might not be desired. To avoid unwanted tax consequences, firms have to issue in the name of the subsidiary. However, this may adversely affect pricing. This cost consideration may steer firms one step closer to a swaps program.

(5) Swaps keep the balance sheet light. Foreign currency borrowings do offset translation exposure. However, borrowings load up both the asset (increased cash) and liability (increased debt) sides of the balance sheet. This so-called balance-sheet ballooning can have some undesired effects on financial ratios; ratios adversely affected include return on assets and debt/equity.

30. Six Ways to Manage Liabilities with Forward Swaps

While currency swaps can improve FX management, interest rate swaps are ideal for interest rate risk. One of the most intriguing forms—and a particularly effective instrument for today's circumstances—is the forward swap.

Forward swaps should be treated as an integral part of a firm's overall debt management strategy. In a forward swap, all the terms of the transaction are set today, but the actual swap commences on a predetermined date some years in the future. To use forward swaps, managers need to develop a strategy based on either an interest rate outlook or the firm's sensitivity to refinancing risk. The scenario should be expressed in three bands—low, high, and medium interest rates. In general, if rates move up to the higher band, the firm will want to shorten its liabilities. If rates drop to the lower band, it will want to lengthen its liabilities.

Using these interest rate bands, managers can define target rates for entering into a forward swap arrangement. For example, when rates are poised to edge up, managers with short-term debt taken at higher rates should have a target interest rate that they consider the bottom of the cycle. At this rate, they can use a forward swap to lengthen the duration of their liabilities. Says a banker with extensive forward swap experience, "Those that have very long maturities should have a target in mind at which they think rates are high enough to shorten maturities. At that target they should consider using a forward swap to convert swaps that were fixed at lower levels to sub-LIBOR funding."

While forward swaps can be used in a wide variety of situations, there are six basic scenarios.

(1) To fix the cost today of funds needed tomorrow. Often managers can anticipate a future funding (or refunding) need. Rather than waiting until the funds are actually required and exposing themselves to the risk that interest rates will rise in the meantime, managers can enter into a forward swap to set their costs now. For example, forward swaps can be used to lock in a refinancing rate on an unswapped callable or maturing bond. If future borrowing needs are less than anticipated, the swaps can be reversed or terminated for a cash settlement.

(2) To reduce refinancing risk by smoothing out the debt maturity schedule. Managers are sometimes faced with the danger of too much debt maturing all at once or too soon. For example, suppose a firm has the following maturity schedule: 1991, $250 million; 1993, $150 million; 1995, $75 million. By arranging a $100 million forward swap commencing in 1991 and maturing in 1993, the effective maturity structure could be converted to this: 1991, $150 million; 1993, $150 million; 1995, $175 million.

The forward swap period would require a new underlying liability starting in 1991, but the interest rate would be set today. So the restructuring would lock in today's low rates for an extended period of time while reducing the risk the borrower would face by having to refinance over 50 percent of its fixed-rate debt in the same year. The alternatives—such as waiting until 1991, taking out a $100 million four-year bond, and using the proceeds to pay down part of the expiring debt—would expose the firm to interest rate movements between 1989 and 1991.

(3) To lengthen debt maturities in low-rate periods. While the two strategies discussed above are for hedging, forward swaps can also be used to manage debt actively by taking advantage of rate cycles. Rather than refinancing a high-cost liability by acquiring new debt, and thus incurring call costs or (if the new debt is taken before the old debt expires) investment carrying costs, firms can use a forward swap to extend an existing liability at a lower rate.

The technique works this way: When rates are high, a firm issues fixed-rate debt at short maturities. Then, when rates come down, it uses a forward swap to effectively lengthen the maturity of the outstanding debt to its target maturity while taking advantage of the lower rates. For example, when rates were topping out at 14 percent, one firm, though interested in seven-year debt, took out a three-year fixed-rate bond. Two years later, when rates had come down, the firm took out a forward swap at about 9 percent and in effect extended the liability's maturity to seven years.

Note that the firm lengthens the maturity of its interest rate risk, not of the specific funding. The actual mechanics are similar to those of the first strategy listed above, but the purpose and strategy are more aggressive. While setting its interest rate costs in advance with the forward swap, the firm could cash out of the swap and refund the three-year liability when it retires with a four-year bond. It could achieve the same goal by issuing floating-rate debt and using the forward swap to convert it to fixed.

(4) To shorten debt maturities in high-rate periods. This strategy requires early planning but yields the reward of sub-LIBOR funding. When rates bottom out, the firm should issue a 10-year fixed-rate liability (either a bond or swap) at, say, 8 percent. Then, two years later, when rates appear to be topping out or are at the top of the firm's target bands, it can do a reverse-forward swap commencing three years before the original maturity date. Instead of paying 8 percent fixed, the firm receives fixed—but at, perhaps, 10 percent due to the general increase in rates—for the forward period (i.e., years 7 to 10) and earns a 200-basis-point spread.

The firm still has fixed-rate debt, but because rates are now high, it has effectively cut the 10-year maturity to 7 years. Since the swap is paying 10 percent fixed versus 8 percent on the original bond, the end result is LIBOR less 200 basis points for the last three years of funding. Australia's TNT, for example, used a forward swap to reduce a seven-year issue to five years at 185 basis points below LIBOR.

(5) To fix the forward take-down schedule of a floating-rate loan. This is an increasingly popular technique for construction and real estate financing. Consider a firm that takes out a $350 million seven-year loan with an 18-month forward take-down schedule required. The firm must borrow floating and then swap into fixed. However, if it waits for two years before swapping the entire amount, it is exposed to interest rate risk before the 6-, 12-, and 18-month drawdowns.

By taking out a series of forward swaps, one commencing at the beginning of each six-month period, the firm can lock in the amount of funding it has drawn down to that point. Some 20–30 forward swaps have been done in this way.

(6) To do all of the above with a forward currency swap. While forward currency swaps are much less common than forward interest rate swaps, they can be very attractive. While unwilling to divulge the details, Security Pacific managed a forward currency swap for PKBanken that generated LIBOR minus 515 basis points.

31. How to Price a Forward Swap

Brokers, bankers, and corporate managers have taken a more cautious approach to the market in forward interest rate swaps recently. To help managers calculate a fair price for these instruments, BI spoke with an expert from Euro Brokers. What follows is a presentation of Euro Brokers' market-based model (using the Hewlett-Packard 12C calculator) for pricing forward swaps.

Brokers and banks are only too happy to quote a rate on a forward swap. In order to fathom their idea of a "fair" price, however, managers must understand the financiers' pricing rationale. As one corporate manager told BI, "There's always the fear that if you're not certain what's going on—how things are priced—you're going to get ripped off."

For the banks, a forward swap is essentially a straight swap with a missing counterparty for the near period. Covering the loss of this counterparty represents a loss for the institution and must therefore be reflected in the swap price. So in addition to the normal swap pricing, the purchaser of the forward swap must expect to pay a premium equal to the time-adjusted cash flow losses incurred by the bank when "standing in" for the missing counterparty.

For example, suppose an MNC wants to stay in floating rates for the next three years but pay fixed rates in years four through seven. To achieve this structure, a firm would need to enter what bankers call a "four-year fixed swap with a three-year forward start."

To build this swap, the financial institution would combine two known swaps: a seven-year floating-to-fixed swap and a three-year fixed-to-floating swap (the latter would be designed to cover the counterparty loss). In the first swap, the bank would be a fixed-rate receiver for seven years. In the second, the bank would arrange to pay a fixed rate for three years—essentially standing in for the missing counterparty. For example, the relevant swap prices (in terms of the bank) are as follows:

	Treasury yield	AAA spread	Pay fixed	Receive fixed
3-year	7.43%	72–77	8.15	8.20
7-year	8.10	86–90	8.96	9.00

Six-month LIBOR: 7.0%

Source: *BIMR* '88, p. 96, provided by Euro Brokers.

The actual spread must be adjusted to account for creditworthiness.

The problem, however, is that one counterparty is missing—the fixed-rate payer in years one, two, and three. Therefore, the bank will require that it be compensated for the loss of cash flow represented by the 85 basis points over three years (i.e., 8.15–9 percent).

Pricing this forward interest rate swap is a matter of constructing a series of cash flow time lines. Using conventionally accepted notation, the numbers above the line are cash payouts; those below the line, receipts. To begin, the seven-year deal may be shown as follows:

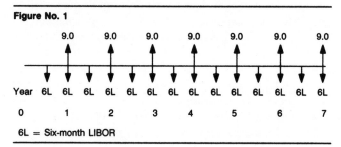

Figure No. 1

6L = Six-month LIBOR

The three-year deal would appear as follows:

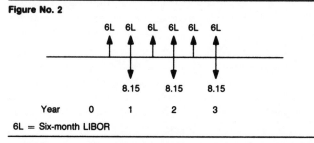

Figure No. 2

6L = Six-month LIBOR

When the diagrams are combined, the LIBOR receipts and payments in years one, two, and three cancel out, resulting in a net cost of 0.85 percent. This diagram represents the cash flows the bank would expect to receive from entering the two plain-vanilla swaps:

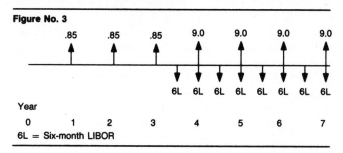

Figure No. 3

6L = Six-month LIBOR

However, the corporate customer wants no cash flow consequences in years one, two, and three—in other words, a three-year forward start. Therefore, the cash flow for the corporation would be equal to that of the final four years of the seven-year deal, adjusted by the net costs incurred by the bank in years one, two, and three. This is the desired (but unknown) swap rate (represented as i):

Figure No. 4

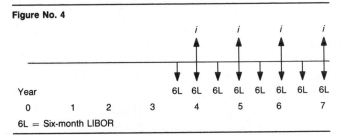

6L = Six-month LIBOR

In an efficient marketplace, the cash flows depicted in Figure No. 3 should be equal to those of Figure No. 4 on a net present value (NPV) basis.

Therefore, the NPV in Figure No. 3 minus the NPV in Figure No. 4 should be equal to zero. The result would look like this:

Figure No. 5

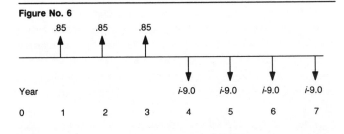

This can be more conveniently shown as the following:

Figure No. 6

The requirement now is to calculate i, where the NPV of Figure No. 6 is equal to zero. This problem can be readily solved with the HP 12C. The first step is to convert the time diagram in Figure No. 6 into a format recognizable to the calculator. Let CF stand for "cash flow." Cash flows one, two, and three are acceptable as they are. However, cash flows four through seven require a simple arithmetical adjustment (as shown):

CF0 = 0	CF4 = $-(i - 9.0) = (9.0 - i)$
CF1 = .85	CF5 = $(9.0 - i)$
CF2 = .85	CF6 = $(9.0 - i)$
CF3 = .85	CF7 = $(9.0 - i)$

Now the task is a relatively simple calculation. The machine is used to calculate the NPV of Figure No. 6 for various values of i. When the NPV is equal to zero, the swap rate i represents a fair market-determined price.

To perform the iteration, begin by guessing the swap rate i. For this example, an initial estimate of 9.5 percent is used. Note that the fixed rate on the seven-year swap, minus the estimate, is the equivalent of cash flows four through seven. (A grid like the one used below is useful.) After estimating i, enter the cash flows into the HP 12C:

f, CLx	clears financial registers
0, g, CF0	enters CF0 (from the table above)
.85, g, CFj	enters CF1
3, g, Nj	repetitive entry for CF1, CF2, CF3
.5, CHS, g, CFj	enters CF4 (9.0 − 9.5 = −.5)
4, g, Nj	repetitive entry for CF4, CF5, CF6, CF7
9.5, i	enters the swap rate estimate
f, NPV	solves for NPV

If the NPV is positive, then i is too low a guess. If the NPV is negative, then i is too high a guess. Adjust cash flows four through seven and i accordingly, and continue to force the absolute value of the NPV closer to zero.

The complete iteration for the swap in this example is shown in the grid below. The final estimate for i results in an NPV of −.001, implying that 9.885 percent is a fair price for the four-year fixed-rate swap with a three-year forward start.

i	9.0 − i	NPV	Comments
9.5%	−.5	.91	NPV is positive; guess higher
10.5	−1.5	−1.39	NPV is negative; guess lower
9.9	−.9	−.4	NPV is negative but close; guess slightly lower
9.875	−.875	.02	Guess higher
9.88	−.88	.01	Guess higher
9.885	−.885	−.001	NPV is sufficiently close to zero; i is the market rate

While the steps depicted above are rather tricky at first, they can be quickly mastered. In any case, the cost of not making the effort—and perhaps taking a swap market bath in the process—far outweighs the cost of learning. Also note that if pricing forward swaps becomes a habit in the office, these steps can be easily programmed. Further, there are a number of iterative procedures that can greatly speed the process.

32. Using Futures to Emulate the Swap

The swap is not the only method of manipulating the yield curve. Corporations can use interest rate futures the same way as interest rate swaps to convert fixed-rate liabilities to floating rates and vice versa. For example, to switch from fixed to floating rates, a company would buy futures. If rates fall as anticipated, the price of the futures contract rises (prices on the most common futures—Eurodollars and T-bills—are quoted as 100 minus the annual interest rate on the underlying instrument; other futures are quoted differently). The end result is that the loss on the fixed-rate debt is offset by the gain on the futures position. Conversely, to move from floating to fixed rates, a company would sell futures.

But corporate managers have never responded to interest rate futures the way developers of this product initially hoped. This is principally because futures are liquid only up to two years. Nevertheless, interest rate futures can be a powerful tool, particularly when combined with an overall swap program. Corporate managers who currently shy away from the instruments should consider the following applications.

(1) **Reverse swaps or portions of swaps.** Futures can be used to counteract the undesired effect of a swap or to delay the effective date of a swap's implementation. By running the short end of a swap into the futures market, a company can effectively create its own forward swap.

This is exactly what Mattel did. The firm knew it faced refinancing risk on a portion of its debt in a par. It wanted to swap out of the risk to take advantage of the current low-rate environment. Instead of going to a bank for a forward swap that would have fixed the cost of the refinancing, the firm created its own. It entered into a long-dated swap and then reversed the first year by buying futures. "It was exactly how the bank would have done it," says the firm's assistant treasurer. "We saved some basis points by doing it ourselves."

(2) **Use futures where the swap market is illiquid.** Most managers see the swap market as a longer-term financing tool. However, by looking at futures as a short-term swap, a number of new applications are immediately available.

For example, futures can be used to hedge inventory carrying costs—a short-term exposure. Firms are exposed in two ways on inventories: on the selling price of the goods and on the interest rate. Commodities firms are especially vulnerable in this area, since the price of their underlying product changes daily in the cash markets of the exchanges.

In general, the spread between the future price of a good and today's price will change if interest rates change. But that change is not necessarily correlated on a one-to-one basis because the current price of the good is also fluctuat-ing. "If I want to protect myself from the interest rate side of that," says the assistant treasurer of the commodities firm Archer Daniels Midland, "I might sell the corresponding amount of Eurodollar futures, depending on the prevailing price of the product."

(3) **Cover short-term risks while looking for a long-term hedge.** The futures market is open to everyone; the swap market may not be. Union Carbide found that out when it was looking to shift a portion of its fixed-rate debt to floating-rate debt to take advantage of a falling rate environment. With its credit rating suffering, "finding counterparties was difficult," says the manager of foreign exchange risk. "The negotiation process was dragging out because of their credit concerns."

As the search for counterparties continued, the firm was left with its debt exposed. It bought futures to hedge in the interim. "We did a few million dollars in futures while we were canvassing the swap market," says the manager. Eventually counterparties presented themselves, and the firm hedged its position through the swap market.

(4) **Hedge bond-issuance risks.** Companies can sell interest rate futures to hedge the risk of adverse price movements during the time it takes to bring a debt issue to market. This is one of the most common futures applications for corporations, according to some futures brokers. "If we write some short-term debt Friday morning, it's difficult to get it done in the afternoon," says the AVP and capital markets director for Sallie Mae (Student Loan Marketing Association). "We have used T-bill and Eurodollar futures to protect ourselves over the weekend."

(5) **Emulate periodic interest rate readjustments.** Firms can use futures to fix the cost of a floating-rate obligation before the rate readjustment takes place. Similarly, they can lock in borrowing rates before the actual borrowing takes place, effectively creating their own forward rate agreement (FRA).

The Federal National Mortgage Association (Fannie Mae), for example, knows it will be in the markets monthly but faces exposure due to the delay between its commitment to buy an asset (i.e., a residential mortgage on the secondary market) and the actual purchase. Since it typically raises funds right before purchase, the firm sells interest rate futures to lock in the cost of its eventual borrowing. It primarily uses futures on 10-year Treasury notes, since it raises long-term funds. Says Fannie Mae's VP asset/liability manager, "The note futures mirror the changes in our funding costs more closely." Fannie Mae is in a special situation. It faces a very short-term set of exposures since its assets fluctuate with the weekly resetting of the 91-day T-bill rate.

Sallie Mae has also used futures for this purpose, but only when there was no alternative. In some cases, Sallie Mae has needed the rate on a debt to vary over a shorter period of time to match its assets. "We can synthesize a weekly reset by doing a strip of T-bill futures and rolling out of a certain number of contracts each week," explains a Sallie Mae capital markets director. Thus if the firm has a rate that will readjust every six months and that it wants to reset every week for the 26 weeks of the period, it would sell the corresponding amount of futures and close out 1/26th of its position each week.

(6) Negotiate prices of derivative bank products. Futures are the raw material from which bankers mold a number of packaged risk management products. By knowing how these products are put together, a company may be able to strike a better deal with its bank when it sits down to negotiate pricing. "With any derivative product, there's a range of prices at which it can be sold," says Union Carbide's manager of FX risk. "We have used the futures market to check the bank's prices and as a negotiating tool."

He admits, however, that the calculation may not be as straightforward as comparing the bank's price for the product with the price of the equivalent transactions in the futures market. "Pricing of the alternative futures transaction is very subjective," he cautions. "Do we want to spend the kind of time and effort necessary to manage the futures position knowing that we probably aren't as skilled in doing so as the banks?"

33. Equal Time: The Drawbacks of Interest Rate Futures

While interest rate futures can add a great deal of flexibility to a company's risk management program, companies have not been avid users of this instrument to date. Before interest rate futures can become part of a company's risk management portfolio, five principal problems need to be addressed.

(1) Futures are an administrative hassle. Unless a company's transaction volume is above a certain threshold, the expense of running a futures position may not be justified. Futures involve many variables, are complicated to use, and require a fair amount of time to understand and implement. Their maturities are set by the exchange and may not mesh with a company's debt profile. One of the main reasons Fannie Mae uses Treasury note futures to hedge its borrowings is that the simpler products, like forward rate agreements, are not available to it. "We're just too big," explains the VP asset/liability manager. "The bank forward market is not a viable technique for us."

For many companies, swaps are a better choice for interest rate risk management because they are much easier to maintain. Says British Petroleum's divisional manager of treasury, who has dabbled, "It is quite a troublesome business to deal in the futures market, compared with some of the alternative ways of obtaining our objectives."

(2) Bank derivatives abound. Given what one treasurer calls "the mess" of managing a futures position, many managers prefer the derivative products offered by banks for short-term interest rate risk management. "In the corporate world of risk management, you're getting many projects thrust in front of you at once," says Union Carbide's manager of FX risk. "It may be beneficial to pay the bank a premium to get a nice product without all the noise around it."

Moreover, some bank products are priced very aggressively to attract corporate business. Admits one futures broker, "If I were a company, I'd look at the market real hard before I went to all the trouble just to save the couple of basis points that the bank charges."

Other futures brokers, however, argue that the derivatives are not as hands-off as they may appear. "Even with bank instruments, you have to be on top of their value if you're going to manage your position correctly," says the director of financial futures and options at the Canadian merchant bank Burns, Fry Ltd. "Why not go directly to the markets yourself?"

(3) Futures affect cash flow. Part of the exchange's role in a futures transaction is to cut out counterparty risk. It does this by requiring that participants post a performance bond and mark their positions to market daily. Companies therefore have to lay aside some cash to play the futures market and meet daily margin calls.

(4) Futures are an imperfect hedge. Despite the high liquidity of the futures market, futures prices may not move exactly in tandem with actual interest rates—a phenomenon called "basis risk." That means the number of contracts that are needed to precisely offset gains or losses from rate movements can vary.

Basis risk may not be a big problem given the kinds of short-term hedging operations most companies execute with futures. "If it's a couple of days, basis risk is bad but not intolerable," says Sallie Mae's AVP and capital markets director. "If you're dealing with a large amount of money for a month or more, then it can really hurt you."

In Union Carbide's case, the benefits of moving even partially from fixed to floating rates made the risk acceptable. "We were in a falling rate environment with too much fixed exposure," says the FX manager. "So even though the basis risk was there, we could tolerate it under these conditions."

(5) Futures are frightening. Many proponents of futures say the main reason corporations have been reluctant to participate is simply because of psychological obstacles. A walk through a Chicago trading floor can deter a good number of treasury managers. In addition, futures have a sullied reputation. Old wives' tales about people losing their shirt in the futures market or ending up with a boxcar of pork bellies have kept some corporate treasurers and many corporate boards from embracing the futures market. "It may be irrational," admits one treasury manager, "but it's no less a hurdle."

34. When It Is Time, How to Unwind Your Swap

A few years ago, terminating a swap was an unusual operation. But as the swap markets have grown in sophistication, corporate managers have begun to look at swaps as a much more flexible commodity product. The financial manager at a major U.S. MNC emphasizes that swap positions today are meant to be managed. Instead of allowing a loss position to continue growing, "you can eliminate it or reduce it by unwinding; just don't let it sit there," he says.

The following checklist provides some options and guidelines for companies ready to adjust or unwind their swap contracts.

● **Enter into a reciprocal swap transaction.** A swap can effectively be neutralized by entering into another swap transaction that is a reciprocal of the original. While this technique solves cash flow problems, it also adds more credit risk to a company's balance sheet because it increases the number of swap counterparties the company has.

● **Unwind the swap.** When a swap is unwound, it is taken completely off the books. Unwinding has a strong appeal to many corporate treasurers, since it reduces the company's total credit risk. "There is a structural advantage to canceling a swap," says the managing director for capital markets operations at Bankers Trust International in London. "It's obviously a lot cleaner." Unwinding can be reasonably cheap as well: Offering an up-front payment to the forgiving counterparty may cost less than the total cash payments made by sticking to the swap. To unwind, though, swappers need their counterparty's cooperation, which is not always forthcoming.

● **Reverse the swap.** Another alternative is to enter a reciprocal swap, and then, if all parties agree, unwind the first swap, leaving the third-party swap partner with your original contract. Unfortunately, reversing a swap by taking on a so-called mirror swap adds a new credit risk and loads up the balance sheet if the swap cannot be passed along to the third party. It also demands extra monitoring. Like unwinding a swap, it involves the difficulty of convincing the original and reverse-swap counterparties to cooperate

(most swap contracts stipulate the right of first refusal for any reassignment). "Many big companies are already up to their necks in exposure to each other and may not want to take on additional credit risk," says one corporate financial manager.

● **Use a bank to ease the process.** Because finding a new counterparty can be so difficult, firms often turn to major banks that manage large swap portfolios. These banks have sophisticated hedging mechanisms that can easily provide unwinding and reversal options for many difficult corporate swaps. Says the Bankers Trust spokesman, "I don't think it costs any more to do a reversal than it does to do any other swap." However, some banks take advantage of this predicament and hold clients for ransom in these deals, knowing that the clients' only alternative is the painful process of finding a counterparty themselves.

● **Sell a profitable swap.** Owning a profitable swap is clearly a happier situation than figuring out how to get out of a losing venture. Managers with a profitable swap can either sit tight or sell it at a premium, especially if its underlying purpose (e.g., a hedged debt) no longer exists. Profitable swaps can also be sold to help reduce the cost of a planned financing. Bankers Trust helped one client do just this through a swap reversal. Instead of keeping the swap and arranging an additional private placement, the spokesman convinced his client to sell the first swap at a premium and enter a new swap, locking in an attractive fixed rate that would hedge the new financing. "What [the manager] avoided was borrowing more money and seeing his balance sheet balloon up," he said. "He also got money at about 70 or 80 basis points less than he would have paid in the market."

● **Don't forget about the underlying exposure after bailing out.** While interest rate shifts are important, managers must remember that when swaps are unloaded, concern must also be focused on the resulting unhedged debt. This may need to be covered through a new swap or another hedging instrument, or possibly eliminated as debt and turned into equity.

Chapter 5
Gaining Maximum Advantage from Global Capital Markets

The deregulation of major international money and capital markets has freed MNCs from the confines of domestic markets. Increasingly, companies are tapping investors worldwide to meet their funding requirements. In addition, financial executives today have a vast array of sophisticated and complex arrangements from which to choose, all designed to take advantage of investor preferences and arbitrage opportunities in different markets.

To help companies derive maximum advantage from the world's capital markets, this chapter's checklists show how the most innovative firms are responding to today's global marketplace. In addition, they describe how sophisticated financial managers evaluate and select from among the plethora of available instruments.

35. How Innovators Tap Global Capital Markets

The explosion of capital markets activity has created a wealth of new opportunities and instruments. These can help companies reduce financing costs and risks. Even so, a sound debt-management strategy must underlie a firm's tactical approach to the capital markets. Below, two firms with well-earned reputations as innovative players—Student Loan Marketing Association (Sallie Mae) and PepsiCo—outline seven maxims for success.

(1) **Stay open-minded.** Opportunities frequently occur in faraway corners of the global marketplace. Innovative issuers take a global approach to the capital markets, seeking optimal funding opportunities anywhere they can. "We believe that the broader the spread of our investor base, the better off the investor base as a whole," says PepsiCo's deputy treasurer.

However, tapping so many varied sources of funds means that companies cannot adhere to any programmed method of issuing. In fact, the philosophy almost necessitates a one-solution-at-a-time approach. Caution should not scare companies away from new concepts. "The key in a lot of these markets is to strike quickly," says the CFO of Sallie Mae. "We won't say no for the sake of saying no."

Such a philosophy also requires that deals be tailored to the individual markets. Innovative issuers are offered a virtually never-ending stream of potential deals, but they almost always need minor adjustments. "You have to twist them a little," one treasurer says. A case in point was PepsiCo's solution to the domestic Swiss market. There are a lot of Swiss franc investors who by law can invest only in Swiss franc securities; they cannot buy dollar-denominated bonds. When it was seen that Swiss investors would support a dual-currency issue, PepsiCo and Credit Suisse structured a deal to meet their currency requirements. The result was a $400 million, Swiss franc-denominated, reverse dual-currency bond—the largest domestic issue ever launched in Switzerland.

Sallie Mae's pioneering issue of yield curve notes exemplifies the same philosophy. Yield curve notes pay a higher coupon as interest rates come down. "It's very logical," says the CFO. "If straight floating-rate securities are a bear market instrument, then maybe the reverse is a bull market instrument." Sallie Mae then entered into a series of swaps to trade the notes' LIBOR risk for a 91-day Treasury-based liability. In the end, the firm's novel yield curve note concept produced cheap funds.

A month later, the CFO saw a research paper that presented a series of elaborate mathematical formulas detailing how and why yield curve notes worked. "We didn't have a clue about any of that when we sold them," he says.

(2) **Work quickly.** Markets change rapidly, so borrowers have to move fast to turn ideas into issues. The negotiations with bankers and counterparties, and the abundance of legal documents that accompany a new deal, often have to be finalized within two or three days to reap the full advantages of the borrowing. "I've gotten calls from the competition and they're literally agog at how fast we hit the market," says Sallie Mae's CFO. "A lot of times we're first with an issue just because we're faster."

PepsiCo's policy is to continually monitor the marketplace so as to always be ready for a market window. "We stay in constant touch with traders," says the deputy treasurer. To help in this task, one treasury staffer takes responsibility for a portfolio of competing securities. Explains the deputy treasurer, "We run a book of Euro-CP—up to $250 million—which we trade continuously to find out what other players in the market are actually trading."

The spokesman believes that PepsiCo's hands-on approach is the only way to get to know a market. While other firms may rely simply on a screen for price quotes, he feels that "you can't trust what's on the screen. The screen is just a screen; it's not the market."

(3) **Take what the market gives.** The potential market for any particular innovative instrument can be fairly thin and can become saturated quickly. But Sallie Mae's philosophy is not to let that deter an issue. For example, there is simply not a sufficiently deep market to absorb a $500 million issue of yield curve notes. If investors will only accept $150 million, asks the CFO, "Do we throw it away or do we take the $150? If you can save 50 basis points on $150 million, that's $750,000 a year. That pays a number of salaries."

However, given the requirement to work quickly, small issues sometimes are not worth the trouble. Explains PepsiCo's deputy treasurer, "There are many times when we'll turn down an issue because the terms are too short or the value is small." For example, PepsiCo was recently approached with an attractive New Zealand dollar opportunity. But the proposed US$25–30 million three-year issue was too small to warrant the needed manpower—at the time. "If someone came to us with one like that today, we might do it. I don't have any live deals in the hopper right now."

(4) **Do not rely on a house bank.** Smaller issues and thin markets have forced innovative firms to broaden their contacts in the investment banking community. Says the Sallie Mae spokesman, "My view of relationship banking is that it's fine—for the investment banker." Although Sallie Mae borrows over $2 billion a year, it generally enters the markets with issues of less than $200 million. It needs to use a number of different investment banks to reach the widest investor base possible. "We'll do business with anyone who's reputable and with anyone who brings us a transaction that will work," explains the CFO.

PepsiCo shares this philosophy. In part, the firm is able to launch so many innovative issues because it gets so many proposals. "We deal regularly with a certain number of name banks, but we don't exclude the others," says the deputy treasurer. "They all know that if they come in with an idea, we'll keep it to ourselves. We won't go shop it. The fact that we're responsive helps us."

(5) Price the issue fairly. A primary tenent of PepsiCo's issuing strategy is to cultivate investors for the long term. It is essential, therefore, to ensure that the investor gets a fair deal. PepsiCo believes that trying to exploit markets makes it more difficult to place paper over the long term. Therefore, it prices a bit less aggressively than some observers feel it should. Pricing fairly not only expands the investor base but also helps the firm line up underwriters and comanagers. "People know that when we ask them to come into a deal, it's reasonably priced." PepsiCo also backs every deal: "In our Euro-CP program, for example," the spokesman explains, "our [dealers] know we're always ready to buy back paper. We think that's important."

PepsiCo also ensures fair pricing by selling directly to investors. Its Euro-CP program sells to end investors exclusively—in any amount or maturity up to five years. Direct contact with investors helps PepsiCo "gain a clear understanding of investors' needs." And since PepsiCo's paper stays out of traders' books, the yields on the ensuing issues stay lower.

When Sallie Mae prices a deal, it focuses on the end result of the transaction. The actual debt issuance can be the most mundane part of highly complex deals. The attractiveness of a foreign currency borrowing, for example, might actually be driven by the quality and price of an accompanying currency swap. "You can actually have the specific issue be a little bit more expensive than you would normally tolerate," says the CFO, "because you've got an advantageous pricing on some other piece of the deal."

(6) Avoid credit exposure. Currency and interest rate swaps entail mutual obligations for both parties. But Sallie Mae will not tolerate any unnecessary credit risk on its books. The firm applies rigorous credit standards, preferring AAA and refusing anything below AA.

In one case, even a quality credit rating was not enough to allay the CFO's worries. After swapping a zero-coupon Australian dollar bond with a high-rated counterparty, Sallie Mae insisted on collateral. Since no interest is paid on the Australian dollar security until maturity, the swap counterparty would accumulate a seven-year liability to Sallie Mae. "That makes me real nervous," says the CFO. "If I'm writing checks for seven years and he's not paying me anything until maturity, I could be out a lot of money."

PepsiCo runs a sophisticated cash/swap market arbitrage program that is dependent on its high credit rating. The firm is able to deal with major financial institutions willing to assume the credit risk.

(7) Know where you're going. Complex deals can involve a number of discrete transactions—the debt, the swap, a currency option, a cap, a floor—and negotiations can bring together a number of different parties. Throughout this process, the borrower must keep a firm eye on its eventual goal.

In Sallie Mae's case, that goal is floating-rate funds at the lowest possible spread to the 91-day T-bill. "We know where we want to end up before we start," says the CFO. "And we don't allow the vagaries of the market to take us to places we don't want to go." At PepsiCo, the decision to issue any deal depends on the all-in cost of funds. In its search for swaps, the firm uses a minimum target rate of commercial paper less 30 basis points. Transactions completed so far have beaten this benchmark.

That sense of focus simplifies complicated deals from the issuer's standpoint. "The new instruments all sound crazier than they really are," says Sallie Mae's CFO. "We always get back to a fairly dull routine—Treasury-based U.S. dollars. We'll continue to do that, and we'll continue to find the least expensive source of funds."

---

36. Financing Alternatives: The Pros and Cons

"Adaptability" is the operational buzzword for today's corporate treasurer—a manager who must consider a multitude of financing alternatives in markets that change virtually from day to day. Below are some of the most common alternative financing techniques—Eurobond financing, commodity-backed bonds, warrants, private placements, and zero-coupon bonds—and a checklist of factors that treasurers should weigh when selecting their funding vehicle.

Eurobond Financing

In a short time, the Eurobond market has blossomed into one of the world's most active markets. Billions of dollars are raised via Eurofinancing every month. The following are the four key questions to be considered before drafting a Eurobond issue.

(1) How do the covenants compare with those in the United States? Eurobond covenants are generally less restrictive than those in the United States.

(2) Can a bond be issued without a rating? Borrowers are not rated, but new issuers require widespread name recognition. Can your firm easily establish its reputation in the Euromarkets?

(3) What time frame can the issue handle? Financing deals in Europe are more rapidly concluded than those in the United States because no SEC registration is required. But offerings tend to have shorter maturities. Can your firm take on more shorter-term liabilities?

(4) Is a European issue cost-effective? Evaluate the market conditions, both in general and for your company's paper in particular. Can you place it at an attractive rate? Watch the fees, as fees are usually higher than in the United States, and U.S. issuers require offshore financing subsidiaries.

Commodity-Backed Bonds

Commodity-backed bonds are typically collateralized with assets thought to be more liquid than the firm's (or sovereign borrower's) fixed assets when the borrower has an overbearing debt position. Recent debt issues have been backed by gold, oil, and even automobiles.

(1) How stable is the commodity's price? An investor can obtain an asset valued much higher than the bond itself, but the value of a volatile commodity might be difficult to estimate. The result is a bond that will be hard to trade in the secondary market. The commodity could also depreciate in value, dragging the value of the bond down with it.

(2) How well defined is the legal right to the commodity? Commodity-linked bonds are often plagued by legal problems. The participants' rights are sometimes ambiguous.

Warrants

Equity-linked offerings, or warrants, can combine the benefits of debt issuance with the flotation of equity. Investors have responded well to Eurobond issues containing warrants, but a firm must evaluate the instrument carefully.

(1) What are the borrower's interest rate expectations? If interest rates rise, the bondholder will not find the warrant to be as attractive. But if interest rates decline, the warrant may be exercised, and the borrower will be forced to honor the warrant at an interest rate above the market rate.

(2) Can the warrant be exercised easily? The legal position of the warrant as a separate entity is often problematic. For example, what happens if the bond is defeased? Is the warrant still valid?

(3) Will the borrower be saddled with too much equity?

Although the borrower gets additional capital when the warrant is exercised, the firm must also grapple with the problem of overissuing equity.

Private Placements

In the United States, private placements are usually cheaper than public offerings. Moreover, they require less documentation and can attract investors who are willing to take on more risk. However, private placement requirements abroad are often another story. Rules are usually very stringent. In fact, the regulations may be more limiting than those for public offerings.

● **Check the hidden costs.** The Japanese Ministry of Finance has a de facto quota for keeping private placements to one-fourth of the Samurai bond market. The issuer's U.S. rating and its ratio of yen bonds to its total portfolio determine the amount a firm can raise and the maximum term. These stipulations make it difficult for even well-known MNCs to make private placements.

Zero-Coupon Bonds

Zero-coupon bonds are issued at a steep discount on their face value and pay no interest for the life of the bond. The issuer must pay the whole face value at maturity, which implies an accrued interest rate.

(1) The borrower's trade-off. For borrowers, zero-coupon bonds offer lower nominal long-term capital costs. But the bond's proceeds are well below the principal due at maturity and may impede its refund.

(2) The investor's trade-off. For investors, zeros probably will not be called before maturity because the call price is at par or at a premium above par. But the yield to maturity is below that of comparable full-coupon bonds and turns off some investors who would rather have current interest income.

---

37. How to Place Global Equity and Avoid Flowback

One of the key changes in the world's capital markets is the emergence of global equity programs. The market for global equities has increased exponentially over the past few years. Corporate finance managers generally cite four reasons to go global with stock issuances. First, firms are freed from limited domestic markets. Second, global issues diversify the investor base. Third, shares receive maximum value, since they are spread among the widest possible number of investors, reducing the chance of market saturation. Finally, making a splash in a local equities market spreads the firm's name in that country.

But the whole point of raising equity capital in the international markets is defeated if shares end up back in the home market. This can occur if a higher price—thanks to greater liquidity or demand on the domestic exchange—

entices overseas investors to sell back their shares. This phenomenon is known as "flowback." In this case, comments the finance manager of a U.S. firm that placed 15 percent of a recent dual-syndicate equity issue overseas, "You won't have placed your shares with foreign investors; all you'll have done is print a pretty tombstone."

While there is no way to eliminate flowback completely, here are four guidelines for stemming the tide.

(1) Watch your syndicate. The flowback problem sometimes lies with the underwriters that have been brought together to distribute the issue on their respective national markets. If the price in the firm's more liquid home market is higher than the price on the underwriter's local market, "There is a temptation not to bother trying to sell the shares to the client base," says the director of a London-based merchant bank. "Instead, they might just sell it back [on the firm's home market] and take the profit."

The solution is to choose and then police your syndicate carefully. Advises the manager of a publishing firm that made its initial public offering on the international markets, "What really matters is where your stock is placed. Is there a sufficiently liquid market for it? Do you have committed market makers in the stock? Is there proper research to track the stock? Those are the essential requirements."

Obviously, experience with the syndicate is also helpful. Many times a company will stipulate certain foreign banks or brokerage houses, with which it has existing relationships, for the syndicate. For example, one U.S. company went to the participants in its permanent overseas debt-underwriting syndicate for its dual-syndicate offering. "The reason we are very confident," says the firm's finance manager, "is that we've used these same people to place well over a billion dollars in debt."

(2) Make sure the foreign market knows who you are. The Catch 22 of international equity offerings is that, while they are preferred for their ability to spread a firm's name, a company already needs a name to place one successfully. Local operations and a local market presence can thus greatly enhance the marketability of an issue. The publishing firm mentioned above has subscribers and advertisers in 130 countries, for example.

However, in spite of its huge size, the U.S. company also cited above has very few overseas operations. Nevertheless, it has made its mark in the international financial markets. Listings on a number of foreign stock exchanges and an off-shore finance company that borrowed over $1 billion on the international markets made the company recognizable to the international financial community. "The dual syndicate was part of a continued drive to develop an overseas investor appetite for our securities and an overseas investor base," says the finance manager at the company.

(3) Emphasize the retail market. A syndicate's ability to tap private individual investors in a market is extremely important for helping an issuer beat flowback. Retail stock buyers typically buy stock as a medium- or long-term investment. Explains the investment bank director, "They tend not to be quick buck takers in the same way as wholesale investors."

Institutions, on the other hand, are large enough to buy a substantial percentage of an overseas issue, making companies vulnerable to institutional sell-offs. This compounds the problems imposed on portfolio managers by their companies' rigorous profit-based performance evaluation. "If you've done a placement outside the domestic market with just a few institutions, you haven't really achieved much," says the spokesman for a brokerage house in London. "If the distribution and placement have been in small lots with lots of investors, on the other hand, you're beginning to create a real base of investors."

(4) List on the national exchange. While not necessary to an international equity deal, a foreign listing gives local investors a place to sell their shares locally. Therefore, they are not forced to rely on the secondary market in the issuer's home country. "Whoever's buying it wants to be able to trade it," says the London investment banker.

Listing is especially important for European companies that have braved Securities and Exchange Commission (SEC) requirements to issue on the U.S. public market. According to a U.S. bank official who has put together a number of U.S. offerings for foreign companies, "A U.S. listing, combined with a strong investor relations program, ensures a strong secondary market. That helps stem flowback."

---

38. Tips on Building a Global Shareholder Base

In today's global equity game, companies cannot simply rely on an AAA credit rating from Moody's or Standard & Poor's to arouse the interest of potential investors. Instead, according to firms skilled in creating a pool of global shareholders, success rests on building a solid presence and image in the minds of prospective share buyers. In addition to the critical factors of timing, share price, and the condition of the firm's income statement and balance sheet, executives cite a well-developed marketing strategy as a key element of any Euro-equity campaign. Positioning a firm for Euro-equity issuance involves four main approaches.

(1) Build and maintain a consistent advertising campaign. For investor-relations experts at GTE Corporation and PepsiCo, providing current and potential shareholders with a steady stream of written and face-to-face information is a crucial ingredient of a successful issue. One of the biggest mistakes companies make in preparing a Euro-equity issue is to stage an elaborate show one or two months prior to the launch and then to forget about investors until they go back to the market with the next issue. Remarked a GTE spokesman, "We find it crucial to keep the GTE name in the mind of the foreign investor. We periodically hold presentations, generally making an annual trip to each foreign financial center and perhaps visiting the major foreign markets two or three times a year."

(2) Tell the market what it wants to know. Target your campaign to the specific information needs of investors in each foreign financial center. One consumer goods manufacturer finds that European investors attach great significance to the continuity of management. Hence, it devotes considerable attention to the stability of the firm's executive corps. "In Japan, we receive the best response from the audience when we emphasize the company's strategies and long-term direction," added the company's treasurer.

(3) Strengthen investor-relations servicing. The role of ongoing investor relations is not to "peddle stock" but to accommodate the increasingly complex needs of a global shareholder base, according to the GTE expert. This means the investor-relations department of a Euro-equities issuer must be adept at presenting the financial highlights, business strategies, and details of the various markets in which the firm operates. Complained the treasurer of one U.S. MNC, "Too many firms beef up their departments with people who can't even read a balance sheet and can't satisfy or stimulate investor interest."

(4) Consider using local consultants. Many MNCs use local consultants or financial institutions. In Japan, this is a must. GTE recommends having a consultant along on visits and at meetings so that foreign clients know there is a local representative on hand to provide information and to call in case of emergencies. Consultants can also be used to investigate and stimulate investor demand for shares prior to issue and to target the appropriate audience.

---

39. Should Foreign Firms List on the Tokyo Stock Exchange?

Increasingly, firms seek the advantages of listing on offshore exchanges; for instance, U.S. firms list on the London Stock Exchange, and U.K. firms list on the New York, American, or OTC exchanges. But the costs and rigors of listing on the Tokyo Stock Exchange (TSE) are dramatically higher than those on any other major exchange.

Nevertheless, firms are prepared to undertake the expense. By end-1989, there were 116 foreign firms listed on the TSE; that number is expected to rise to over 200 by the end of 1990. This surge is remarkable considering that only 11 foreign stocks were quoted on the TSE as of end-1984. BI spoke with executives from four major NYSE- and TSE-quoted firms to find out the reason for this trend.

(1) Building a name to facilitate future borrowing. The principal goal of many foreign companies listing their stocks in Japan is often to enhance their name recognition in Japan and hence their borrowing capabilities in Japanese debt markets. One Chrysler Corporation executive said he hoped that his corporation's TSE listing would "pave the way to borrowing short- and medium-term funds on the Tokyo capital market."

(2) Developing market awareness of the company and its products. The listing and eventual trading of a company's stock makes the company's name and business known to Japanese investors and consumers. As Japan increasingly opens its consumer markets, pioneering issuers hope that investors will become motivated consumers. In addition, issuers hope that the presence of a firm's name on the local exchanges will eventually enhance its image on the shelves.

(3) Compensating for increasing yen-based income. Another reason for companies to list on the TSE is to balance their rising yen-based income with yen-based equity.

(4) Facilitating equity-linked borrowing. Once a company has its stock listed on either Tokyo or Osaka or both, it can contemplate equity-linked debt issues to raise funds. Equity-linked issues were by far the lowest-cost source of funds for Japanese firms during the 1980s.

---

40. How to List on the Tokyo Stock Exchange

TSE listing procedures are significantly more cumbersome than those of comparable U.S. or European exchanges. To help firms decide whether a TSE listing is worth the effort, the following checklist warns of the obstacles firms will need to overcome.

(1) Only common shares can be listed. Currently, the Ministry of Finance (MoF) employs a very narrow description of securities, eliminating the listing of nonvoting shares on domestic exchanges. Hence, foreign shares listed on the TSE must be common voting shares. Whether the MoF will relax its listing criteria and admit nonvoting shares is uncertain.

(2) The combination of formal and informal listing costs is significant. The cost of a TSE listing is considerable and can be divided into two principal categories.

● **Administrative costs levied by the TSE.** Corporations listing stocks on a domestic Japanese exchange face one-time and annual fees. The cost of the initial listing is Y2.5 million plus a per share fee ranging from Y0.0045 to Y0.0225, depending on the proportion of total shares held in Japan. Annual listing fees are about Y150,000, again depending on the number of shares held in Japan.

● **Public relations and promotion.** Though the actual fees for a listing are manageable, the real cost of a listing comes in the translation of the prospectus and company data and in the promotional entertaining that is required to sell the listing to the market. One firm estimated that its listing—including brokers' fees, promotional cocktail parties, printing the annual report in Japanese, public relations, and miscellaneous paperwork—cost roughly US$500,000.

(3) The total listing process takes six months. The total time period required for a listing of foreign stocks in Japan is approximately six months, with three months required for the preparation of the documents and three months for the TSE/MoF evaluations. Key events are:

- Day 1. Board of directors starts listing procedures. Auditing by a Japanese CPA begins.
- Day 80. Submission of application and translated and certified documents to TSE.
- Day 125. TSE hearing (two to three days).
- Day 140. TSE approval. Submission to MoF.
- Day 180. MoF approval. Listing and start of trading.

(4) Japan has extensive listing criteria. The following criteria must be met in the listing of stock on the TSE (similar rules apply to the Osaka exchange).

- Number of shares listed. A minimum of 20,000 shares must be listed for each trading unit. Hence, if the share will trade in units of one, then 20,000 shares must be listed. If the share is to trade in units of 1,000, then 20 million shares must be listed.
- Home market. The share must enjoy a fair and efficient home market.
- Number of shareholders. The issue should be aimed at a minimum of 1,000 shareholders in the market.

- Past performance. The company must have a history of at least five years of continuous operation.
- Minimum shareholder equity. This must be Y10 billion or more.
- Minimum net before tax profits. This must be Y2 billion in each of the last three years.
- Dividend performance. The company must have paid a dividend in the last three years.
- Dividend prospects. The company must be able to show good prospects of paying future dividends.

(5) Extensive documentation is required. The following documents must be provided at some point in the application process for a listing on the TSE: Application for Listing, Securities Report for the Application for Listing, Sections I and II; stock listing agreement; certification by legal counsel; documentation of appointment of shareholder services agent and dividend-paying bank; copies of documents filed with the respective authorities in the country of origin; articles of incorporation; minutes of the board resolution to list; specimen stock certificates; proof of listing in the home country; proof that the signator of the application for listing has the proper authority.

41. Defending a Stock's Price from the Whims of a Fickle FX Market

As equity share prices become increasingly sensitive to currency movements, money managers must anticipate the impact of currency fluctuations on reported corporate earnings. Unfortunately, the market often reacts irrationally to currency news because investors find it difficult to assess how currency trends will affect the complex multicurrency revenue and cost structure of a typical MNC. Can a corporate treasurer protect shareholder wealth from the fickle reactions of the investment community in today's volatile FX environment? BI interviewed several equity portfolio managers to find out what they think treasurers should and should not do to keep the market on their side.

- **Disclose your pretax geographical and currency cost/ revenue profiles.** All managers polled agreed that the more information they have about a company's cost and revenue profiles, the better. "We like to see a breakdown of sales and profits by geographical area," says a spokesman for Aetna Montagu. "Some companies just give a breakdown of sales, but one doesn't know whether they are running an overseas operation for historical reasons or whether it actually makes them any money."

A spokesman for American Express Asset Management explains why money managers like to know the currency in which revenues are denominated. "Take the case of Mercedes Benz. We do a breakdown of its pretax profits—how much came from Saudi Arabia, how much from the United States and from Hong Kong. Then we make some judgment

in our own mind about whether the deutsche mark will appreciate and by how much against the dollar, the riyal, and the Hong Kong dollar." The spokesman uses this information to estimate the impact currency translation will have on Mercedes' future reported earnings.

But according to Cigna's spokesman, market participants don't always know what to make of income translation gains and losses. "The international investment game is too young for there to be any standards," he said. "Let's say a U.K. company's revenues have grown 20 percent in dollar terms and yet are down in sterling terms. Investors often don't really know how to evaluate that." Although the portfolio manager examines currency transaction and translation gains and losses, he is most concerned about real growth. "What I want to know is, has the company sold more spanners this year than last, and have their margins improved? That is the only way to evaluate the true performance of a company."

- **Disclose your hedging policies.** A money manager cannot accurately assess the effects of currency movements on earnings without some knowledge of a firm's hedging policies: what currencies it is hedging and at what rates it has locked in its cover. "A company that discloses more information about its hedging strategies will have a leg up on one that doesn't," says the American Express spokesman. "Treasurers should be as open as possible about what they are doing on the hedging front. To the extent that the portfolio manager is aware of what is going on, he will have more comfort with his ability to predict performance. This should translate into a less volatile stock price and a relatively higher multiple than would otherwise be the case." He says that the standard of reporting on hedging practices is much lower in the United States than in most major European markets. "Philips' Lamp provides a much more exhaustive discussion of hedging techniques than IBM," he notes.

● **But do not expect to always be understood.** Even those firms that keep the markets abreast of their current management practices may not be rewarded for their candor. A case in point is Jaguar. The company hedged its dollar revenues during a period when the greenback was strengthening. When the company reported lower earnings than the market expected, its stock price suffered. "A lot of people assumed it was a dollar play last year and were betting on increased dollar earnings," says Aetna spokesman. "But they hedged all their dollar sales and didn't have the windfall profits people were expecting." However, as a money manager for Baimco International notes, "The firm reported that it had been hedging its earnings all along, but the investment community didn't listen."

Disclosing hedging policies can backfire for other reasons as well. For example, the Baimco spokesman reports that, given current market conditions, he would place his bets on a company that covered all its nondollar costs but left a portion of its nondollar revenues open. A firm that disclosed a contrary strategy might not gain his favor.

● **Aim for predictability, not flashiness.** Most portfolio managers polled said that they look more for predictability than for spectacular but unrealizable results from corporate currency managers. "A company isn't necessarily in the business of beating currency markets all the time," Aetna's spokesman remarks. "We like to see them concentrating their activity on core business rather than trying to outguess the currency markets. We appreciate caution and conservative currency management so that we can predict within a reasonable range what a company's earnings will be."

The Baimco expert agrees. "I am generally against the idea of treasuries as profit centers. Treasurers aren't soothsayers any more than professional forecasters have turned out to be. If I am looking for currency speculation, I will buy currencies, and if I am investing in earnings from currency transactions, I will buy a bank, not a drug company."

● **Do not expect a lot of credit for active hedging.** The market generally gives little credit to firms that engage in active currency hedging. "I think investors prefer to look at a company and say, this one is a deutsche mark play and this one a sterling play," says Cigna's spokesman. "They'll give those companies a lot of credit when the currencies are going their way and punish them when they aren't." A company's hedging profits may well go unnoticed by the market, but its losses are sure to get plenty of press.

However, innovative financing and currency management are not wasted on some money managers. "We do give credit for creative financing when we evaluate a company," Cigna's spokesman reports. "As for treasury as a profit center, we have no strong feelings. We are just interested to see if they can consistently make a profit out of their treasury operations. But if we see great volatility of results, then we wonder what risks have been taken."

● **Do not expect your share price to benefit if the local currency appreciates.** A growing, sophisticated minority of international money managers regard investment in a company and investment in a currency as two separate decisions. For example, a manager who is bullish on the deutsche mark would not necessarily buy equity in a German company. Instead, he might hedge his U.S. equity position with a forward purchase of deutsche marks or with deutsche mark call options.

On the other hand, Cigna's spokesman explains, "A program of competitive devaluation may be beneficial for the stocks of exporters but bad for the currency. As an investor, you might want to take advantage of both aspects, say, by buying U.K. stocks and also owning put options on sterling."

42. Four Ways to Issue Europaper

Just about all Euro-commercial paper (Euro-CP) programs have one thing in common: Issuers, even those who allow direct access to U.S. investors, rely on dealers in Europe. "It's just a different market here," explains a U.K. CP dealer. "That's the way things are done."

But issuers vary in their view of the optimal number of dealers for a given program. The following is a checklist of four different optimal distribution structures derived from the practices of a number of Euro-CP issuers and international bank dealers.

(1) Use a tender panel of 10–20 banks. The tender panel structure is a feature common to all Note Insurance Facilities (NIFs). This distribution method, it is thought, appeals to Euromarket investors because it gives the appearance of a flourishing secondary market.

However, according to one U.S. firm's assistant treasurer, this appearance is probably just that—an appearance. The dealer refers to "hero bidding" and says that prices on the secondary market bear no relation to the prices at which the tender panel strikes. "That's due to the fact that so many people are involved. It's not in anyone's interest to protect the price singlehandedly. Panel members know they have no power over the others."

(2) Use a sole dealership. At the opposite end of the spectrum is the sole dealership. The idea behind this arrangement is that the underwriter's obligation is very clear.

"With a sole dealership, you know exactly who you're dealing with—who's responsible," says a U.K. banker. "This arrangement ensures that the paper will be traded realistically at all times." A U.S. issuer of Euro-CP agrees: "It's got to be easier dealing with just one bank instead of the tender panel zoo."

However, a New York Euro-CP trader is against the sole dealership approach, as he considers the market too fragmented to reach all segments through one market maker.

(3) For a modest CP program, use three dealers. The New York Euro-CP dealer recommends that "for a program north of $75 million in terms of anticipated usage, employ three, maybe four dealers."

(4) But do not use more than six. Even the largest programs—the dealer cites intended placements of $300 million and up—should have five or, at most, six participants. He cites a case in point: "GMAC is up to $600 million with only four dealers."

Chapter 6
Building an Efficient Cash Management Function

The previous chapter highlighted strategies and tactics that can help raise capital at the lowest cost. But just as critical as raising capital efficiently is the need to put funds already on hand to optimum use. In short, treasury managers need to ensure that their firm's local and headquarters staffs are taking all the necessary steps to promote effective cash management.

BI interviews demonstrate that proactive managers can save their companies millions of dollars annually through refinements of cash management. Audits of current corporate practice often show dozens of inefficiencies, from idle bank balances, undue collection delays, and unwarranted transaction charges to completely unwarranted currency exposure. The following checklists will provide the treasury manager with a solid barometer for measuring the effectiveness of current practice. In addition, they will help managers decide whether a complete cash management audit is warranted, and whether that audit should be conducted by company personnel or outside consultants.

43. How to Audit Current Cash Management Practice

Companies conducting thorough reviews of their cash management systems in specific country environments frequently meet with stunning success: One U.S. financial services company expects to save over US$7 million in Canada alone as a result of a recent evaluation of its cash management procedures there. A U.S. high-tech company, which conducts intracountry cash management studies of its operations around the world, estimates that it saves about 1 percent of each subsidiary's sales through this practice. The following checklist, based on extensive interviews with corporate managers and cash management consultants, outlines the key steps needed to develop and implement an effective cash management audit.

● **Decide which cash management functions will be reviewed.** The first step in undertaking a review of your company's cash management system is to set the scope and terms of reference. This involves two issues.

First, determine which of the seven key areas of cash management need to be reviewed: cash reporting; credit and collection, including export receivables; payables management; banking relations; short-term investment; short-term borrowing; and cross-border cash management. Further, decide if there are any key related areas on which the study should focus, such as currency management, export financing, or automated systems.

Second, decide which countries and subsidiaries should be covered. Should the study examine only the parent company's domestic and cross-border cash flow, or should it review intracountry cash management systems developed by local subsidiaries? Which areas will lead to the biggest savings?

In general, firms should consider their largest operations first. Once these are defined, an effective rule of thumb is to concentrate first on the problem countries—those with inefficient banking systems, slow mail systems, or high local funding costs. High on consultants' recommended lists are Italy, France, Brazil, Mexico, Argentina, Venezuela, the Philippines, and—because of its unique practices—Japan.

● **Gather all relevant internal company information.** Once the scope of the review is set, the next step is to collect information. The simplest way to do this is to gather existing reports and information from subsidiaries held by various departments at regional and parent headquarters. Once sufficient data have been collected, the firm can formulate a game plan and focus the impending audit.

While the quality of available data will vary, firms should strive to obtain such information as procedure and policy manuals; previous audit reports; bank analyses and statements; bank account data and related information on banking networks; copies of daily cash position sheets; cash flow or financial diagrams; organizational charts; job descriptions and responsibilities; annual reports, financial statements, and 10Ks; five-year plans and budgets; and borrowing and investment data.

● **Learn the operating environment.** While cash managers should always strive for peak efficiency, they will have to do so within the confines of the local reality. That is, any strategy must blend with local banking services, payment practices, postal systems, exchange controls, and tax regulations.

It is essential for managers conducting the audit to become familiar with local practice. Explained one corporate cash manager: "You have to gain the [local] company's confidence and project credibility before you can make recommendations." Discussions with consultants and managers from other companies and examination of consulting studies conducted for other firms are the best means of getting to know local practice.

● **Involve both local managers . . .** For a study to succeed, it is critical to involve local management. If local managers are not approached early in the process, a cash management audit can easily become a struggle rather than a cooperative effort.

Depending on the scope of the study, it may be useful to involve the local personnel with the following functional responsibilities: treasury, accounting and control, financial planning, marketing, purchasing, credit and collection, payables, information management (EDP), and any senior management.

● **. . . and senior headquarters management.** It is equally important to demonstrate to local managers that the project has a clear, unqualified mandate from senior management at the parent level—for instance, the CFO. BI has uncovered more than one system review that received less than total cooperation due to a nonexistent nod of senior management approval. If senior managers are not committed to conducting the review and implementing its recommendations, it is often better not to conduct the review at all.

● **Observe the existing system on site.** Said one seasoned system auditor: "We go on site and find out what is going on—talking to the people involved in each step. Although this process may be time-consuming—it can take several weeks—it is vital to the success of your study."

It is critical to work with the "Indians" and not just the "chiefs." A cash management consultant cautions: "You don't want only the supervisor, because many times he tells you what he thinks you want to hear. You really have to go to the unit itself and see how the checks are brought in from the mailroom, when they are brought in, and what the clerk does with them."

The on-site review should be an exercise in minutiae. For example, to analyze a collections system, the audit team should examine the elapsed time between a sale and the receipt of the order; between receipt of the order and receipt of the invoice; between receipt of the invoice and receipt of the payment; between receipt of the payment and receipt of the payment's deposit in the bank; and, finally, between the deposit and credit to the company's account.

- **Document the existing system.** The final step of the system audit is the documentation of existing procedures. This should clearly describe the cash management practices as currently understood, including work flowcharts. This will serve as the benchmark against which any cost-benefit analysis of improvements can be measured.

- **Compare your cash management practices with local standards.** After documenting the existing system, procedures should be reviewed and assessed in light of sound cash management practices and standards in the country or countries under investigation. The examination of local practice conducted earlier in the audit may prove sufficient at this point. However, most firms will find it desirable to revisit this step, taking full advantage of the newly acquired insights into local practice.

- **Develop new, more effective cash management procedures—if warranted.** With the system's weak points identified, the next step is to devise improvements.

However, as one cash management consultant remarked: "We're not going to make a change just for the sake of making a change. Change to increase efficiency or cost-effectiveness or to generate some cash gains for the company. Otherwise, try to change the system as little as possible."

- **Put the recommendations in writing.** Many companies underestimate the time it takes to write up the findings and recommendations. The process may take from several weeks to several months, depending on the depth of the study. But the document must be thorough and clear if the recommendations are to be successfully implemented. Finally, since most senior executives do not have the time to read a lengthy document, be prepared to make an oral presentation of the findings.

44. Should You Use a Consultant?

Not all companies have the resources to conduct their own internal reviews of a cash management system. The alternative is to hire an outside consultant. Before deciding on this route, however, be sure to consider the following points.

- **Do you have the in-house expertise to conduct a cash management study?** A cash management study not only requires in-depth knowledge of the latest cash management strategies, but also intimate familiarity with the environments under examination—including local banking systems and services, financial regulations, tax rules, and country-specific cash management techniques. This expertise is best gained through experience.

Consultants offer the advantage that they are usually conversant with both local practice and the cash management practices of adjacent countries. Further, they are often familiar with the cross-border techniques available in the region. Finally, they are apt to have a better overview of what other companies are doing and what the banks have to offer.

Companies can combine the use of a consultant with the strengthening of in-house capability. For example, they can use a consultant for the first one or two audits while training company personnel for any future assessments.

However, some firms prefer to go it alone. The CFO of one French company pointed out: "Any company that keeps going to the banks for help will never know how to run its own treasury function. If you don't understand how to solve problems and build systems, how can you hope to manage your cash effectively and to make improvements when new situations arise?"

- **Do you have the time to spend on a cash management study?** A cash management review can be a tedious process. According to a seasoned cash management consultant, "A standard intracountry study for us would take three people, who would spend 10 days on site averaging 14 to 18 hours per day and an additional 10 man-days back here refining the analysis. That includes the writing. So with one person, it would take up to three months of eight-hour days. If the company's records are in shambles, we work 18-hour days instead of 12."

Of course, a cash management audit need not be so expensive. Many firms simply send a treasury manager to make a quick review. Explained a cash manager of a leading consumer goods producer: "I fly in for a few days and look over what we are doing. I discuss procedures with the local treasurer. I bring up approaches that have been used successfully in other countries and discuss the merits of using them in this country. It's not as thorough as what the banks might do, but I believe in the 80/20 rule—80 percent of the savings will result from 20 percent of the effort."

- **Will the budget allow for the cost of an outside consultant?** Proprietary cash management studies can be exorbitantly expensive—ranging from $30,000 for a small intracountry review to hundreds of thousands of dollars for a full-blown study of global operations. "For that price," explained one treasury manager, "we can make it on our own."

To avoid paying out high fees for studies that may not provide concrete results, some firms negotiate contracts with private consultants whereby fees are tied to the actual savings generated by the study. For instance, a Swedish capital goods producer used this pricing approach on several intracountry studies conducted by a U.S. bank. Says the firm's treasurer, "In the end, I think we wound up paying more money, but at least we knew we got good value."

- **Can you be objective in your assessment of subsidiary**

operations? It can be difficult for the patient to cure himself. If internal staff members are not objective, the study will reflect their bias.

Objectivity is the main reason a giant Swiss pharmaceuticals firm hires outside consultants for cash management studies. An executive explains, "It is very delicate when you, as a representative of the parent company, go to the subsidiaries and look into their books. They don't like it when you say, 'Here is a mistake' and 'Here your duty is not fulfilled correctly.' When you go with an external expert, they more easily accept his advice and knowledge."

● **How long will it take an outside consultant to get to know your firm's business?** Internal staff have one key advantage over external consultants: They understand the company. Consultants can spend one-third or more of their time just learning your business and operations. This step is eliminated if someone in house conducts the audit.

45. How to Choose a Consultant

Deciding to use a consultant is relatively easy. Selecting a consultant requires significant effort. The trick is to find a consultant who is knowledgeable, cost-effective, and blends well with your firm's culture. Although the field is narrowing (the number of banks active in the consulting game is falling rapidly), companies should weigh the following points in making their choice.

● **Objectivity.** A key reason companies turn to outside consultants is to obtain an objective opinion. However, this must be balanced against the consultant's own particular bias. For example, a bank's consultant may be primarily interested in selling his institution's systems and services. For this reason, many companies prefer to use consultants from management accounting firms or private companies rather than from banks.

However, many bank consultants are aware of these corporate concerns and go to great lengths to preserve their objectivity. "Our job is to improve their system," said one. "We try not to push our products. But if our product will do the job, we tell them. We have to fight very hard to promote ourselves as objective."

● **Reputation.** Although some companies question banks' objectivity, most are convinced of their ability to handle cash management studies. As a U.S. treasurer said: "In the area of cash management—and treasury management in general—the banks have an edge. They know the business inside and out and have the most expertise."

However, a bank consultant may not be the best qualified for all countries. In particular, banks may not have the necessary expertise in the minor Third World countries. In these instances, local representatives of major accounting and management consulting firms probably have the upper hand. This can also hold true for some developed countries. Said one treasurer of the Netherlands, "Banks have not specialized in this part of the world."

● **Qualifications.** The reputation of the institution is not enough: The bottom line is the qualification of the individual consultant who will work on your project. "Some consultants in a bank are better than others. You have to size up the individual who will do the study," warned an assistant treasurer of a leading consumer goods company.

● **Price.** Consultants usually charge on a per diem basis—roughly $1,000 per day. While a number of banks are involved in cash management, they often approach it from two different perspectives. Some see consulting as a profit center; others see it as a service. The latter group has the flexibility to set very competitive prices for targeted customers.

In particular, firms should consider taking bids from banks with which they have no relationship. These banks are often hungry for business and will conduct a best-effort audit at a break-even price.

Further, firms should look at individual consultants—not just institutions (with their high overheads). In particular, look for individuals with proven track records who have only recently moved out on their own.

● **Quality of the proposal.** Companies should go to several consultants and get a written proposal. They should examine the proposals not only for price but also for such key issues as methodology and duration. A cash management consultant asked, "Does the methodology suit your purposes? You look to see if they are competent and their methods sound."

Furthermore, a good consultant should be willing to tailor the study to your needs. In judging the proposal, make sure that the consultant has full understanding of your concerns and has geared the project to suit your firm's unique situation. Also check to see if the proposal includes details on other relevant assignments handled by the consultant, as well as an estimate of fees and expenses that is broken down by project phase.

● **Confidentiality.** Companies should be extremely careful that information supplied to the consultant remains confidential. For this reason, corporate treasurers are sometimes uneasy about giving banks access to the information needed for a cash management review.

As one Dutch financial manager said: "With a bank, there is a natural reluctance to really open up our books to scrutiny. It would be difficult to be candid with them."

Of course, a major fear is that bank consultants will give the data to lending officers. Interestingly, a bank consultant felt that these suspicions were sometimes justified: "It's not meant to happen. But the people selling products are often the same people who are the account officers."

- **Willingness to work closely with you.** The most successful reviews are those that closely involve corporate financial staff. As one cash management consultant advised: "If a company can free up an individual and get him out in the field, it will benefit internally, because all the knowledge is going to be in his head as well as in the report."

Many consultants encourage this approach. One bank consultant said: "We prefer to have someone from your organization dedicated to the project team. We may uncover something very obvious that you can correct without waiting a year for the report. If we have one of your people there, we can pick something up and get it implemented while we continue with the routine audit. That's how you benefit. We benefit by having better interaction with the company."

- **Compatibility.** Finally, you have to "click" with the consultant. As one cash management consultant remarked, "It's people. You've got to feel comfortable. That's a difficult thing to put in a document. You can't write it down. It's similar to interviewing two or three people for a job. Two or three have very much the same resume, but one really turns you on; you are comfortable with him."

46. The Key Questions to Ask During a Credit and Collection Review

A major portion of savings from any cash management audit will arise from improvements in the credit and collections cycle. To get receivables management into shape, a review team can start by asking each subsidiary the following questions.

- Do you have any procedure manuals or guidelines you could share with us?

- How many customers do you have? With which companies are your major accounts, and what percentage of receivables do they represent? Where are they located? What is the value of receipts by location?

- Who is responsible for collections, billing, credit, terms, and sales? Who reports to whom?

- From where are bills sent? Where are they collected?

- Are collections part of the performance review of salesmen? Is compensation tied to collections rather than sales?

- How do you monitor your receivables? Are your systems automated? Does your monitoring system update receipts and pinpoint outstanding accounts without delay?

- What is the format of receivables reports? Does your assessment of collection performance include days' sales outstanding (DSO), days' delinquent outstanding, aging of receivables, and current receivables levels? Are these reports adequate for efficient credit and collection management? How would you improve them?

- Do you conduct regular checks on all customers through local credit agencies, bank and supplier references, personal visits to customers' facilities, and other sources of credit information?

- Do you have many delinquent accounts? How much bad debt do you encounter? If there are problems, what are the reasons?

- What are the established credit limits by customer? How are these limits monitored?

- What are the standard terms of sale? Are there many exceptions? Does the finance department have input into the decision making?

- Do you impose penalty fees for late payment? Do you offer discounts for early payment? How do you judge the effectiveness of these terms?

- What steps have you taken to make sure credit terms are not too tight or too lenient? Have you compared your terms with those of other companies in your industry?

- Do you negotiate tighter credit terms or raise prices to compensate for long terms?

- Does your standard invoice clearly state the due date, payment instrument to be used, and the account to receive payment? Is the due date based on the goods' delivery date or the date of the invoice?

- What is the process from the time an order is received to the time the invoice is sent out? How long does each step take? What are the main delays? How efficient is the system, and how could it be improved?

- Have you automated the entire collections process—from creating the invoice to dunning late payers to recording receipts—to minimize internal float?

- What payment instruments do you receive (checks, drafts, transfers) in terms of percentage of total receipts? For each instrument, how long does it take from the time an invoice is sent out until funds are credited to your account?

- Do you encourage customers to use the fastest clearing instrument available? Have you asked customers to permit you to debit their accounts directly or to use Automated Clearing House (ACH) or other electronic funds-transfer systems?

- Do you use courier services, in-house messengers, or sales representatives to collect payment from customers and speed documents to the banks before value-dating cutoff times?

- Have you considered using lockboxes or intercept points to accelerate collections? Are you pooling cash or using concentration accounts to speed cash to an investment pool?

- Which banks are used as collecting agents? Where are they located? What are your average daily receipts at each bank?
- What are the bank costs—by bank—for processing drafts, transfers, and checks?
- Do you use the same banks as your customers to speed clearing or, in countries with multiple clearing systems, do you use banks within the same network?
- Do you regularly try to negotiate better value-dating and clearing times with your collection banks?
- When do you receive notification that funds have been deposited and credited by bank and payment instrument? How is the information received—by telephone, mail, telex? How could this process be accelerated?
- Have you established formal dunning procedures? How do you dun customers (letters, telephone, telex)? When do you start dunning a customer? Who does the actual dunning?
- Is your sales force prepared to eliminate credit terms or even stop shipment to delinquent customers? Do the marketing and finance departments work closely together to ensure that sales are collectible?

47. Building a Manual: Nine Guidelines to Sounder International Credit Policies

Local managers need to know what is expected from headquarters. However, it is virtually impossible to create an all-purpose document that effectively serves every situation.

One area where this is particularly true is international credit policy. Controlled credit and collections policies and systems are absolutely essential to effective cash management. Because credit terms set the pace for the collection cycle, companies should reevaluate these regularly with the aim of reducing DSO.

However, cash management objectives must be balanced against the realities of the competitive market: Terms that are too short will quite simply undermine a company's competitiveness. To help managers develop a manual that addresses these and other trade-offs, the following checklist presents the advice of experienced MNC practitioners.

(1) **Be flexible.** Do not tie affiliates to any rigid across-the-board strictures, but conclude terms on an individual case basis, according to the affiliates' levels of cash and capitalization.

(2) **Use credit in preference to money transfers.** Extend credit terms rather than ship money into and out of a foreign subsidiary, since transfers will incur bank charges, stamp duties, and the like. However, credit terms should be extended only when an economic slump or sudden government credit squeeze creates a problem for the subsidiary. If the subsidiary is undercapitalized, it would be better to resolve this problem rather than to gloss over it by extending credit.

(3) **Monitor subsidiary cash.** If it is well capitalized, have the subsidiary pay intercompany accounts promptly.

(4) **Examine local regulations.** Take legal problems into account. Requirements such as prior import deposits may justify longer than normal terms to affiliates.

(5) **Watch local interest rates.** Avoid local borrowing when the cost would be prohibitive.

(6) **Take account of competition and local customs.** Sales subsidiaries in Latin America need either more capital or extended terms to cope with the following situations: fierce credit competition from European (especially German) and Japanese companies and the local custom of regularly failing to meet due dates.

(7) **Say it with a smile.** Do not forget to build good relations with an affiliate, much as you would with an independent customer. On the other hand, be prepared to be firm—in the knowledge that "a friend will repay a loan in a hurry; your brother will take his time."

(8) **Know your firm's cyclical variations.** Take into account business cycles affecting your products, be it the weather, seasonal variations in demand, or others. One firm that is fairly strict about its 90-day terms allows 180 days for a product sold to farmers with semiannual crop cycles.

(9) **Keep an eye on collections.** If the subsidiary is not sufficiently strict, crack down by insisting on prompt payment.

48. The Key Payables Audit Questions

All too often, disbursement management—the flip side of credit and collection—is a weak link in corporate cash management systems. An experienced consultant offers this advice: "You need to review payables if you can't, without a lot of trouble, get your hands on answers to the following questions: What are my cash disbursements outstanding [CDO], broken down by operation and country? What percentage of my payments are made by which instruments? And what float am I realizing from various payments? If your reporting system makes it difficult to retrieve information on payables, you've got a problem." Here are the key questions for a payables audit.

- Are local managers getting enough information to manage payables efficiently?

- Have adequate lines of communication been opened with all relevant departments, e.g., purchasing and production units?
- Are order and invoice data reported regularly to the accounts payable staff?
- Are reports prepared frequently enough to provide a basis for aggressive disbursement management?
- Are you carefully tracking disbursement float?
- Are you using such measurements as CDO and aging of payables to assess the effectiveness of payables practices?
- Are major cash outflows—e.g., dividends, tax and supplier payments—forecast to plan for funding?

- How are forecasts made?
- Do you forecast payments by supplier, amount, and currency?
- How frequently are forecasts prepared?
- Are forecasts measured against actual results and evaluated for accuracy?
- What actions do you take based on your reports and forecasts?
- Are payables reports and forecasts transmitted via the most cost-effective and expeditious methods?
- Have you explored the cost advantages of automating local payables reporting and forecasting systems?

49. How to Maximize Your Self-Financing Capability

Improving internal cash flow involves much more than speeding receivables and slowing down payables. This summary checklist presents steps that can help companies improve their self-financing capabilities. (Of course, the most effective way to boost self-financing is to increase profits.)

- **Consider increasing the ratio of retained profits for reinvestment and decreasing the distribution of profits.** Although the local partners in joint ventures may be opposed, there is often enough room to negotiate utilization of profits for capital requirements. If a distribution must be made, a company may change its mode of paying dividends by switching from a percentage of profits to a fixed dividend.
- **Leave the dividends with the subsidiary as a loan if profits are to be distributed.** This will avoid creating a drain on the subsidiary's cash position. Similarly, royalties due the parent can be lent to the subsidiary. Investigate the possibilities for converting dividends into equity.
- **Replace a cash dividend with a stock dividend.** This has been a widespread U.S. practice and could well be extended to operations elsewhere.
- **Utilize incentives offered by foreign governments** in the form of easy credits, lower interest rates, subsidies for locating plants in certain areas, and tax incentives or tax holidays.
- **Stretch out tax payments.** Defer payment of taxes and customs duties until the deadline. In some countries, an extension of the payment period is possible.
- **Move some activities to specialized subsidiaries in certain countries.** A captive financing subsidiary often has a better chance of obtaining funds and maximizing interest or fees than the parent manufacturing firm.
- **Lease out unused space or machinery.**
- **Maximize allowable rates of depreciation.** Any improved terms may require negotiation with the government or governments in question, but companies should not shy away from such efforts.
- **Consider self-financing factors in selecting sites for new plants.** Besides the possibility of capital and tax incentives, one location may offer better depreciation rates than another. Compare tax, transportation, and wage costs.

- **Institute a centralized international cash management policy** including a regular and detailed reporting system. Have local management file cash flow reports and forecasts with corporate headquarters or a designated central cash management point abroad. Have them file monthly or more frequently, even daily, if operations are large enough to warrant the extra work.
- **Hold subsidiary cash positions to the minimum required to carry on operations.** Invest local funds in short-term paper only if there is no better place to use the money within the corporate family or to invest at a higher yield (and/or safety). Compute exchange commissions and possible taxes on money movements and consider exchange control guidelines.
- **Speed up collections.** Make sure that payments from customers and others that owe you money are received as quickly as possible. Consider offering discounts for prompt payment. Use person-to-person collection methods in countries with poor mailing systems.
- **Delay your own payments to suppliers and creditors until the due date.**
- **Make maximum use of "leads and lags" when currency markets are unstable.** Prepayment of imports makes a lot of sense if the currency in which the goods are billed is likely to be revalued.
- **Reduce or eliminate the float** (i.e., the period of time during which funds are in transit between banks). A fast method of funds transfer from subsidiaries to the parent or to a designated collection point is essential. A netting system among subsidiaries in a given country is one possibility (see Checklist 53).
- **Negotiate an agreement with an international bank** that ensures close cooperation or offers you a tailor-made system of international money mobilization and management. A bank may offer a large MNC a complete package covering collection and disbursement of funds with the use of central mobilization points. This greatly accelerates transfers and cuts the cost to the company. Some banks also offer a "cash pooling" function whereby each subsidiary of a corporate group keeps an account. This permits easy

washouts of intracompany accounts and pulls all excess funds into a single point from which they can be disbursed or invested on a day-to-day basis.

● **Improve the management and control of inventories,** if possible by unified regional systems (e.g., for all of Europe). Determining the right size of inventories for raw materials, components, and finished products is a formidable task—one that some companies use econometric systems to accomplish—but the resulting savings are worth the effort. Also, many companies have switched over from first in, first out (FIFO) to last in, first out (LIFO) accounting, which, in a period of rising prices, reduces taxable income. This, in turn, reduces current tax payments, conserves cash, and allows the company to rely on internal sources of funds.

● **Consider setting up a reinvoicing center in an overseas location with minimal exchange controls and low tax rates** (e.g., Switzerland or Bermuda). Such a center can facilitate international cash management, particularly netting, leading, and lagging.

● **Consider the possibility of presenting supplementary financial accounts adjusted for changing prices.** By displaying inflation-reduced profits, companies may be better able to resist excessive wage increases and reduce dividend payments. In countries that impose price controls, inflation accounting may put firms in a better position to argue for price increases and thus to improve their profitability.

● **Institute an exposure-management system to identify and hedge currency positions.**

● **Analyze all new projects for ways to cut capital costs, but keep in mind long-term needs.** Cutting the capital requirement to the bone has its merits, but only if anticipated expansion will not be endangered by too small a capital cover.

● **Do not overestimate the potential of self-financing** and have standby arrangements for external funds if they are needed. If borrowed funds are not needed within a relatively short period, they can always be invested. Normally, yields can be obtained that are only slightly below borrowing costs.

● **Rent land and buildings and work out leaseback arrangements.** Insurance companies and similar institutions in Europe have shown considerable willingness to invest in leaseback arrangements.

● **Lease equipment.** The cost of leasing can often be less than that of borrowing because of tax and depreciation benefits.

● **Subcontract production** when other firms can offer quality output, and when investment costs are high or payout periods are long.

● **Avoid tying up funds in assets that are illiquid or hard to move.**

● **Calculate carefully the cost of capital.** Internal funds are not free, and their cost should be compared with the cost of external funds or with opportunity costs.

---

50. Motivating and Directing Local Cash Managers

Even efficient companies should take steps to keep the organization in trim. An effective way to keep local managers thinking about cash management—even after the audit team leaves—is to let them know that headquarters is watching. The following checklist details some of the issues that must be addressed in order to sow the seeds of sound cash management at the local level.

● Have adequate cash management guidelines and procedures been established and disseminated?

● Are incentives provided—in the form of raises or prizes—for superior cash management performance?

● Is competition encouraged among subsidiaries to achieve reductions in DSO levels and improvements in other key cash management areas?

● Is your firm hiring local workers experienced in cash management?

● Can local staffs communicate effectively in English?

● Are local staffs being shown the principles of efficient cash management through training programs, seminars, consulting studies, or published materials?

● Do you issue formal systems manuals that spell out standard financial procedures to prevent disruptions resulting from employee turnover?

● Does the finance department set credit and sales terms in conjunction with the marketing staff?

● Have responsibilities for such functions as credit and collection, money market investments, and banking relations been clearly defined?

● Is interest income included when evaluating the performance of the foreign subsidiary or local manager?

Chapter 7
Building a Cross-Border Cash Management System

Chapter 6 shows MNC managers how to build liquidity from the ground up through effective local cash management. This chapter presents the basics of global cash management. The checklists are designed to help managers determine the ultimate level of sophistication their operations require.

More and more firms are turning to global cash management vehicles to reduce financial costs and upgrade managerial control. The following checklists will help treasury managers determine which systems they need, sell the system concept to both senior managers and local operations, and eventually implement their global cash management system.

51. How Sophisticated a Cross-Border System Do You Need?

Companies with a complex web of complementary cash, currency, and tax positions in different countries often find that a cross-border treasury system is a powerful tool for improving treasury management. But many treasury problems can be solved by a simple netting or pooling system, without resorting to the process of setting up a reinvoicing center or similar finance company. To get a clearer picture of whether a simple system will suffice or whether a full-scale treasury vehicle is required, managers should consider the following points.

(1) Do you need to protect your subsidiaries from excessive foreign exchange exposure? Executives need to decide if centralized exposure management—for example, through a reinvoicing center or factoring company—is an important concern. By concentrating expertise, dealing in volume, and identifying natural offsets, the treasury vehicle can manage exposure far more efficiently and at less cost than the subsidiaries can achieve individually.

If hedging efficiency or control is not required, however, a netting system may be sufficient. For small to midsized operations, a netting system—which cuts FX costs through a reduction in the number of currency transfers and conversions—will probably provide most of the savings available from a treasury vehicle, and at reduced start-up costs.

(2) Do you have substantial and complex intracompany cross-border trade? Smaller firms can easily develop procedures for an informal manual netting system. However, $50 million in annual intracompany flows is generally considered a minimum threshold for a formal automated cross-border netting system or for a treasury vehicle.

(3) Do your subsidiaries have cash surpluses and deficits between countries or over a period of time? If so, then a treasury vehicle can facilitate the pooling and shifting of cash. If surpluses and deficits are predictable, you will need a less sophisticated system. For complex situations with volatile local liquidities, your firm will probably need a reinvoicing center or other finance vehicle to manage liquidity.

(4) Do the tax positions of subsidiaries vary in a predictable way? A treasury vehicle can offer tax arbitrage benefits. The vehicle can be used both to shift interest income to subsidiaries in a loss position and to move interest expense to profitable tax-paying subsidiaries.

Further, a factoring or reinvoicing center can legitimately charge a significant markup on the transactions it processes. This can be very helpful in managing an excess foreign tax credit position (see Chapter 9 for more on the tax advantages of treasury vehicles).

(5) Can you benefit from economies of scale in finance and investing? A treasury vehicle allows companies to divide up a Euromarket issue among several subsidiaries, financing all of them at a lower rate than individual borrowings. Similarly, by pooling cash, subsidiaries can boost their yields on excess cash investments. By centralizing exposure, the cost of forward cover can be greatly reduced. Finally, centralizing financial management eliminates the need for duplicate functions at local levels.

(6) Is there resistance among your subsidiaries to centralizing the finance function? Parent company finance managers planning to centralize the finance function can often use a treasury vehicle to overcome resistance from subsidiaries. Local managers may resist the idea of loss of control, but they will find it hard to refute the benefits of a treasury vehicle. Further, they may see the vehicle as less threatening if it is located outside the parent's home country. For example, a reinvoicing center of a U.S. MNC in Europe centralizes control over European operations without removing the locus of power from the region.

(7) Do you have a manager capable of developing and running a treasury vehicle? Building a treasury vehicle requires not only financial expertise but also negotiation and interpersonal skills. The manager who heads the project must inspire confidence and enlist the support of local managers during the development phase. Moreover, these qualities are equally important once the system is in operation: For a treasury vehicle to be fully successful, it must always remain a cooperative venture with local subsidiaries.

52. Selling a System Concept: One Manager's Experience with Netting

Company A is the perfect candidate for a netting system. Its four Asian manufacturing sites—Malaysia, the Philippines, Taiwan, and Hong Kong—export products to sales subsidiaries in the United Kingdom, France, Italy, Germany, Canada, and Australia, as well as to its U.S. parent. This results in considerable intracompany transfers. Further, its Italian subsidiary not only sells but also manufactures some of the company's larger products and supplies them to the other sales subsidiaries, creating yet another channel of interdivisional cash flow. The company's assistant treasurer realized that the firm needed a netting system to link these multiple operations.

He soon found, however, that his most critical task was to convince headquarters and foreign management of this fact. Despite the clear need for the system, it took a full year to design it, to convince management of its merits, to educate foreign controllers, and, finally, to implement. The following checklist shows how the assistant treasurer went about selling the idea within the company. These points should help other managers overcome internal resistance.

(1) Submit a formal proposal. Convinced of the merits of a netting system, the assistant treasurer submitted a formal proposal to senior company officials. "Everyone in management had different concerns about the system," he commented. Three concerns were voiced immediately by the corporate treasurer:

● **Effect on subsidiaries' borrowing requirements.** This proved a difficult question to answer. Since the firm was changing its product lines, the assistant treasurer's year-old data were not fully applicable. "I had to make a lot of assumptions to answer him," the assistant treasurer said. "But eventually he was convinced that any problems could be handled."

● **Possible resistance by local controllers.** The assistant treasurer responded by talking up the advantages the system would offer to local controllers. He pointed out that netting would facilitate cash planning and forecasting by local staff, reduce the paperwork involved in paying and receiving invoices, and give subsidiaries a consistent set of records that would identify all important exports and imports.

● **Exchange control problems.** The assistant treasurer turned to experts at Citibank to resolve this concern. "We went country by country, and they told us the difficulties in each and how they could help us gain government permission to net."

For example, the bank's cash management experts pointed out that Italy allows netting only with special permission. However, they also knew how to meet Italian requirements. Said the assistant treasurer, "All I had to do was send our controller to the bank, and they showed him the forms that had to be filled out. It took three months to get permission from the central bank in Italy."

(2) Convince the CFO. Once the treasurer was sold on netting, the CFO had to be convinced. Commented the assistant treasurer, "We knew what he wanted. It was control. So we just hit on the control issues, showing him how netting would improve his control of global cash movements, invoicing, and shipping." The CFO was delighted and gave his approval.

(3) Convince headquarters . . . Next, treasury had to present the system to headquarters' operating management. The main selling points for the operating managers were the same as those that persuaded the foreign subsidiaries—ease of planning and predictability of cash flows.

(4) . . . and local subsidiaries. Getting the support of foreign subsidiary managers took longer than winning over headquarters. Eventually, the subsidiary managers saw the benefits to local operations. European subsidiaries responded favorably to the fact that the system would ease their borrowing requirements. The Asian subsidiaries were ultimately sold by the fact that netting would cut down the time needed to track payments.

53. The Nine Advantages of Netting

The following checklist highlights the nine most frequently mentioned benefits to be derived from netting. This should help managers decide if a netting system is warranted. If so, the checklist also provides the basic arguments that will help sell the concept within the company.

(1) Reduced currency-conversion costs due to fewer FX transactions. One U.S. computer company slashed the number of currency deals from approximately 75 a month to fewer than 30. The firm's treasurer proclaimed, "We made $500,000 in annual savings by more than halving the number of FX transactions."

(2) Finer FX spreads as a result of centralized FX trading. The treasury manager of the German regional office of a U.S. company explains: "We get an enormous amount of efficiency and savings because of more competitive bidding."

(3) Reduced funds-transfer costs because of fewer transactions. "What's the advantage? Fewer funds transfers and therefore lower costs," said one finance director.

(4) Minimal float due to same-day value of transfers. "A vital part of the system is the fact that all funds are transferred with same-day value, eliminating float," commented one company's assistant treasurer.

(5) More effective planning and forecasting of cash flows. "The biggest advantages are qualitative," in the view of one Swiss corporate executive. "It has allowed everybody to plan much better on transfers and, therefore, on needs. If you know on a certain day of the month that you're going to pay out francs, you can take advantage of the short-term money markets by investing until exactly that date."

(6) Greater control over group settlement and reconciliation. This benefit was best described by the treasurer of a Swiss electronics firm. "Prior to implementation of the system, the companies dealt with one another. We would hear funny stories. The manager from one company would say, 'This company has not paid us,' to which the other firm would reply, 'We're not paying until they pay us for some other invoice,' and so on. The netting system put a stop to the whole thing by saying, 'Everybody pays on one date, and what's due is due.'"

(7) Reduced administrative work load for subsidiary managers. "Netting allows my subsidiaries to refine and streamline their operations and reduce their overall burden," reported the treasurer of the U.K. regional office of a U.S. automotive maker.

(8) Better control over cash and exposure management. The group treasurer of a Swiss MNC commented on this point: "Before our netting system, it was an incredible situation, because one day we were receiving a currency, and the next day we were needing that currency. We were selling it one day, buying it back the next. Netting has allowed for a very rational system of exposure management."

(9) Better and more consistent banking transfer channels. One U.S. MNC interviewed by BI has established a worldwide netting program that channels all funds transfers through the global branch network of a single bank. "We find the transfers go easier by having each subsidiary transfer or receive its funds at a branch of bank X or one of its correspondent banks," said the firm's treasurer.

54. How to Set Up a Cash-Pooling System

Cash-pooling systems siphon cash from local operating units in various countries to a single concentration point. From this central operation, surplus funds can be invested for higher yields or onlended, thus transferring excess intercompany liquidity from cash-rich to cash-poor subsidiaries.

Cash pooling is a basic building block of any cross-border system. But it requires a great deal of effort to put into operation in the initial stages. To implement an effective system, managers will need to address each of the following organizational issues.

(1) Establish daily reporting procedures. Participating units should report daily, via telephone or telex, their expected receipts and disbursements for that day. This step is essential for allowing the corporate "money desk" to determine its cash position for the day. Early and accurate information will help the firm to achieve higher interest on investments and enable it to manage intercompany liquidity more effectively.

(2) Make sure the bank involved communicates the company's daily balance reports. This information can be calculated to determine the cash position of each subsidiary, thus minimizing the firm's overall borrowing needs and optimizing returns on short-term investments.

(3) The subsidiaries must send all surplus funds to the company's central account. In this way, payments can be netted and the firm can benefit from economies of scale on borrowing and investing.

(4) Offer an advantageous interest rate to subsidiaries. A favorable rate will attract subsidiary participation to borrow money or invest through the central account.

(5) Negotiate for the best rates with the bank handling the account. Because the central account will hold a significant amount, a company can negotiate lower bank transaction costs.

(6) Subsidiaries should submit detailed cash forecasts. If supplied on a monthly and a yearly basis, these projections will help refine central management borrowing and investment decisions.

(7) Consider combining cash pooling with domestic netting to reap greater savings. A French manufacturer set up a cash-pooling system and expanded its domestic netting system. The operating units could hold no excess cash and had to come to the central treasury for their funding requirements. The central treasury calculated the whole group's position and transferred only the net amount, thus reducing funds-transfer costs and simplifying reconciliation procedures. Through its cash-pooling and netting arrangements, the firm's treasury headquarters has become a form of central bank, i.e., by shifting funds, making loans, and investing surplus cash.

55. The Benefits of Reinvoicing

By concentrating cross-border trade flows in one entity, a reinvoicing company is well positioned to exercise direct control over a broad range of treasury functions, including cash management, bank balance management, tax planning, FX trading, and hedging. Managers conducting a cost-benefit analysis of such a vehicle should weigh the start-up costs against these 10 key advantages.

(1) By centralizing currency exposure, the center removes risks from subsidiaries. Typically, the reinvoicing center is billed in the exporter's local currency and reinvoices in the importer's local currency, thereby assuming the exposure. This improves the quality and reduces the costs of any hedging program.

(2) Upgrades monitoring and control of cash and trade flows. Because billing is handled centrally, reinvoicing companies can simplify the tracking and analysis of intracompany payables and receivables. Just as important, they impose discipline on intracompany billing practices and observance of credit terms. Said one executive, "The reinvoicing center gave us the systems we needed to control our cash flows."

(3) Centralizes cash and exposure management expertise. Treasury management is an area best handled in a consistent and efficient manner. Said the financial manager of a U.S. food and beverage firm, "When you have a decentralized system with lots of people coming in and out—and they're handling FX—the philosophy becomes inconsistent. Things are tried, mistakes are made. Sometimes mistakes have to be made in order for people to learn, but the point is, you don't want to see those same learning mistakes made year after year. Therefore, having one center with continuity of expertise and philosophy is a big plus. With FX, one mistake can wipe out the value of a million cases of milk."

(4) Facilitates liquidity management. Reinvoicing gives a company greater flexibility in shifting liquidity between subsidiaries through the leading and lagging of intracompany payments. For example, if both the exporting and importing subsidiaries need funds, simultaneous leading and lagging can be accomplished through a reinvoicing center.

(5) Cuts borrowing costs and increases investment yield. A company has more clout if it handles all bank borrowing through a reinvoicing center than if each subsidiary raises its own financing. Similarly, by pooling cash resources at the reinvoicing center, a company will be able to maximize investment yields. According to a U.S. finance executive, "We pool cash through our intracompany trade accounts via our reinvoicing center and invest at a higher rate."

(6) Opens arbitrage opportunities. Centralizing both cash and financial expertise allows firms the luxury of careful financial analysis. Explains one company's treasurer, "With everything centralized, we find it's often worth the effort to compare an investment in Australian dollars, with a forward contract back to U.S. dollars, to a straight U.S. dollar placement. We couldn't afford to maintain this level of expertise at the local level, and the size of the deposits would be almost trivial—not worth the effort."

(7) Improves export trading. A major benefit of reinvoicing is that it enables firms to concentrate the expertise needed to trade successfully with low-volume, highly complex countries. "It's better to have one organization that deals with these exotic countries—one credit and collection department that knows the procedures on how to sell to Eastern Europe or Nigeria," contends the treasurer of a major chemicals firm.

Reinvoicing centers also give exporters a marketing edge, since imports can be billed in local currencies. "One reason Japanese trading companies have been so successful is their ability to bill in local currency," one reinvoicing company's manager remarked.

(8) Improves trade finance. Banks are more willing to provide export finance for higher-risk countries if the business is offset by export finance (and other transactions) to lower-risk countries. A centralized facility can build a more attractive volume of business than can subsidiaries acting on their own. Firms that have used a reinvoicing center to centralize trade finance have found that, in general, their increased clout gets them better rates—and more high-risk financing—at any given bank.

(9) Acts as central purchasing agent on behalf of the company's subsidiaries. "Our reinvoicing center buys commodities needed by the subsidiaries to manufacture their products," explains a U.K. treasury manager. "We have more clout because we purchase large quantities, and we have the expertise to determine when to enter the market and how to hedge our exposure."

(10) Provides tax advantages. Reinvoicing centers provide a legitimate means of increasing transfer prices. The services provided have real value; hence, they may be billed. Since reinvoicing centers are typically located in low-tax jurisdictions, this can be of significant benefit to a firm's excess foreign-tax credit position.

56. The Benefits of Factoring vs. Reinvoicing

Factoring has become popular because it is a relatively simple means of gaining the advantages of reinvoicing with significantly fewer operational complexities. It is important to note, however, that there are varying degrees of complexity among both factoring and reinvoicing companies. In their most sophisticated forms, the two systems are virtually indistinguishable.

Bear in mind that in its basic form a factoring center can be the most efficient means of improving global cash management. The benefits of factoring are the following.

(1) Factoring centers are usually simpler and less costly to establish and operate than reinvoicing centers. Only one invoice is required for factoring, rather than the two needed for reinvoicing. Therefore, administrative costs are reduced.

(2) Factoring reduces transfer-pricing problems and legal hurdles. Because factoring is merely the discounting of trade receivables, not the transfer of title, it avoids many of the transfer-pricing problems of reinvoicing. "Factoring does not have the stigma of transfer pricing—profit shifting," says one executive. He maintains that factoring is far simpler to implement because it is subject to less stringent government scrutiny.

(3) Like a reinvoicing center, in-house factoring centralizes exposure. By paying an exporting subsidiary in its own currency and receiving payment in the currency of the importing subsidiary, the centralized factoring unit assumes and manages the FX risk.

(4) Factoring reduces funds-transfer and currency-conversion costs. Because factoring units handle financial transactions centrally, they have increased leverage with banks and they can negotiate low transfer costs and narrow FX spreads.

(5) Factoring companies can shift liquidity. Factoring companies can lead and lag much like a reinvoicing center. Factoring is slightly less flexible, however, since credit terms must be established up front and cannot be adjusted.

(6) Factoring cuts borrowing costs and increases investment yields. Like reinvoicing companies, a centralized factoring entity can achieve lower borrowing costs and higher yields resulting from economies of scale.

(7) Factoring avoids the need for a separate legal entity. "If you can avoid it, there's no point in creating a whole new company," says one company's Netherlands-based spokesman.

(8) Factoring offers tax benefits. Although the spreads that can be earned through factoring are lower than those earned through reinvoicing, a reinvoicing center that takes legal ownership performs more functions. Nonetheless, a factoring facility essentially offers the same tax benefits as a reinvoicing center.

(9) Factoring is ideal for export financing. "If your primary reason for setting up a cross-border vehicle is export financing," explains one treasury consultant, "you should probably choose an in-house factoring company." In general, a factoring company offers the same exporting advantages as a reinvoicing company.

57. Automating a Full Treasury Vehicle: An Information Checklist

The most sophisticated factoring or reinvoicing centers integrate subsystems such as pooling, netting, leading, and lagging. To do so, they need adequate information and computer support. The following checklist identifies the accounting information and computer capabilities necessary for a state-of-the-art treasury vehicle.

Raw Data

(1) Get information on purchases to determine cash and currency outflows and the status of payments. Ensure that you have the following details:
- Selling company's name;
- Invoice number (or description), date, and due date;
- Currency and amount;
- Special terms (e.g., discount for prompt or early payment, interest rates, charges on late payments); and
- Ultimate purchaser (i.e., company actually receiving the goods).

(2) Get information on sales to determine cash and currency inflows and the status of receivables. This should include:
- Purchasing company's name, country, and paying bank;
- Invoice number (or description), date, and due date;
- Currency and amount; and
- Special terms.

(3) Enter information on exchange rates and interest rates. This should include:
- Book rates;
- Market spot rates (actual);
- Market forward rates (and forecast spot rates);
- Interest rates; and
- Standardized 360- or 365-day basis.

(4) Keep track of other pertinent accounting data. These will include:
- Nontrade receipts;
- Nontrade payables;
- Borrowings;
- Investments;
- Forward contracts;
- Operating expenses and taxes;
- Capital infusions; and
- Dividends.

Computer Requirements

The above information can be processed using one of the following:
- The on-site computers of the finance center;
- A sister company's computers, with each export having a subledger that is managed on behalf of the center; or
- An outside vendor's computer.

The choice will be determined by what is available at the sister company level, how it can be adapted, and how information can be communicated between the computer center and the finance center. Alternatively, use of on-site accounting and management information systems will depend on the funds available and the time that can be spent on start-up.

The following is a list of typical reports that can be generated:

Reports

(1) Detailed list of purchases—month to date:

Date	Seller	Invoice No.	Due Date	Currency	Amount

(2) Summary list of purchases—month to date and year to date:

Seller	Currency	Amount	Exchange Rate	Base Currency Equiv.

(3) Detailed list of sales—month to date:

Date	Purchaser	Invoice No.	Due Date	Currency	Amount

(4) Summary of sales—month to date and year to date:

Purchaser	Currency	Amount	Exchange Rates	Base Currency Equiv.

(5) Summary list of inventory:

Seller	Currency	Amount	Exchange Rate	Base Currency Equiv.

(6) Calculations of the price of purchases and sales:

Purchases				Sales		
Invoice No.	Currency	Amount	Ex. Rate	Currency	Amount	Invoice No.

(7) Accounts receivable by company:

Company	Currency	Amount	Exchange Rate	Base Currency Equiv.

(8) Accounts receivable aging (in days):

Company	0–30	31–60	61–90	90–180	No. Days

(9) Accounts receivable by currency:

Currency	Amount	Exchange Rate	Base Currency Equiv.

(10) Accounts payable by company:

Company	Currency	Amount	Exchange Rate	Base Currency Equiv.

(11) Accounts payable aging (in days):

Company	0–30	31–60	61–90	90–180	No. Days

(12) Accounts payable by currency:

Currency	Amount	Exchange Rate	Base Currency Equiv.

(13) Accounts receivable by currency and due date:

Currency	Current	1 Month	3 Months	6 Months

(14) Accounts payable by currency and due date:

Currency	Current	1 Month	3 Months	6 Months

(15) Detailed list of borrowings:

Currency	Amount	Date	Maturity	Interest Rate	Owed	Bank

(16) Detailed list of investments:

Currency	Amount	Date	Maturity	Interest Rate	Owed	Bank

(17) Detailed list of FX contracts:

Currency Bought	Amount	Currency Sold	Amount	Date	Maturity	Bank

(18) Currency exposure statement:

Period	1	2	3	4	5	6	Total
+ Receivables							
− Payables							
= Trading exposure							
+ Investment and cash							
− Borrowings							
+ FX purchases							
− FX sales							
= Total exposure							

Base currency equiv. _____

(19) Currency exposure statement summary (by currency or base equiv.):

Currency	Period 1	2	3	4	5	6	Total
US$							
£							
Dm							
Ffr							
L							
etc.							

(20) Hedging tactics analysis:

Currency	Amount	Spot Rate	Hedged Rate	Earnings (Costs)

(21) Summary of hedging earnings (costs):

Currency	Earnings	Base Currency Equiv.

Computer Calculations

The calculations that produce these figures are the following.

(1) Sales equivalent of purchases—determined by multiplying purchases by the exchange rate applicable to ultimate purchases.

(2) Accounts receivable by currency and company—determined by adding sales and deducting receipts.

(3) Accounts payable by currency and company—determined by adding purchases and deducting payments.

(4) Inventory or stock in hand—determined by adding purchases and deducting sales after converting to base-currency equivalents.

(5) Borrowings outstanding by currency—determined by adding borrowings and deducting repayments.

(6) Investments outstanding by currency—determined by adding investments bought and deducting investments sold or matured.

(7) Forward purchase contracts by currency—determined by adding forward purchase contracts and deducting contracts matured.

(8) Forward sales contracts by currency—determined by adding forward sales contracts and deducting contracts matured.

(9) Aggregate exposure by currency—determined by adding items 2, 6, and 7 above and deducting items 3, 5, and 8.

(10) Exposure by currency and date—determined by adding items 2, 6, and 7 above and deducting items, 3, 5, and 8.

(11) Base currency or currency of domicile—determined by multiplying any of the above by the appropriate exchange rates.

(12) Revenue:

(a) By currency—determined by adding sales, exchange gains, and interest income.

(b) By base currency or currency of domicile—determined by multiplying revenue by exchange rate.

(13) Expenses:

    (a) By currency—determined by adding the cost of goods sold (purchases have been reinvoiced), interest expense, exchange losses, and operating expenses.

    (b) By base currency or currency of domicile—determined by multiplying expense by exchange rate.

(14) Profit (loss) by currency, base currency, or currency of domicile—determined by subtracting expense (13a or 13b) from revenue (12a or 12b).

(15) Net financial cost or earnings of hedging transactions—determined by converting the forward exchange premium or discount profits into an annual percentage, and then dividing by the spot rate and annualizing.

(16) Earnings or costs of hedging—determined by multiplying aggregate exposure (9), or exposure by date (10), by net financial cost or earnings.

(17) Accounts receivable aging by currency and company—determined at the user's option from the invoice date or due date, applying gross amounts to time periods.

(18) Accounts payable aging—determined as in item 17.

(19) Balance sheet—determined by converting assets and liabilities to base currency or currency of domicile.

---

58. Choosing the Best Country for Siting a Treasury Vehicle

The final problem (or, in some cases, the initial problem) for a treasury manager to solve is where to site a treasury vehicle. The right location can yield savings on FX and borrowing costs and strengthen the company's negotiating position with banks. But companies that choose the wrong location risk bureaucratic hassles with the central bank, burdensome taxes, and problematic exchange controls. To help firms pick the best location, the following checklist pinpoints the eight critical factors to examine when siting a treasury vehicle.

(1) **Is a subsidiary already operating in the country?** Using staff and facilities at an existing subsidiary can help reduce start-up and operating costs. "We set up our reinvoicing company in Geneva because we already had a subsidiary in that city serving as our regional headquarters," said the treasurer of a U.S. manufacturing MNC. "Sharing facilities saved us a lot."

(2) **Are labor costs reasonable?** Skilled clerical and financial employees cost more in Switzerland than in most other European countries. Some companies split their operations, maintaining a small staff in, for instance, Switzerland and a larger staff—typically computer and other support operations—in another country (the Netherlands is a popular support location).

Corporate residence requirements, which vary by country, may restrict this strategy. Some governments demand a high proportion of managerial or operational functions to be performed in the country of incorporation.

(3) **Are banking costs reasonable?** The cost of taking forward cover, funds transfers, borrowing, and maintaining accounts differs by country. For example, banking costs in the United Kingdom are reputed to be lower than those in Switzerland. "We get better rates in the United Kingdom than in Switzerland because there's more competition," noted one financial executive.

(4) **Is the location convenient to a money center?** The vehicle must be either in a major money center, such as London, or in a country that has good communications with—and is in a similar time zone as—a major money center.

This point is especially important for U.S. MNCs with European operations. If U.S. tax is the main consideration, the finance vehicle would be best placed in the United States. But for day-to-day operations in Europe, such an entity would only have a two- or three-hour communications window for obtaining and acting on European information.

Compounding this problem is the fact that the window opens late in the operating day of European financial markets. Thus, practical requirements call for a vehicle to be established in the same time zone in which it is going to operate, unless a company intends to set up a 24-hour treasury function.

(5) **Is the country's financial infrastructure adequate?** The country should have a financial infrastructure capable of absorbing large transactions and providing efficient communication. The banks must be able to offer multiple-currency-denominated accounts for the collection of third-party receivables, for payments to third parties, and for the flow of intracompany funds. These accounts will be required to support FX transactions.

Most companies choose to locate multiple-currency operating accounts in a major money center, usually London, even though the vehicle may be incorporated in another country.

The vehicle's ability to use offshore bank accounts is a prime consideration when determining its country of incorporation.

(6) **What tax rate will apply to the vehicle?** This is not necessarily the local corporate tax rate. Belgium, for example, has offered a 10-year tax holiday to firms that establish finance and factoring companies. The local rates often vary depending on the size of the operation, the number of employees, and the tax status of existing subsidiaries within the country. Given the low margin associated with treasury vehicles, tax authorities frequently levy tax on a percentage of turnover or operating expenses.

(7) **How will the tax-treaty network affect withholding taxes?** More important than the local tax rate is the network of tax treaties in a country. According to a financial

executive of one reinvoicing company, "Our goal is to make sure that there are tax treaties that will reduce withholding taxes on payments of interest, royalties, and license fees."

There are a number of countries offering low or nonexistent corporate tax rates that have become traditional sites for financial vehicles. "Brass plate" companies, with no actual substance, can be established in these tax havens, with management and operational functions performed offshore. Nevertheless, some governments—notably those of the United States and United Kingdom—are seeking ways to tighten control over such operations.

(8) Are exchange controls flexible? Whenever possible, a treasury vehicle should be located in a country with non-existent, or at least negligible, exchange controls. Firms should look not only at the current situation but also at the government's track record.

Chapter 8
Finding the Best Deals in Export Finance

The worldwide financial crisis and the accompanying local credit and hard currency crunches have heightened the risks of exporting and made it much more difficult for exporters to find the trade financing needed to sell overseas. Still, with the fierce competition in evidence throughout the world, companies are finding that financing has, more often than not, become the most critical element in making a sale: Companies than can offer low-cost financing today have a clear competitive edge.

The treasury manager is ideally suited for leadership in this fundamental area. A principal link in both the credit and collections processes, as well as in banking relations, the treasury manager should make every effort to help his firm identify and utilize the various sources of export credit. The following checklists will help managers in this vein. First, the chapter highlights the key sources of trade finance; second, it delineates how firms should work with various financial intermediaries to get the best deal and the best access to risky market financing. Finally, the checklists show how a treasury manager can keep his own house in order by building an efficient international collections function.

59. Seven Steps to Better Export Financing

Companies that would like to increase their exports should be prepared to examine all avenues of trade finance. The treasury manager can assist in this effort by making sure that all local operators are aware of, and are pursuing, all of the various opportunities. The following checklist is a primer of how the most successful firms go after export financing:

(1) Tap official export programs whenever possible. Exporters should explore the full range of export credit programs and pick the ones that best suit their needs. The most common include Eximbank, the Foreign Credit Insurance Association (FCIA), the Agency for International Development (AID), the Overseas Private Investment Corporation (OPIC), the Commodity Credit Corporation (CCC), and the Small Business Administration (SBA).

International agencies, such as the World Bank, and various regional development banks are also potential sources of financing. Exporters able to source from foreign subsidiaries should always try to tap foreign export credit programs, because they offer the cheapest money available in the world. Foreign countries such as the United Kingdom, France, Germany, Italy, Canada, Brazil, and Mexico have their own export credit programs. Even if the funds are not needed to support trade, they can be swapped through today's capital market into any major world currency.

(2) Investigate all private sources of export credit. Exporters can benefit from a wide array of private suppliers of export credit, including money center banks, regional banks, U.S. branches of foreign banks, Edge Act banks, factoring companies, trade finance companies, leasing companies, forfait houses, export trading companies, and private insurers. As traditional private sources of credit dry up, exporters must become familiar with forfait houses and other new sources of export financing. Exporters who wish to sell to risky countries or customers may prefer the flexibility of private insurance over official programs.

(3) Take a fresh look at export payment terms. Payment terms used in the past may not be appropriate in today's risky environment. To choose the best payment terms, exporters must consider the trade-off between cost, risk, and marketing considerations, as well as local country and industry practices.

(4) Know all the financing techniques available to your firm. Exporters can choose from myriad techniques to finance export, ranging from discounting receivables and factoring to banker's acceptances, bank lines of credit, leasing, and forfaiting.

(5) Adapt to countertrade regulations and other new exporting ground rules. Because of the worldwide financial crisis and the resulting shortages of hard currency, an increasing number of countries are establishing official or unofficial requirements for countertrade, arrangements under which exporters must take products from the importing country to make the sale. Obviously, exporters who wish to penetrate or maintain these export markets, such as Indonesia and the Philippines, must become familiar with countertrade and must formulate effective export policies and strategies.

(6) Take advantage of advanced export financing vehicles. Exporters may benefit from export-oriented vehicles such as export trading companies, reinvoicing centers, finance companies, export factoring companies, and DISCs. These vehicles not only facilitate export financing but also simplify other related activities, such as export collections, currency exposure management, billing practices, tax management, and countertrade.

(7) Understand your firm's limitations in trade financing. Small and medium-sized exporters clearly face more problems in financing exports than do large, sophisticated exporters. While small companies may have to try harder, perseverance will pay off by producing many ways to finance exports successfully.

60. How to Get Export Financing in Risky Markets

Tight local credit and intense competition (particularly from Japanese and German firms, which regularly obtain low-cost government-sponsored financing) make Third World markets a tough sell. In many cases, the only way for capital goods exporters to win these incremental sales is to offer flexible, deferred credit terms to foreign importers or accept countertrade.

However, one way to make this situation palatable is to offer these terms and then transfer the payment risk to a nonrecourse export financing entity. With nonrecourse financing, the supplier sells his receivables at a steep discount. The mechanism transfers the payment risk from the supplier to the bank (or other institution) and allows the exporter to receive payment in cash up front.

Although nonrecourse financing is expensive, limited, and sometimes almost nonexistent (currently the situation), for risk-averse firms it is often the only solution. When looking for nonrecourse financing, exporters should explore the following avenues:

(1) The forfait market. Many banks and finance companies based in London, Vienna, Zurich, Frankfurt, and New York are frequent participants in forfait, nonrecourse discounting of trade bills guaranteed by a bank in the importer's country. The draft, discounted at a fixed rate, can run anywhere from three months to five years. All FX, interest rate, commercial, and political risks are assumed by the forfait house.

When the forfaiter (a commercial bank or specialized trade financing company) purchases the exporter's claims, these are usually "avalized," or irrevocably guaranteed by a government agency or prime bank in the importer's country. But since the definition of the aval is not the same in all countries, the document should stipulate under which nation's laws the guarantee is enforceable. The exporter must verify that the importer's country recognizes an unconditional guarantee.

(2) The private insurance market. Another nonrecourse financing technique is to purchase insurance in the private political-risk market in New York or London. Political-risk insurers include the American Foreign Insurance Association (AFIA), American Investors Group (AIG), Political Risk Inc., Chubb, and Lloyd's of London. Exporters are advised to see a broker who specializes in private insurance.

(3) Foreign export credit programs. In addition to the private insurance market, exporters can benefit from official foreign programs. Although government insurance programs have become more restrictive in the areas of political and commercial risk, some are more flexible than others. For example, the United Kingdom's Export Credit Guarantee Department (ECGD) can be especially useful for insuring exports that do not originate in the United Kingdom.

(4) Export finance companies. Export finance companies are generally connected with a European bank and provide financing directly to importers. Although most credits are contracted on short terms, some companies will provide medium-term nonrecourse financing. The package is based on the creditworthiness of the importer, and the exporter is paid upon presentation of papers showing that the goods have been shipped.

(5) Bankers acceptances (BAs). BAs are usually drawn with some recourse to the exporter. Although exporters are not responsible for credit risk, they seek banks that take on the country risk. Exporters may find BA credit to developing countries drying up suddenly. An exporter who ships to the Middle East notes: "The U.S. bank might suddenly become uncomfortable with the issuing bank because of political circumstances, and all at once it might cut you off from accepting the drafts. We had that problem in Iraq."

(6) Receivables purchase. A bank may buy the exporter's trade receivables, but if the bank cannot collect, some risk to the exporter remains. To reduce commercial and political risks, exporters can buy insurance from organizations such as the FCIA, AIG, and AFIA.

(7) Buyer credit arranged by supplier. The bank arranging the buyer credit may ask that the exporter buy insurance to cover the bank's receivables from the importer. However, the policy might not cover nonacceptance of goods by the importer or might be invalidated by the exporter's failure to comply with the terms of the contract. The bank might then seek indemnification from the exporter.

(8) Bank line of credit. If the importer's government controls the allocation of FX, the bank must be assured that FX will be available to service the loan. Convertibility insurance may be required by the bank, but the bank may help the exporter line up coverage through official export incentive programs.

61. Export Finance: Finding the Best Bank to Get the Best Deal

The hard currency shortages and exchange controls inspired by the debt crisis have made finding optimal sources of export financing more difficult than ever. However, in most cases, the first place to look is the commercial banks. To help firms narrow the search for the right bank to work with, exporters should consider the following points:

(1) How sophisticated is the bank in export financing? Make sure that the bank's export finance department has extensive experience and that the individual you deal with is knowledgeable. Discuss your company's needs with a representative from the export finance group, rather than with a banking generalist.

(2) Does it offer the products and services you need? It doesn't matter how knowledgeable or efficient a bank is if its products and services do not match the exporter's needs. If your company is frequently faced with countertrade requirements, for example, look for a bank with an export trading company.

(3) Is financing truly available? Look around for the bank most willing to finance deals for a particular country.

Find out where various banks have branches, representative offices, or correspondent banks and where they want to continue to do business. This is a function of a bank's level of involvement in a country, including its willingness to operate in a risky environment. Supply financing to a particular country—especially a risky one—changes over time, depending on the bank's exposure in each country and its perception of risk. Exporters must try several banks and other financial institutions to locate the one or two that have open windows.

(4) Are there any restrictions on your exports? Some banks, as a matter of policy, will not finance sales of certain types of goods.

(5) How responsive is the bank? Look for banks that will give you a financing decision quickly and execute the arrangement promptly. "We had one bank that delayed confirming a letter of credit for weeks, and the goods just sat in the warehouse," remarked one unhappy exporter. "Their inefficiency was costly."

(6) How much risk will the bank take? Look for banks

that do not demand that the exporter provide guarantees or insurance on riskier exports.

(7) Stress the overall relationship. A transaction is profitable to a commercial bank only if it is in the million-dollar range. But even large exporters will fill small export orders—which are not profitable in themselves—if the exporter has a well-developed relationship with the bank. In other words, companies should seek export financing at banks where they maintain large balances and do other business. By stressing the relationship value of the financing to the bank, the exporter may be able to negotiate a small trade credit.

(8) Provide sufficient information. Banks have confidence in informed, sophisticated exporters, and sophisticated exporters prepare documentation thoroughly. Specifically, exporters should provide information on the buyer or importer so that the bank can make an evaluation.

(9) Buy insurance. Faced with increased risk, many banks require that the exporter be insured. One banker explained it this way: "The availability of political and commercial risk insurance can do two things for exporters. One, of course, is just to insure against catastrophic loss. The second is to make it easier to gain access to bank financing that might not otherwise be available for a given transaction."

(10) Negotiate. Terms and rates are almost always negotiable. One exporter suggests that companies "try to interest several banks in the same deal and seek the best rate from each."

But some exporters disagree with this approach. One major exporter uses what it calls a "lead bank approach," under which it gives a specific bank preference on all its financing needs in a particular country. The company believes that this system results in better treatment from its chosen bank.

(11) Accept recourse. When all else fails, an exporter may have to accept recourse on a deal that the bank considers risky. Remarks one banker: "Even with government insurance, there is a certain amount of export risk retention. Exporters have to be prepared to take that risk rather than try to lay the whole amount on the bank."

---

62. How to Cut Float Time on Export Collections

Payment float on export sales can cost millions of dollars every year. To reduce losses caused by inefficient payment patterns, firms should take the following 10 steps to speed export payments.

(1) Choose the best method of transfer. Probably the single most useful step is to bring payments in by express money transfer rather than by the ordinary methods of mail transfer or bank draft. For most amounts, the fees required for express payments are less than the savings generated by putting the money to use more quickly.

(2) Provide full bank account information. Many transfers cannot be credited directly to the exporter's bank account by the bank's international center because account details are missing. By providing your account number and your bank's name, branch address, and sort code on the transfer instructions to the importer, you can save up to a week in some cases. The money can be transferred to your bank account the same day from the clearing bank via automated clearinghouse systems.

(3) Cut the banking chain to a minimum. An international money transfer can pass through a surprisingly large number of banks between the time it is initiated by the customer and the time the money arrives at the exporter's local branch. A careful examination of the routing with your bank, the customer, and the customer's bank can often reveal quicker routes. For larger customers, it may even be worthwhile for both of you to hold accounts with the same bank or with banks that are full correspondents.

(4) Use banking services to the fullest. Assess your bank's strength in and knowledge of your main markets, where it should preferably have its own offices or at least first-class correspondents. It may be necessary to use the services of different banks if no one bank meets all your needs.

(5) Evaluate where you exchange or hold currencies. Conversion of the customer's payment into the exporter's home currency usually occurs in the exporter's country. Sometimes, however, it is quicker to exchange the money at a financial center in the importer's country when the exchange rate is competitive. Some exporters also find it useful to maintain accounts in several foreign currencies either at home or overseas, although variations in exchange and interest rates must be taken into consideration.

(6) Don't ignore low-value transfers. As a basic rule, the lower the value, the slower the transfer. Delays and losses may be significant if the exporter's business consists of large numbers of small consignments. In such cases, it is useful to give the bank standing instructions—for example, to place receipts on deposit and group individual amounts until transfer becomes worthwhile.

(7) Pay close attention to high-value transfers. For high values, every day saved can avoid substantial interest payments. It is worthwhile to make arrangements with customers not only to transfer the money by the fastest means possible but also to avoid initiating the transfer immediately before a weekend or public holiday—the point being that one of you should have use of the money. Discuss with your bank any special arrangements to avoid missing cutoff times.

(8) Tighten up internal responsibilities. Make someone responsible for controlling float time, which may be overlooked if responsibility falls between departments. Improve coordination across the company to make certain that all avoidable delays are in fact avoided. Allocate a due date to every export invoice and make regular checks to identify delays. Finally, encourage your staff to work closely with their counterparts in the banks and to become attuned to the financial costs of dead time.

(9) Monitor improvements. Only in this way can an accurate measure be made of the tangible benefits of better export receivables management. Monitoring will also reveal where such benefits have not materialized and where improvements are still needed.

(10) Institute a plan of action if the money is missing. If you know that the customer has paid but you have not received the money, make certain that the customer followed payment instructions. Some customers are known for their skill and innovation in slowing down payments, using cheap, slower methods instead of those requested by the exporter. Get the name of the initiating bank and the transfer reference number and date, and pass that information on to your local bank. Finally, ask the customer to investigate from his end.

---

63. Seventeen Proven Methods to Speed Export Collections

International credit and cash managers must cut through a thicket of difficulties when collecting export proceeds, particularly from the world's developing nations. Among the most common snarls are cumbersome trade regulations, FX conversion problems, government red tape and corruption, high country risk, customer delays and bankruptcies, and inefficient mail and banking systems. But there are tactics to improve in-house payments and funds transfers, as this final checklist reveals.

(1) Train employees fully. The key to effective export collections is well-trained personnel; any carelessness gives customers and banks an excuse to delay payment. One potential tool is a systems manual that spells out internal procedures. Some firms have instituted in-house training programs to educate export staff in efficient cash management.

(2) Maintain adequate backup documentation. Customers often withhold payment until documentation questions are resolved. These delays can be minimized by maintaining good files on the terms of the transactions, copies of invoices, and other data that can be easily accessed.

(3) Communicate payment instructions clearly. To ensure that importers pay via the most cost-effective payment mechanism, exporters should print instructions conspicuously. A major U.S. chemicals company uses a big red stamp on the face of its invoices to communicate payment instructions. If possible, instructions should be given in the importer's language.

(4) Cultivate good relations in the importer's country. Time spent nurturing relations with local embassies, consulates, central banks, commerce ministries, and trade associations pays off handsomely by curbing red tape and speeding government approvals for trade and foreign exchange.

(5) Tighten credit terms to reduce receivables levels. This is easier said than done, especially in smaller companies that do not have enough clout with their importers. But several firms of all sizes are waging campaigns to bring down worldwide DSO levels by shortening terms across the board.

(6) Use discounts and penalty fees where possible. While the practice of offering discounts for early payment is common, slapping interest charges on overdue accounts is a controversial technique. Nonetheless, a substantial minority of firms in all parts of the world have used this tactic effectively without loss of sales.

(7) Set tight collection targets and even consider linking salesmen's commissions to collections to provide them with an incentive to reduce DSOs. For example, the Singapore regional headquarters of a U.S. consumer products manufacturer pays its salesmen 50 percent of commissions when the sale is made and the other 50 percent after payment is received.

(8) Implement systematic dunning procedures. All companies should have standard procedures to handle their overdue accounts. When a customer's payment is late, the credit and collection department should initiate a series of actions that includes telexes, telephone calls, letters, and even personal visits.

(9) Instruct customers to pay via the quickest method. The most common way to accelerate export collections is to have importers remit payments via cable (or telex) transfers. While cable transfers are the fastest way to move funds, companies must weigh the expense against that of using slower payment mechanisms like bank drafts and checks. Also, firms must guard against mishandled wire transfers—a frequent mishap in less developed regions.

(10) Discount drafts to obtain funds sooner. With this method, an exporter simply takes a trade draft of a promissory note to its bank and receives the value of the draft, minus an interest charge. Similarly, firms may use factoring—selling receivables at a discount to banks or factoring companies—to accelerate the receipt of funds.

(11) Negotiate faster check-clearing and value-dating times. For example, a U.S. exporter of clothing managed to get its main bank to reduce funds' availability on transfers from between five and seven days to just one or two days simply by pointing out that other banks were offering those terms.

(12) Utilize direct collection systems under which the exporter sends documents directly to the importer's bank rather than through its own bank, thus accelerating the flow of documentation through the banking system.

(13) Take advantage of courier services offered by banks and independent firms to speed up the clearing of foreign currency checks.

(14) Set up lockboxes or intercept points to reduce mail delays. This method allows customers to mail checks to a post office box operated by the exporter's bank. For example, a U.S. pharmaceuticals company established a lockbox in Hong Kong to cut down on the float generated by having Asian customers mail checks directly to New York.

(15) Establish foreign currency accounts to accumulate export proceeds. Also known as "hold accounts," these versatile cash management tools are simply foreign-currency-denominated bank accounts held locally or overseas by the exporter. The benefits of such accounts include reduced FX costs, reduced currency exposure, and short-ened float delays. However, the use of hold accounts is restricted in a number of countries.

(16) Look closely at netting, reinvoicing, and other cross-border cash management vehicles to control intracompany trade. Netting, or the offsetting of creditor and debtor positions within a corporate group, accelerates export sales by eliminating bank float. Reinvoicing centers, which buy products from manufacturing subsidiaries and resell them to sales subsidiaries, can be used to centralize intracompany export management, as well as for exposure and liquidity management.

(17) Consider setting up a trading company to concentrate trade activities and expertise, carry out consistent pricing and marketing plans, and improve cash and exposure management. Trading companies are widely used in the Far East, especially in Hong Kong, Japan, Korea, Singapore, and Taiwan.

Chapter 9
Treasury in the Era of Tax Reform

With tax reform in the United States and abroad affecting nearly all phases of MNC activity, treasury managers must review their current operations and future plans. In particular, firms should reconsider their use of currency and capital markets, cash management, and other financial techniques in light of new regulations. In fact, to manage a global treasury effectively in the era of tax reform, MNC treasurers and their staffs need an unprecedented level of working knowledge on taxes.

The following checklists will help accomplish two objectives. First, they will alert managers to the key provisions of U.S. tax reform affecting international profitability—specifically, the changes in the U.S. foreign tax credit system. Second, they will provide a practical, systematic approach for saving tax dollars both at home and abroad. Armed with this information, the treasury manager can move to build tax-effective treasury operations, as well as educate and influence managers with line responsibilities.

(Though this chapter takes the perspective of a U.S. MNC, the checklists also provide numerous tax-saving hints for foreign MNC managers operating in the United States and abroad.)

64. Taking the Plunge into New Tax-Saving Strategies

Even the most sophisticated firms must prepare themselves for managing international tax in the era of tax reform. How can companies best accomplish this? BI's research indicates taking the following steps.

(1) Evaluate your firm's staffing requirements. More than ever before, MNCs are in need of talented and motivated tax experts. The savings or loss of millions of dollars depends on the effectiveness and initiative of tax managers in dealing with changing tax realities.

Firms should review their current staffing on at least three points:

● **Does your tax manager at U.S. headquarters have adequate support?** If it seems that the manager spends too much time dealing with compliance and related filing issues—and not enough on special projects or strategic planning—then additions to staff are clearly in order.

● **Is your tax manager climbing the learning curve?** To develop an effective response to the novel reforms created by the Tax Reform Act of 1986 (TRA86), tax managers should read everything available. They should also speak with accounting-firm tax partners, attend seminars and workshops, and trade ideas with peers from other MNCs.

● **Is your firm as well equipped to deal with TRA86 locally as it is at headquarters?** Firms should reevaluate the strength of local tax management—particularly in countries where the tax rate is higher than at home. At the same time, companies will want to redefine local job descriptions to include more attention to tax matters and alter performance-evaluation standards to reflect the new strategies under TRA86.

When necessary, firms should consider adding some tax experts. In countries where this is not economically feasible, firms can pool benefits by jointly employing a regional tax director.

(2) Survey your firm's tax flows. The next step in preparing for TRA86's foreign tax credit provision is to build a comprehensive diagram of all cash flows with tax implications. Firms need to understand fully where cash flows originate, whether the income is foreign or United States sourced, and what underlying activity actually generated the income. Only after a firm is certain of its current taxable flows can it identify and initiate the changes needed under TRA86.

(3) Build a simulation model. To aid tax-planning efforts, many firms find it helpful to build a tax simulation model. To gauge TRA86's effects using a model, some firms evaluate the impact on the cash flows for the last two or three years, plus forecasted cash flows for the next year or two. The tax manager for a major consumer goods MNC used the previous five years' operating figures and one year's projected sales and expenses.

Other MNCs, particularly those with earnings closely tied to commodities prices or interest rates, might want to run a much longer simulation to reach a more "economic" assessment. According to a major U.S. oil company's tax manager, "these last years, with low oil prices and almost no exploration, are *not* representative." Therefore, the firm is conducting its analysis of the new rules based on operating figures for the past 10 years. Another oil company spokesman is using 10 years' past data and 2 years' pro forma.

(4) Examine your firm's mix of TRA86 variables. No matter how difficult the exercise may seem, firms should evaluate the tax laws with an eye to determining their precise tax-credit position for each country of operation, for each 10–50 percent corporation, and for each of the remaining baskets. Once the tax position is assessed, firms can begin toying with variables to see how a change in one component affects the others. Without question, this endeavor requires a clear understanding of the tax reform's effects.

The exercise is particularly important as a basis for discerning where the greatest tax problems lie. For instance, some unleveraged or locally funded firms may find they have plenty of room within the tax credit limitations. But they may also find they have simply paid so much in foreign taxes that they have ended up with excess credits. These firms will want to focus their initial efforts on reducing the local tax bill. Others may find they are losing the deductibility of tax credits as a direct result of the expense-allocation rules and the Federal Trade Commission (FTC) limitation. These firms should focus on moving interest and R&D expense overseas and finding ways to generate additional foreign-sourced income.

(5) Build or buy tax management decision-support systems. Managing hundreds of income baskets and facing dozens of tax rates will force MNCs to automate the planning process. Says one tax manager based in New Jersey, "There's no way we can maximize mechanically." Remarks another, "We either triple the staff or write some spreadsheets." While companies are free to build programs and spreadsheets of their own, it may be advantageous to purchase the software available from various accounting firms and other vendors. As with any major systems software purchase, insist on references.

(6) Involve local managers . . . Right from the start, MNCs need to talk to local managers and bring them up to date on the firm's problems and objectives. Many of the solutions that should be implemented under TRA86 are at odds with traditional local objectives. Country managers must understand that changes that may have a negative impact at the local level are being instituted for the overall corporate well-being. Furthermore, managers need to feel that they are part of the decision-making process. If these steps are followed, the quality of decisions may actually improve.

(7) . . . and line managers. Many of the best responses to TRA86 would come from operating and line managers if they were involved in the process of evaluation. Managers close to production, warehousing, distribution, and so on, could easily make suggestions based on their experiences if they knew the broad objectives. For instance, an experienced line manager might be aware that the firm is billing intercompany far below the industry average for a particular service. This simple piece of information could be used in making a case for raising a transfer price to an overseas affiliate and thus reduce local taxes at the foreign subsidiary. In any event, line managers should be active participants in the process known as "functional analysis" (explained below).

(8) Begin to monitor local tax developments. In the era of global tax reform, keeping on top of tax changes in local jurisdictions has become essential; in fact, a full 61 percent of respondents surveyed intend to do just that. Firms may take a number of routes in this direction. One simple step is to ask local managers to keep headquarters informed of any anticipated or implemented changes. This practice may be carried out on an informal, as-needed basis or formalized into an annual—or even quarterly in volatile environments—management report. Questions that should be regularly discussed include the following:

● Is the local government contemplating any major changes in tax rates or key provisions? If so, what are they?

● What incentives does the country (or do areas of the country) offer for new employment, capital formation, and so on?

● What favorable accounting techniques are currently available in the country?

● What is the attitude of local authorities to changes in intercompany transfer prices, royalties, or other charges?

In any case, headquarters' renewed interest in these and other local tax developments should be stressed.

At the same time, headquarters management should also aim to keep abreast of local tax regulations, with an eye to the global tax picture. One way is to subscribe to various tax newsletters or information services. Speaking with accounting-firm tax partners and corporate peers is also desirable. Another is, again, simply to stay in touch with local managers and make sure they keep tabs on the situation.

(9) Review potential strategies with tax authorities. In general, firms should treat their responses to TRA86 as a set of possible alternatives. For companies with very cautious policies, each strategy, in turn, can be checked by the firm's public accountants in each country affected. On an even more cautious note, whenever the tax precedent is unclear, firms may want to ask the authorities of the pertinent jurisdiction for a ruling.

This procedure is designed to avoid major problems in the future. "There are wide variations in how local authorities react to various tax-savings strategies," notes Hewlett-Packard's spokesman. So before a firm proceeds with certain tax plans, he suggests taking the time to meet with local authorities.

He has found that in some cases it pays to speak with officials forthrightly. "In some countries, we were highly successful despite precedent." In Spain, for example, Hewlett-Packard managed to negotiate significant increases in the royalty structure. He says, "As a result, I think we were the first U.S. company to get substantial royalty rates out of Spain."

The spokesman concedes that in certain regions the exercise has its limitations. "The Latin American governments are still in a 'no-no' mood," he explains. But he won't give up: "We're negotiating with the Mexican government. Eventually, I think we'll sell them *all* on the idea—one at a time."

65. Managing Foreign Tax Credits in the Era of Tax Reform

Of all the provisions in TRA86, none is causing greater concern for MNCs than those relating to foreign tax credits (FTCs). Simply stated, a company with excess FTCs is not receiving full credit for the income and withholding taxes paid to foreign governments. Under the old tax rules, most U.S. MNCs managed to avoid accumulating excess FTCs. Instead they maintained the position known as "excess limitation" (i.e., their FTCs were fully creditable against U.S. taxes).

For the most part, even those that *did* have excess FTCs were not that far under water. But with the adoption of the new U.S. tax code, many more MNCs will be thrust deeply into the ocean of excess FTCs. The following checklist outlines how the new regulations are affecting firms' tax positions and is the basis for further analysis in coping with TRA86.

● **Dealing with a new, lower tax rate.** With the U.S. corporate tax rate falling to 34 percent, the greater differential between U.S. and foreign statutory rates will add to excess tax credits. Taking his own firm's mix into account,

a Boston-based tax manager of a consumer goods concern explains, "Most of my income will be generated in countries with a significantly higher tax rate; yes, I'll be accumulating credits."

The problem would have been worse if most of the major domiciles of MNC activity had not responded to TRA86 with rate cuts of their own. Canada, Japan, Germany, France, the United Kingdom, and even Mexico have all effected their own tax reforms. The difference—at least in statutory rates—has been narrowed a good deal. But none of these reforms were as extensive as TRA86, so U.S. MNCs are now learning to live with the reality of fast-accumulating FTCs.

● **TRA86 introduces four new income baskets.** U.S. MNCs have always had to deal with income baskets, which are the launching pads for all subsequent FTC calculations. Essentially, any income returned to the United States is segregated into a specific basket. Within each basket, firms receive credit for foreign taxes paid. To the extent that the foreign tax exceeds the U.S. tax on comparable income, a firm will realize an excess FTC. To the extent that the foreign tax is less than the comparable U.S. tax, a firm has to pay the difference in the form of U.S. taxes. Within each basket, firms can use income that has generated an FTC to offset income that has resulted in a U.S. tax liability.

In the past, there were six income baskets. These included passive interest, DISC dividends, foreign trade income of foreign-sales corporations, foreign-sales corporation dividends, and foreign-oil and gas-extraction income baskets. Finally, there was an all-other category, often called the "overall" or "active" basket, where the income from principal business lines collected.

What TRA86 has done for corporate treasuries is to add four additional baskets: high-withholding-tax interest income, financial-services income, shipping and aircraft income, and dividends from each individual 10 percent- to 50 percent-owned foreign corporation (the minority-held basket). Each of these isolates a different type of income and creates what Price Waterhouse's director of international tax services calls an accounting and tax-planning "nightmare."

In more detail, the new baskets are:

● **The high-withholding-tax interest income basket.** This basket segregates any income subject to a foreign withholding tax of 5 percent or more.

● **The financial-services income basket.** This comprises banking, insurance, and financial income from business abroad.

● **The shipping and aircraft income basket.** This category includes income from the use of aircraft or other shipping vessels in the conduct of international business.

● **The minority-held basket.** This segregates the repatriated earnings from all minority-held (also known as "noncontrolled foreign corporation," or "non-CFC") income. A minority-held firm or non-CFC is defined as any venture where the U.S. parent holds 10 percent or more, but 50 percent or less, of either the voting rights or value. Because minority ownership is so prevalent among MNCs in new markets or developing countries, this basket is the real backbreaker for many firms.

Why these particular baskets? The legislative intent, according to a spokesman for Price Waterhouse, was to eliminate the investment of MNCs' excess cash abroad (thereby effectively encouraging U.S. investment). In the past, cash-rich overseas subsidiaries of U.S. MNCs found it desirable to invest their excess cash in businesses that typically generated low-tax income. Such income then could be averaged with the high-tax income from mainstream operations. "What Congress did," says the Price Waterhouse spokesman, "was close down what it perceived to be the areas of abuse."

● **"Look-through" rules defy "tax gaming."** Inextricably linked to the income baskets are the new "look-through" rules. These, as the name implies, enable the IRS to "look through" any income received (e.g., in the form of a dividend or interest) to determine the actual economic origin of that income.

For example, a U.K. subsidiary might pay a dividend to the U.S. parent. But if 10 percent of the U.K. subsidiary's income can be attributed to a dividend from a downstream 10–50 percent operation in Italy, then a corresponding 10 percent of the dividend to the parent would be placed in the minority-held basket. Because the look-through rules defy the multitiered repatriation channels of many MNCs, a Coopers and Lybrand senior tax partner explained their effect as the elimination of "tax gaming."

● **Expense-allocation rules disrupt borrowing strategies.** Lower rates, more baskets, and the look-through rules will cause FTCs to accumulate faster than ever. But without question, the new expense-allocation rules will have the most dramatic effect on the way MNCs conduct international business.

Basically, the IRS is taking a much more punitive view of the way interest expense is allocated within related companies. For purposes of the U.S. tax computation, TRA86 is forcing MNCs to allot interest expense incurred by the parent or controlled financing companies to the books of overseas subsidiaries. This practice results in a drastic reduction in calculated foreign-sourced income, which in turn can shrink allowable tax credits by means of the FTC limitation.

In a nutshell, TRA86 has turned the expense-allocation methodology upside down. In the past, MNCs were able to segregate specific expenses, such as borrowing costs, within specific subsidiaries' foreign-sourced income. For instance, a finance company could incur all of a firm's debt and pay all of its interest. Any cash flow from the finance company to the parent or related subsidiary could be classified as a dividend.

However, under the new rules, for the purposes of the U.S. tax book, any interest, R&D, or similarly defined expense incurred by the parent (or its captive finance companies) must be allocated to all related parties. The allocation is based on a ratio of local assets to total assets and is performed for each foreign subsidiary. The following formula is used:

$$\frac{\text{Foreign subsidiary assets}}{\text{Total assets firmwide}} \times \begin{array}{c}\text{Total allocable} \\ \text{expenses incurred} \\ \text{by parent}\end{array} = \begin{array}{c}\text{Expense allocation} \\ \text{for} \\ \text{FTC limitation}\end{array}$$

The effect of the added expense allocation is a dramatic decrease in foreign-sourced income—the numerator in the FTC limitation calculation. This, in turn, can substantially reduce the availability of otherwise useful tax credits.

For companies with very high levels of interest expense at the parent level, this expense allocation, with its attendant reduction in allowable tax credits, requires a cardinal financial repositioning. The expense-allocation rules are, in effect, forcing firms to reexamine and restructure their corporatewide funding strategies, their debt-equity ratios, and even their basic reasons for operating as an MNC. Additionally, for R&D-intensive companies, these changes are fundamentally altering the economics of conducting research in the United States.

Reducing Excess FTCs

The next three checklists offer different approaches to reducing excess FTCs. The first deals with measures to be taken at the local or operating level. The second deals with transfer-pricing strategies—particularly intangible charges. The third lays out strategies to be planned and implemented by the parent.

---

66. Tax Strategies for the Local Level

Once a firm has defined its tax position and objectives, local and headquarters managements can begin formulating specific responses. Given the new environment for FTC planning, MNCs need to evaluate the tactics available. One approach to relieving FTC problems is to stop excess FTCs at the onset by using strategies and techniques that lower foreign taxes at the local level.

● **Consolidate same-country loss subsidiaries with profitable ones.** This technique is designed to take advantage of operating loss carryforwards. Under TRA86, the value of tax-loss carryforwards will be greatly eroded. By combining gainers with losers, firms can exploit not only existing loss carryforwards but also current-year deficits; moreover they can effectively defer payment of U.S. taxes on current-year, Subpart F earnings.

● **Identify and utilize the most beneficial accounting techniques.** While precise accounting methodologies are often prescribed by local law, in some countries MNCs may choose from among local standards to obtain the most beneficial tax results. Firms can, for example, use local generally accepted accounting principles (GAAP) to calculate local taxes and then convert to U.S. GAAP for consolidated shareholder reporting. Thus, companies can lower their local tax burdens with no detrimental effects on their consolidated profits for U.S. shareholder reporting.

For example, certain countries allow firms to deduct reserves held for pensions, inventories, and accrued expenses, thus reducing reported local profit (and subsequently taxes). However, these deductions are not always available under U.S. GAAP. In this case, the firm should use local GAAP on the local return (increasing expenses and reducing local taxes) and U.S. GAAP for shareholder reporting.

While using multiple accounting standards can be very profitable, it can also be difficult to administer. First, a keen knowledge of local accounting practices is needed. The tax manager must be aware of what is allowed and expected. Second, the practice of running extra books requires a relatively competent systems capability and a high level of support from corporate and local accounting departments. Warns the inveterate dual GAAP practitioner for a major U.S. MNC, "It plays hell with your accounting."

● **Bill employee stock options to other countries.** The discount employees enjoy from incentive stock options is no longer a deductible expense in the United States. However, it *is* still deductible in many foreign jurisdictions. One computer maker's corporate tax director discovered "that in Austria, France, Holland, Germany, the United Kingdom, and possibly Switzerland, there is very favorable legislation or rulings with regard to stock options." By billing stock options to its European affiliates, the firm has managed to create a substantial deduction on the local books.

● **Identify and utilize local incentives.** To stimulate a specifically desired activity or to attract employment to depressed areas, foreign jurisdictions often create tax incentives. Now, under TRA86, awareness and utilization of these incentives have become more critical than ever. Firms should constantly be on the watch for tax-advantageous opportunities offered in every country of operation. They should also be open to examining new locations where substantial investment incentives are available.

But firms should be warned that the best incentives are not always widely advertised. "It's often very difficult to get information on these incentives," one U.S. MNC's tax director advises. Worthwhile information is virtually impossible to collect, he says, without a tax expert "working on your behalf within the country"; nonetheless, he acknowledges that such tax incentives have proven very significant. For example, his firm is now benefiting from Italy's wage credits for creation of jobs in regions of high unemployment. The manager points out that plans, like his firm's in Italy, can also include liberal depreciation schedules and incentives for purchasing materials locally.

Another MNC interviewed also aggressively seeks local incentives. After some research, the company learned it could benefit doubly by buying space for its local facility instead of extending its lease. "In any analysis, the price was very good," says the tax director. "But by increasing our capital spending in the country, we received an investment tax credit on our Spanish tax bill."

● **Assume more debt at the local level.** As a fundamental response to TRA86, over half the MNCs surveyed (52 percent) will be leveraging their overseas subsidiaries. Because of the expense-allocation rules, debt incurred by the parent will reduce foreign-sourced income in the FTC limitation calculation. Further, with higher tax rates overseas, an interest deduction has more value outside the United States. Therefore, in order to achieve higher deductions and lessen the expense-allocation effect, firms will want to finance locally whenever possible.

This move implies a change in current performance-evaluation criteria or targets. To begin with, a local manager cannot finance as efficiently as the parent and will automatically be paying a premium of a few basis points. But also, as local debt-equity ratios climb, the marginal cost of each borrowed dollar will inevitably rise. As local financing costs increase, profit margins will fall. Local managers will need to be shown that this phenomenon is being factored into their performance evaluation. (For more on how firms are changing their borrowing strategies, see Chapter 5.)

● **Maximize sources of external financing.** Financing at the local level does not necessarily mean new debt issues or bank borrowing. Local operations in high-tax jurisdictions should make every effort to use supplier credit and other nonbank financing. This type of short-term financing, if utilized at every opportunity, can have a significant effect on the level of required funding.

● **Review all transfer prices to overseas affiliates.** In general, companies should take a fresh look at *all* transfer prices to foreign subsidiaries, especially those in high-tax jurisdictions. Companies should be looking for charges that, for whatever reason, are now lower than actual market conditions.

Of course, raising a transfer price can be a difficult task. Local tax authorities require justification for a price change. Certain countries, Germany for example, are notorious for the rigorous scrutiny that any price change undergoes. Firms must therefore prepare their cases for price hikes carefully. Documentation should include examples of competitors' pricing for similar products and outside vendors' charges for similar services. In addition, analyses of profit margins for similar goods or overall profitability of the subsidiary can be compelling and should be clearly presented.

In some cases, however, no price rise will be allowed unless a fundamental change in the product or service is initiated. In the past, firms have managed to deal with this event by subtle means, such as upgrading a single component or adding a feature to an electronic device and then changing the model number. But again, certain countries may assume a defensive posture; be prepared.

An MNC manager based in New England says the magnitude of the U.S. rate change will force his firm to reevaluate and, when possible, raise transfer prices. In the past, the odd 4 or 5 percent differential in tax rates was not worth the administrative effort of negotiating with the various tax agencies. "At 46 percent, we had no incentive," the manager explains. But now he believes that no matter how difficult such changes may be to implement, the exercise is absolutely essential.

● **Try a cost-plus approach to raise transfer prices.** Cost-plus accounting can be extremely tax effective whenever the goal is to reduce local profit. For example, Company A, an $800 million, high-tech U.S. firm, converted to a cost-plus system to shrink income in its West German assembly plant.

In the past, this U.S. firm *sold* partially completed components to its wholly owned German assembly plant. However, under a TRA86-motivated arrangement, the U.S. parent now retains legal ownership of the components and essentially contracts with the German plant to create a finished product. Basically, the parent contracts with the German subsidiary for labor, rent, and machinery.

By retaining ownership of the inventory, the U.S. parent takes on the risk of inventory obsolescence—which is significant in Company A's high-tech product lines. This added burden on the U.S. parent justifies an increased transfer price to the German subsidiary, which lowers the German profits (and therefore German taxes). While the subsidiary must still earn an arm's-length margin for the services performed, this strategy significantly reduces those services. The subsidiary now realizes a 15–20 percent margin over costs.

In this particular case, the technique gives Company A a significant tax deferral. Taxes on inventory sales are now postponed until the final sale to the consumer, rather than being assessed at the time the goods are transferred to the German plant. (To ensure that this strategy was workable, the company took the precaution of getting a private ruling from the IRS.)

● **Change the terms of sale.** MNCs can substantially shrink excess FTCs simply by altering the terms of sale, paying close attention to the rules of title passage. The goal is to ensure that passage of title occurs overseas. Therefore, the profit the sale generates represents foreign-sourced income.

Under TRA86, the determination of ownership is based on a simple question: Who assumes the risk of loss? By structuring transactions to make certain that the U.S. parent is the party at risk until the material arrives in good condition overseas, firms can easily satisfy this requirement.

This tactic can be accomplished with both third and related parties. However, when the buyer is a related party, firms can do even better by transferring as many expenses as possible to the importer. Local expenses are increased by billing the importer for such items as freight, and the local tax bill thereby is reduced. (Similarly, firms can again hike foreign-sourced income by reversing the strategy on exports *to* the United States from a foreign subsidiary.)

However, one expense *must* be borne by the U.S. exporter to ensure overseas title passage—insurance. Insurance is a key test of ownership; it is reasoned that the party at risk pays the cost of insurance and is the beneficiary. If the importer is billed for insurance, then title must have passed in the United States—implying the income from the transaction is United States sourced.

67. Increasing Intangible Charges

Measures taken at the local level are only the first step in reducing the global tax bite. The next is to review any intangible charges that can be adjusted to lessen the local tax liability in high-tax jurisdictions and increase global profits.

● **Document and charge for the use of creative intangibles.** When an overseas subsidiary is making use of creative devices developed in the United States, a firm is entitled to bill for an intangible. A U.S. firm may, for example, charge subsidiaries for advertising slogans and campaigns designed in the United States if the development costs of the campaign can be clearly documented. In that instance, the foreign jurisdiction will recognize the charge, and the parent can earn foreign-sourced income. But firms should be forewarned: They are not earning the full intangible charge, but only the net after actual costs.

● **Redouble efforts to increase R&D charges.** Firms need to concentrate their efforts on R&D charges. Under the expense-allocation rules, unreimbursed R&D activity in the United States will be allocated against foreign-sourced income. Therefore, firms will want to ensure that they are charging their overseas operations in high-tax jurisdictions the maximum allowable. Unfortunately, raising a charge for something as intangible as R&D can be a very difficult sell with local tax authorities.

● **Increase R&D charges through cost sharing.** In some countries, firms can accelerate R&D charges through a vehicle called "cost sharing." Says a senior Peat Marwick Main tax partner, "The idea of cost sharing is to spread a portion of current R&D cost to the foreign subsidiaries while the product is still in the developmental stages."

Cost sharing is a desirable option for firms with operations in high-tax jurisdictions that want to charge the maximum allowable for R&D. This not only decreases the R&D expense borne by the parent (with attending FTC limitation expense allocations) but also results in a local deduction.

While the concept of cost sharing has been accepted by tax authorities in Germany and Canada, other jurisdictions may not be open-minded. Says the partner, "Keep in mind that the problem is convincing authorities why the local operation will be paying for research that may never bear any fruit." A particularly sticky issue is the determination of where to draw the line on costs. Explains one corporate practitioner, "It's difficult to implement on a start-up basis because it is not always clear when product-specific research commences."

No matter how clear the arguments, some countries may have unique motivations for denying the cost-sharing charge. Japan, for example, is an R&D-intensive nation where the cost-sharing argument has been slow to catch on. The tax partner says, "They feel you should be conducting R&D there."

In any case, before instituting a cost-sharing program, firms need to understand the limitations of the technique. For example, local subsidiaries will experience an initial period of "doubling up" on R&D expenses during the transition; the subsidiaries will still be paying the existing royalties when the cost-sharing royalty kicks in. This action will result in a cash flow drain on the company's operations abroad. In addition, cost-sharing agreements can be difficult, time-consuming, and expensive to draw up, especially when minority shareholders are involved.

● **Increase royalty charges.** Royalty charges are among the most difficult to estimate. It is nearly impossible to establish up front the ultimate value of a technology or product. But under TRA86, firms are under increased pressure to err on the side of too high a charge for three reasons.

First, royalties paid to the U.S. parent represent foreign-sourced income—a valuable commodity under TRA86. Second, any charge that can transfer value to the U.S. parent from a high-tax jurisdiction will result in lower local taxes and fewer excess tax credits. Third, a royalty charge that is too low runs the risk of being eventually overturned by the TRA86's super-royalty clause. This may ultimately mean double taxation, as the larger royalty U.S. authorities impute can prove unacceptable to local tax authorities.

Although an uphill battle, collecting higher royalties for new products and renegotiating existing royalties are essential tasks for U.S. MNCs. Says the tax manager for a major New England consumer products firm, "The costs of doing nothing in this case are far greater than the risk of meeting with only marginal success. It just has to be done."

One firm that experienced success negotiating higher royalties with foreign jurisdictions (particularly European ones) used a macro approach. The firm's tax manager examined the R&D costs incurred in the United States against the products sold abroad. His analysis "suggested that perhaps we were transferring technology for inadequate compensation."

Firms must be careful in structuring their royalty system to ensure that the royalty stream is classified as foreign sourced under U.S. tax laws. If instead the stream is classified as domestic income, it will lower the FTC limitation and increase the company's excess FTCs. To accomplish this objective, transfer of technology must be done either through licensing or through a sale that is contingent on the usefulness of the intangible to the buyer. Both noncontingent sales and transfers of technology as a contribution to capital by a U.S. company generally will generate domestic-sourced income.

● **Begin billing for a service mark.** The "service mark," a relatively new concept, is essentially a trademark tailored for the service industry. Firms may be surprised at the opportunities available under the service mark.

For example, when a major high-tech and computer manufacturer reexamined the functions its U.S. staff was performing, it realized that all the service manuals being used by technical representatives overseas were developed and written in the United States. It also found that the company's logo, when appearing on a service contract, enabled the foreign subsidiaries to charge a premium over contracts similar in other respects.

Under the concept of the service mark, the local operations could be billed a royalty for the aforementioned services. Some local tax jurisdictions have since recognized the firm's "codified" service mark. They allow an intercompany royalty of 2–4 percent for the development of manuals and know-how. But this particular company has decided against using this strategy because of exchange controls and the fact that the lack of tax deductibility in certain countries makes it impossible to administer uniformly worldwide.

● **Establish management-fee agreements.** Billing for management effort and expertise can net firms two major benefits. It creates a tax deduction for the local operations, and it generates foreign-sourced income for the parent. Essentially, firms can bill for the U.S. headquarters' time spent attending to foreign affiliates' matters, such as advising on marketing, manufacturing, and distribution. Rigorous diary keeping and the drawing up of formal contracts are vital steps in this process, as is finding out exactly which charges local tax authorities will allow as deductions. Firms must also realize that they will earn foreign-sourced income only to the extent that the management fee exceeds the actual U.S. expenses associated with the activity. (Further, it is essential that an arm's-length standard be observed at all times.)

68. Strategies for the U.S. Parent

The final checklist in this series examines the steps to be taken at the parent level to mitigate the negative consequences of tax reform. Firms should consider the following 14 techniques:

● **Use more equity—and preferred stock.** Because parent borrowing ultimately affects foreign-sourced income via the FTC limitation, firms should take a harder look at equity financing. If the potential cost of equity seems too great, firms should consider adding additional preferred stock, since it blends the favorable tax consequences of equity (no hits to the FTC limitation) with the advantages of debt (fixed cost).

● **Accelerate dividends where tax rates are expected to fall.** The world is now in a state of tax-rate volatility. Still, as part of the local monitoring effort, MNC managers should have a good idea of the direction in which individual countries' tax rates are headed. Where it appears that tax rates are about to fall, MNCs should consider accelerating dividends so that the higher taxes paid can be credited with the income.

● **Use consent dividends.** One technique for accelerating dividends and avoiding withholding taxes at the same time is to opt for a consent dividend. The consent dividend is a simple election on the U.S. tax return, with no actual cash flows. What the election accomplishes is the conversion of the subsidiary's retained earnings to its capital base. Technically, since the dividend was never actually remitted, it is not subject to foreign withholding tax. (Be aware that this technique is currently under IRS scrutiny.)

● **Issue guidelines specifying the desired character of income.** Tax management at the corporate level should monitor the income baskets and issue guidelines to foreign subsidiaries regarding the character and timing of income. Although the amount of maneuvering that can be achieved within the baskets is relatively limited, *any* success along these lines flows through to the bottom line.

If informed, managers can often accelerate or delay ac-

tions. Thus, they can affect the mix of income in the baskets. In some cases, the character of the income may actually be manageable. For example, one leading MNC found it would be realizing excess FTCs in its passive basket for 1987. The corporate tax manager reacted by issuing a general directive to each of the MNC's 21 foreign subsidiaries, asking that they avoid earning passive income in the current year whenever possible.

However, in issuing such guidelines, headquarters managers need to understand the potential conflict with local managers' goals. For instance, suppose that near the end of a reporting period, a firm learns it should avoid earning passive income from investments. A local manager with significant cash on hand will want to maximize his earnings within the current period. Given the choice of a passive investment with interest earned in the current period or an investment for the longer term, the local manager may need some gentle encouragement to choose the latter.

● **Avoid the $1 million passive-income threshold; keep cash to a minimum.** MNCs whose subsidiaries have significant cash at the local level need to monitor an additional income basket provision: When a single subsidiary earns more than $1 million from passive investments (or 5 percent of gross income), that subsidiary's passive income is generally segregated into the passive basket. Local finance and line managers should therefore be made aware of the need to avoid excessive passive income.

The best idea may be to simply avoid accumulating excessive cash. Since most firms are funding locally to a greater extent under TRA86, it becomes all the more important that any excess cash be used to pay off borrowings.

● **Move R&D overseas.** A sure method for avoiding expense allocations against foreign-sourced income—and, for that matter, the super-royalty provisions—is to move R&D operations overseas. In fact, a number of likely candidates (e.g., the Netherlands, France, Australia, and Canada) are offering substantial tax incentives to attract such activities. However, such a move is clearly fundamental to a firm's future product development and is therefore not to be taken lightly. Before adjusting the location of R&D activity, firms will have to examine their particular needs and markets.

● **Transfer technology to foreign affiliates.** The transfer of technology to an overseas subsidiary, if structured carefully, can mean a significant increase in ongoing foreign-sourced income flows. It can also provide significant deductions for the subsidiary. For example, TRA86 was a principal reason why one major U.S. chemical maker has sold its patents and manufacturing processes to a German subsidiary.

Such decisions must mesh with the overall way an organization conducts business. They should be weighed more for strategic impact than for tax considerations. Still, technology transfers can have a profound effect on the FTC position and should be considered by all MNCs.

● **When passage of title can still be realized overseas, consider leaving high-tax jurisdictions.** MNCs dodged a bullet when a key component of HR3838 (tax reform's identity as a proposed bill in the Senate) did not make it to the actual TRA86 package. HR3838 initially attempted to categorize more U.S. manufacturing income as U.S.-sourced even though title to the goods passed to an overseas sales subsidiary. This provision would have further cut MNCs' foreign-sourced income, thus further lowering the FTC limitation. After much debate, the traditional view, which held that foreign title passage entitles a firm to foreign-sourced income, was left intact.

This has enabled MNCs to analyze foreign manufacturing operations on more of a cost and less of a source-of-income basis. A major New Jersey-based pharmaceutical maker, for example, is now able to reduce its manufacturing presence in high-tax European jurisdictions without losing significant foreign-sourced income. Whenever operationally feasible, the firm now plans to manufacture from the United States—not locally. Because the title passage rules have remained intact, the firm managed to focus on the cost of operations (wages, rents, etc.) and the all-in tax rates (including withholding). *It is also important to note that the weak dollar is just as responsible for lower costs as are the new tax-rate differentials. This was a principal factor in the firm's decision.*

● **Renegotiate joint ventures (JVs) to lower the number of 10–50 percent baskets.** Under TRA86, the income from each minority-held company resides in its own basket for FTC purposes. "In other words," says the Merck & Co. international tax counsel, "When the foreign corporation is half-owned or less, the parent is in the unenviable position of paying the higher of the U.S. or foreign taxes on the dividends from the foreign corporation."

Still, it is a rare MNC that has no JVs among its portfolio of businesses. Firms with JVs are now left with two options for managing them: Managers can simply live with the more punitive tax treatment, or they can renegotiate with their partners in each country for majority control. While the latter task may seem herculean, it may not be so. Actually, TRA86 rules for control of a foreign corporation (which negates the separate basket requirement) are rather flexible. Managers may, in fact, be able to negotiate an agreement for control that satisfies both TRA86 and the local partner.

● **Incorporate foreign branches.** The corporate tax director of a large electronics MNC says, "Under TRA86, there's absolutely no U.S. tax advantage to having a branch. If both the branch and the parent company are consistently profitable, the best that happens is that the branch won't hurt the company."

The problem with branches stems from the character of their income; branch earnings currently are taxed as though they were earned in the United States. Branch income "gets offset against the U.S. loss," explains the tax director. "There's no way we'll ever get credit for the foreign taxes we pay on the branch's profits." To avoid current taxes, branches should be converted to subsidiary status.

● **Conduct a functional analysis.** Some MNCs may be overlooking activities that could be used to reduce excess FTCs. For example, a major computer maker found that foreign service personnel were using manuals written by U.S. staff. The firm has since instituted a royalty for technical support, thus decreasing local taxes and generating foreign-sourced income. However, the opportunity would never have materialized had the firm not taken a critical look at current operations using the technique known as "functional analysis."

Functional analysis is based on the theory that an entity's share of global income should be commensurate with the economic significance of the functions it performs. To the extent that an MNC wishes to shift income from high-tax jurisdictions to those with low taxes, it can first list and review each of the functions that are now or could be performed. Then it can identify those to be transferred from one entity to another.

The technique, tax managers will be amused to learn, was actually developed and perfected by the IRS. The IRS, in fact, actually maintains checklists of economically significant activities, which it uses as a means to challenge corporations' internal transfers of products and services. These checklists are provided to international examiners as part of an IRS training program (and to purchasers of this book; see Checklists 70, 71, and 72).

● **Consider new lines of business; try export financing.** Functional analysis is one way for firms to identify new ways to bill for existing activity. However, in response to TRA86, firms will also want to pinpoint new activities that both complement existing business and enhance the tax equation.

For example, some firms might consider financing their products for overseas markets—a valuable marketing strategy in itself. Under TRA86, income from export financing is placed in the *active* income basket. Since such income is taxed at relatively low rates in most jurisdictions, this service can provide valuable low-tax income for averaging in the active basket.

● **Build a "superdistributorship."** Firms can earn foreign-sourced income or gain local deductions by concentrating activities in an overseas regional headquarters. One leading MNC has established a foreign-based company to act as a "superdistributor" for European sales. The entity now handles regional sales activities (such as marketing and administration), assumes inventory risk (including price fluctuations, obsolescence, or general unsalability), and manages cash flows (working capital, customer credit, and currency risk). Because of the value-added nature of its activities, the center is able to increase charges to local operations and at the same time generate foreign-sourced income (see Chapter 5 for an examination of closely related entities such as treasury vehicles and finance companies).

One caveat in setting up such centers, warns a Price Waterhouse spokesman, is that "local tax burdens can attach to the movement of business assets and functions out of local tax jurisdictions." He suggests that this and other potential tax risks be fully investigated before one proceeds with a superdistributorship.

● **Factor tax into the headquarters-locating decision.** MNCs can further enhance the superdistributorship step (or, for that matter, the treasury vehicle or finance company route) by siting their new vehicle in regions where tax incentives are offered. For example, by locating its U.K. sales and financing headquarters offshore, one company managed to arrange taxation based on a percentage of its overhead expenses, enabling it to do $75 million of business in the United Kingdom (normally a high-tax jurisdiction) at an effective tax rate of only 8 percent. Firms can find similar benefits from incentives offered by, for instance, Belgium and Singapore.

69. Responding to Tax Reform: How to Adjust Transfer Pricing

The volatility in worldwide tax rates makes it imperative that firms review their transfer-pricing strategies with the aim of finding the ideal policy—one flexible enough to allow for price adjustments in response to the changing environment yet at the same time resistant to challenge from local tax authorities. The following checklists will highlight the key theories for determining an acceptable transfer price and provide managers with the means to analyze any proposed changes.

The Four Main Approaches

In conversations with tax directors of MNCs, BI has found that there are four widely used approaches to setting transfer prices when third-party market prices are not readily available. All four are intended to optimize the company's overall tax position while providing an accurate arm's-length transaction price that is defensible against attack by any and all of the countries in which the company does business.

(1) Calculate the cost of each function separately. Some MNCs attempt to build a "bottom-up" product cost by using individual activities or functions as cost building blocks. This enables them to maintain a consistent policy but gives them the flexibility to alter individual-country profits by moving the functions from one country to another. Among the more mobile functions are regional sales, marketing, and administration; inventory-risk management; financing; credit-risk management; and FX-risk management. Such functions can often be centralized at trading companies or superdistributorships, which take title to goods before the goods are shipped on to their ultimate destinations.

(2) Use industry averages to target gross profit percentages. MNCs that use the cost-plus method often start with a functional analysis to ensure an accurate transfer price

and then reevaluate that price to see if it provides a sufficient profit for their sales subsidiaries. To determine if profits are sufficient, gross profit margins for each country in which the MNC does business are compared with industry averages once a year—usually at the time the budget or operating plan is finalized. If profits would otherwise be less than the industry standard, the particular transfer prices involved are adjusted downward to compensate.

(3) Apply a uniform percentage discount to the list-less method. MNCs that use the resale-price or "list-less" method often allow resale prices to fluctuate freely, while a uniform percentage is applied to calculate the discount from the resale price to arrive at the transfer price. One major chemical firm has developed a sophisticated computerized system to track changes in transfer prices. As an executive there remarked: "The most important thing today is to have an objective and defensible system in place. Ours was expensive to develop, but we think the cost will be more than justified by the time saved avoiding nuisance audits."

A computer firm opted for a less expensive solution. Comments an executive there: "We do all our intercompany sales through a trading company. Our transfer prices on sales into the trading company are calculated using the cost-plus method; sales out of the trading company are calculated using the uniform percentage-discount list-less method."

(4) Use a negotiated price. Other MNCs negotiate transfer prices with their foreign subsidiaries as part of the planning process. "The general managers of our foreign subsidiaries all have bonus plans based on their profits," explains the corporate tax director of a leading MNC. "Once we hammer out a price through our internal negotiation process, that price is about as close to arm's length as anything any local tax authority could ever devise."

Choosing the Best Policy

Transfer-pricing decisions are extremely subjective, and the exact percentages and averages used are specific to each industry. In general, however, a company's choice of transfer-pricing policies will require detailed study and an in-depth knowledge of both the official statutes and the actual practices in force in the countries in which a company does business. The following checklist of key questions should receive special attention.

● **What is the latest official posture of the local tax authorities?** To learn the answer, companies look first to official statutes. Most industrialized countries have their own equivalents of Section 482 of the Internal Revenue Code, and just as the United States expects to issue a white paper on its official posture on transfer pricing in the near future, so other countries often update theirs. For example, Section 485 of the United Kingdom's Income and Corporation Tax Act (ICTA) of 1970 recently became Section 770 of the 1988 Tax Act.

While the concept of "arm's length" is firmly established in the official statutes of most countries, allowable methods of calculating transfer prices vary. For example, Italian regulations permit not only the use of "normal-value" methods (calculated using cost-plus, list-less, or customs value) but also the comparable-profits method and those methods using return on capital invested and gross margins of the economic sector.

● **What are the documentation requirements?** In addition to specific invoicing rules, formal written transfer-pricing policies are often required. For example, in Germany, documentation must include evidence that the transfer prices were negotiated with the management of the German subsidiary and that the subsidiary agreed to accept the price increases. Additionally, local authorities in some countries (e.g., France) say MNCs will have an easier time adjusting their transfer prices if they include information on the billing currency (or otherwise provide for revisions due to currency fluctuations), as well as specifics on such subjects as the treatment of auxiliary costs, such as insurance and transportation.

● **Where will the local authorities turn for comparable-price ammunition?** When local tax authorities challenge an MNC's transfer prices, they often rely on particular sources for the benchmark data they use in their accusation. Some local tax authorities use customs data; others are at odds with customs authorities. The tax director of a leading computer company told BI he was surprised to find the French tax authorities challenging his transfer price into France on the grounds that it was too low. He obligingly adjusted the price upward, only to find his firm slapped with a customs audit and a penalty.

In addition to customs data, tax authorities in some countries (e.g., Japan and Germany) maintain their own data bases. Growing numbers are using the European Community's Mutual Assistance Regulations and the Organiza-tion for Economic Cooperation and Operation (OECD)'s Multilateral Convention on Mutual Assistance.

● **How do the local authorities view base companies, such as superdistributorships and trading companies?** As transfers of information become more readily available to tax authorities around the world, the question of how they view base companies is taking on increasing significance in connection with functional analysis. In France, for example, Article 238 of the General Tax Code deals with transfers of profits to tax-haven countries. The French tax authorities apply that provision to intercompany sales that are conducted through base companies. If the authorities view the role of such companies as being limited to invoicing centers, they generally attempt to identify and reject the margin these companies take.

● **What arguments are effective for raising transfer prices?** In certain countries, some arguments are more effective than others. Some local tax authorities, for example, accept and even initiate their own functional analysis. Other countries are more willing to accept industry standards, and still others will accept special arguments.

For example, in France an MNC may be able to prove that its transfer price is in the best interest of the French company. In Spain, which joined the European Community in 1986 and has experienced dramatic declines in tariffs since then, a company may argue that it accepted artificially low transfer prices for a while to compete in the protected Spanish market, but now it wants to bring its profitability up to world-market levels by raising its transfer prices.

● **What are the penalties for a transfer price that is found to be too high?** If a company's transfer price is found to be too high, this means the company has not reported enough profit in the country and has not paid enough taxes. In addition to back taxes, companies are liable to incur penalties in the form of nondeductible interest, taxes on constructive-profit distributions to the parent company, customs penalties, nondeductible profit-sharing distributions to employees (in the case of France), and (especially in Italy) criminal penalties.

● **Is it possible or desirable to get an advance ruling?** Unlike the United States, tax authorities in many countries do not give local rulings or do not give them on a no-name basis. Additionally, in some countries, approaching the authorities can call attention to a transfer price that would otherwise go unchallenged.

● **What recourse is available in the event of an audit adjustment?** While many countries have tax treaties with the United States that provide for an appeal to the competent authority should one country successfully challenge an MNC's transfer prices, the treaties are not strictly enforced. Speaking about U.K. tax law, a local attorney explains: "If a company has been challenged by the IRS, the Inland Revenue will look at the case. If they disagree with the IRS's decision, though, the company can proceed no further." Additionally, appeals to competent authorities can require an extended amount of time. One MNC speaks of 10 years as a not uncommon time frame for dealing with the German tax authorities.

● **How, if at all, does actual practice differ from official posture?** Last, in deciding which transfer approach to use, MNCs need to know the extent to which actual practice differs from the letter of the law. As a generalization, in some countries with high unemployment, transfer-pricing policies may not be strictly enforced. A partner in a Spanish accounting firm points out: "With a 21 percent unemployment rate, Spain is more interested in making MNCs feel welcome than it is in finding domestic tax cheats."

Conducting a Functional Analysis

As noted in the checklists above, functional analysis allows firms to identify new functions for which overseas operations can and should be legitimately charged. By comparing functional analysis worksheets with current operations, managers should find new charges, or at least identify functions that could easily be shifted, thereby creating new charges. The next three checklists offer a functional analysis for marketing, manufacturing, and general, administrative, and selling activities.

Managers who have used the functional analysis approach caution that the active involvement and support of line managers is a key ingredient for its successful implementation. The negotiations and explanations that usually accompany the analysis can result in a time-consuming process—one that might be too time-consuming for some of today's thinly staffed MNCs. Firms will need to gauge their own need to use the analysis based on their level of excess tax credits and their own preliminary analyses.

---

70. Functional Analysis for Marketing

	Parent	Sub		Parent	Sub
	(check one)			(check one)	
(1) Supervises marketing activities	☐	☐	(11) Plans and develops other promotional material, such as brochures, catalogs, display advertising	☐	☐
(2) Develops new promotional themes for advertising and product promotion	☐	☐	(12) Plans trade conventions and shows	☐	☐
(3) Develops training materials and trains personnel	☐	☐	(13) Determines personnel needs	☐	☐
(4) Develops marketing plans for new products and guidelines for such marketing	☐	☐	(14) Establishes compensation and other personnel incentives	☐	☐
(5) Coordinates the execution of planned marketing strategies of foreign subsidiaries	☐	☐	(15) Determines pricing and pricing policy and coordinates policy with foreign subsidiaries	☐	☐
(6) Approves new products	☐	☐	(16) Establishes credit terms	☐	☐
(7) Designs and develops packaging material to implement marketing strategy and effort	☐	☐	(17) Is responsible for customer contact	☐	☐
(8) Plans and develops TV commercials	☐	☐	(18) Supervises sales force	☐	☐
(9) Plans and develops advertising formats and determines the media to be used, i.e., magazines, newspapers, etc.	☐	☐	(19) Does market research and develops new markets	☐	☐
			(20) Identifies need for product modification	☐	☐
			(21) Warehouses finished product	☐	☐
(10) Coordinates production schedules with sales	☐	☐	(22) Ships the product and provides insurance coverage	☐	☐
			(23) Warrants the product	☐	☐

---

71. Functional Analysis for Manufacturing Activities

	Parent	Sub		Parent	Sub
	(check one)			(check one)	
(1) Develops products	☐	☐	(5) Purchases capital equipment	☐	☐
(2) Develops manufacturing process and know-how	☐	☐	(6) Supervises construction of manufacturing plants and other buildings	☐	☐
(3) Develops product specification design plant	☐	☐	(7) Determines need for raw material and other supplies	☐	☐
(4) Designs manufacturing plant, machinery, and equipment	☐	☐	(8) Develops source of raw materials purchases	☐	☐

	Parent	Sub		Parent	Sub
(9) Purchases raw materials	☐	☐	(21) Manufactures finished goods	☐	☐
(10) Warehouses raw materials and supplies	☐	☐	(22) Provides engineering for manufacturing	☐	☐
(11) Develops raw materials flow technique	☐	☐	(23) Determines factory personnel needs	☐	☐
(12) Controls flow of raw materials	☐	☐	(24) Does hiring and training of factory personnel	☐	☐
(13) Arranges for freight and insurance on purchases	☐	☐	(25) Supervises the different manufacturing operations	☐	☐
(14) Plans production schedules and output	☐	☐	(26) Does maintenance of factory buildings, grounds, and equipment	☐	☐
(15) Coordinates production and selling	☐	☐	(27) Does packaging and labeling of products	☐	☐
(16) Develops cost standards	☐	☐	(28) Plans investments in plant and equipment and handles financial needs of manufacturing functions	☐	☐
(17) Develops quality-control standards	☐	☐			
(18) Performs quality-control functions	☐	☐			
(19) Manufactures components	☐	☐			
(20) Manufactures other raw materials	☐	☐			

72. Functional Analysis for General, Administrative, and Selling Activities

	Parent	Sub		Parent	Sub
	(check one)			(check one)	
(1) Develops financial needs and budgets for the group	☐	☐	manufacturing design, and manufactures point-of-display advertising	☐	☐
(2) Plans investments and makes investment decisions	☐	☐	(20) Plans trade conventions and shows	☐	☐
(3) Develops overall marketing strategy	☐	☐	(21) Supervises sales force and does customer contact	☐	☐
(4) Plans, coordinates, and supervises market policy	☐	☐	(22) Designs and develops packaging material	☐	☐
(5) Does market research	☐	☐	(23) Manufactures packaging material	☐	☐
(6) Determines advertising and marketing policy	☐	☐	(24) Designs material for and develops catalogs	☐	☐
(7) Supervises advertising and marketing	☐	☐	(25) Coordinates production schedules with sales	☐	☐
(8) Determines the needs for general, administrative, and selling personnel	☐	☐	(26) Does purchasing of finished goods	☐	☐
(9) Hires personnel	☐	☐	(27) Supervises purchasing and shipping of finished goods	☐	☐
(10) Develops training materials	☐	☐	(28) Does warehousing of finished goods	☐	☐
(11) Supervises training of personnel	☐	☐	(29) Does inventory control	☐	☐
(12) Does training of general, administrative, and sales personnel	☐	☐	(30) Does shipping of finished goods	☐	☐
(13) Determines compensation of personnel	☐	☐	(31) Provides insurance coverage	☐	☐
(14) Determines pricing and pricing policy	☐	☐	(32) Warrants products	☐	☐
(15) Establishes credit terms	☐	☐	(33) Handles patent and trademark protection	☐	☐
(16) Develops advertising formats and translations	☐	☐	(34) Assumes inventory risk	☐	☐
(17) Determines media in which advertising is to be placed and places advertising	☐	☐	(35) Assumes credit risk	☐	☐
(18) Plans and develops TV commercials	☐	☐	(36) Develops accounting systems and software	☐	☐
(19) Plans sales promotion and develops promotional materials, i.e., designs point-of-display advertising, engineers			(37) Maintains accounting records	☐	☐
			(38) Does tax planning and administration	☐	☐
			(39) Handles customers' complaints	☐	☐
			(40) Does billing and collection	☐	☐
			(41) Handles government matters	☐	☐
			(42) Prepares statistical data and financial reports	☐	☐

73. Solving Tax Reform's Funding Equation

The corporate response to tax reform has partly been to adjust the global borrowing structure. Generally speaking, TRA86 punishes firms that continue to fund offshore operations with debt incurred in the United States. However, the analysis is not as simple as it might appear. The following checklist, provided by Peat Marwick Main's treasury management consulting principal, will help firms determine an optimal funding portfolio.

The general perception is that TRA86 will require companies to reconsider their methods for financing foreign operations. But tax implications are only the start: Development of a financing strategy is a complex process in which several issues—both financial and nonfinancial—need to be evaluated, often simultaneously. In many cases, there is no right decision. Rather, firms will need to evaluate collectively the numerous factors that affect foreign financing. The issues to be balanced include:

● **Leverage issues.** In determining the financing of local operations, firms should first look to the desired capital structure for a given entity seeking to reduce the cost of capital on an after-tax and risk-adjusted basis. However, firms must also include growth expectations for both foreign and domestic operations and their liquidity needs over short- and long-term horizons. In addition, industry norms

Figure 1
The Peat Marwick Main Decision Model*

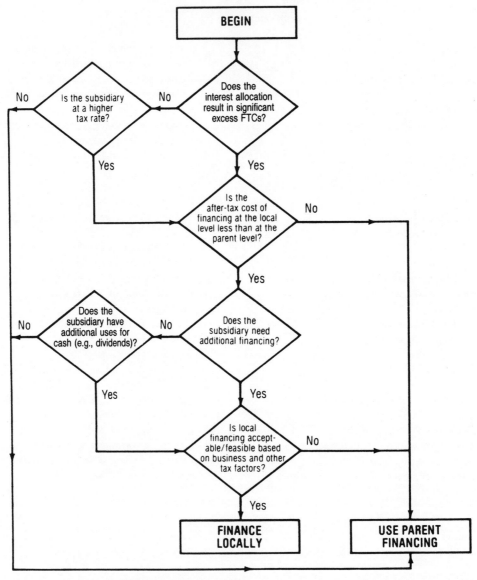

*The above model has been simplified for discussion purposes.

for financial leverage as measured by debt-equity ratios need to be considered. Finally, country-specific regulations (if any) for maximum debt-equity ratios need to be observed.

- **Economic and political issues.** Local risk needs to be analyzed to answer this question: Is the use of local debt a viable means for hedging inflation? Also, political-risk evaluation often affects the amount of equity a company will contribute to a given business. These political and economic factors should be evaluated and become part of a risk-adjusted cost-of-capital analysis.

- **FX exposure.** The use of local debt is an effective method for hedging foreign currency exposures. However, in some cases, a firm's local currency receipts and disbursements might already be reasonably balanced, and additional local debt might actually add to exchange risk. Alternative financial and operational techniques can prove to be more effective hedges, and other solutions for local currency financing will need to be considered as well.

- **Tax issues.** These are no less simple to resolve. While the apparent effect of TRA86 is to encourage MNCs to directly finance foreign operations locally, many MNCs will find that their foreign subsidiaries do not require added financing under the calculations of the allocation method required by TRA86. Furthermore, incurring such financing could trigger a large dividend distribution with its own tax consequences. Also, local tax authorities could challenge the deductibility of interest at the local level. Finally, many companies could find that reducing foreign assets and repaying parent-company debt is an equally effective solution.

The PMM Model

To help MNCs make decisions on the tax aspects of foreign financing, Peat Marwick Main offers the simplified decision-making model shown here. This model is based on the observation that a fundamental downward shift in the value of a deduction for U.S. interest has occurred under the TRA86 provisions. A further tax-based analysis is necessary to determine if the added interest deduction would be used and/or be of greater value if incurred in another taxing jurisdiction. A failure to satisfy this test would seem to indicate that a change in financing is not warranted. If these initial tests are passed, an MNC treasurer would need to conduct a foreign subsidiary financing evaluation, assessing the qualitative and risk factors identified above.

For the purpose of this analysis, the U.S. effective tax rate should be adjusted to allow for the diminished and/or non-deductibility of interest expense related to international operations. The use of this revised effective tax rate specific to financing could prove to have a dramatic impact on decisions regarding foreign financing.

74. Bank of America Explains How TRA86 Affects FX Management

Of particular interest to treasury managers are the ways in which TRA86 alters the tax consequences of certain FX transactions, especially those related to foreign currency loans that are combined with forward contracts, options, or swaps. "Under the old law," explains the vice president and senior tax manager for Bank of America, "it was easier to structure FX transactions so that any gains would be capital taxed at 28 percent (or not taxed at all) and any losses would be currently deductible. Now it's a lot harder." To illustrate how the new tax law affects FX gains or losses, he outlines the effects on a variety of FX transactions.

- **Loan plus investment straddles.** The classic straddle, he says, is a U.S. company borrowing deutsche marks for five years: "Assuming that the company doesn't need to spend the funds right away or that the funds are to be used for arbitrage purposes, they're placed in a six-month deutsche mark deposit. If the mark appreciates, the exchange loss on the loan won't be deductible until the full five years are up and the loan is repaid." But the gain on the deutsche mark deposit will become taxable under Section 988 *as soon as the six months are up and the deposit matures.* In effect, the transaction eliminates currency exposure for the first six months, but it creates a tax exposure.

The Bank of America spokesman goes on to say: "Equally adverse are the tax consequences if the mark de-values. Then the Section 1092 straddle rules apply, and the loss on the deposit isn't deductible because it's offset by the unrealized gain of the loan." He concludes, "If the company has a gain on the deposit, it pays taxes to the IRS at the full 34 percent rate. And if it has a loss, it can't deduct the loss. In other words: heads, the IRS wins; tails, the company loses."

- **Loan plus forward contracts.** If the above company takes the proceeds from its five-year Dm500 million loan and (instead of making a six-month deutsche mark deposit) buys U.S. dollars spot and sells forward into deutsche marks, then a different set of rules apply.

A deutsche mark forward contract is in one of the currencies that is treated as a regulated futures contract under Section 1256. The consequences of being a regulated futures contract are that the contract has to be marked to market at the end of the company's fiscal year and any gain or loss must be treated as a capital gain or loss. Not only is the character of the forward (capital) different from the loan being hedged (ordinary), but the taxation event for the forward (mark to market) and the loan (realization) are markedly out of step. As in the example above, the straddle rules of Section 1092 apply, so that if the forward produces a loss, this cannot be recognized for tax purposes because of the unrealized gain in the loan.

The capital classification works against most companies because the lower tax rate for capital gains was eliminated by TRA86. However, the restrictions against the deductibility of capital losses are still in effect: Capital losses can be deducted only to the extent to which they offset capital gains. To avoid the characterization as a capital gain, a company can choose to make a 1256(e) election—which is what a company with the loan plus forward contract position described above would want to do.

The Peat Marwick spokesman points out that "if the forward contract had been in one of the currencies that is not traded on a recognized exchange, then Section 1256 would never have entered the picture, so you wouldn't have to worry about any elections." And what is the logic behind this? As he reveals, it's "for some reason totally unexplained in anything I have read. Congress [simply] chose to treat contracts in some currencies differently from others."

● **Loan plus options.** Similarly, gains or losses on exchange-traded nonequity options used for the purpose of a hedge are considered Section 1256 contracts and must be marked to market. Gains or losses on other options are covered under Section 1234, which dictates that premiums paid on call options, for example, are not currently deductible. Instead the premiums are rolled back into the basis of the asset. They are not recognized until the currency is disposed of through the exercise of options. If the options are allowed to expire, the gain or loss is either capital or ordinary, depending on how it is used. If used for hedging purposes, the gain or loss will be capital.

● **Loan plus a swap.** If a firm immediately swapped the entire proceeds of its deutsche mark loan into U.S. dollars, the company could make a 988(d) hedge election. This treats the transaction as if the company had borrowed U.S. dollars. That election, which will become operative when the related IRS regulations are issued, works only if the *entire* proceeds and all anticipated interest payments are *immediately* swapped into U.S. dollars.

● **FAS 52 or translation hedges.** When an MNC chooses to hedge its net investment in a foreign subsidiary, the treatment of the hedge for tax purposes will depend on what instrument is used to hedge. The Peat Marwick spokesman says: "If an MNC uses a forward contract or exchange-traded option in one of the traded currencies, then the gain or loss will be capital, with no possibility of making any elections. However, in the event that a currency swap is used or the currency is not one of those traded, then the gain or loss will be ordinary."

● **Speculative hedges.** If the MNC decides to enter into a speculative transaction in the exchange-traded currencies, any gain or loss will be capital in nature, with no hedge elections. However, if the transaction is in a minor currency, the MNC can control the character of either the gain or the loss—which will be ordinary unless the "speculators' election" of Section 988(a)(1)(b) is made, in which case the gain or loss will be capital.

75. The Effect of TRA86 on Foreign-Based MNCs

For foreign-owned firms with U.S. operations, TRA86 offers good news and bad news. First, the good news: The tax law offers an incentive to foreign firms in the form of a lower tax rate. With nominal corporate tax rates falling from 46 to 34 percent, foreign corporations stand to make a significant windfall from the U.S. market.

Now for the bad news: Since TRA86 relates to any firm doing business in the United States, foreign MNCs will also suffer from the loss of the investment tax credit and changes in other capital incentives (e.g., loss of capital gains tax and extended depreciation schedules). Making matters worse, TRA86 singles out foreign-owned companies for special treatment through six key provisions. As a result, on balance, TRA86 may actually raise the taxes of foreign-based MNCs despite offering lower nominal tax rates.

To help foreign firms assess the tax implications of their forays into the U.S. market, this checklist presents the eight provisions of TRA86 that are specifically targeted to their operations and is followed by two important provisions that, though not aimed at foreign MNCs, could have a critical impact on their operations.

● **Imposition of a branch-level tax (BLT) on profits and interest.** Foreign firms doing business in the United States as branches are now subject to a 30 percent tax rate on both branch profits and interest. Either tax, however, can be reduced or eliminated when a treaty applies. This BLT provision essentially equates U.S. branches of a foreign firm with full-fledged U.S. subsidiaries. Both will be subject (in the absence of an applicable treaty) to a tax rate of 30 percent on corporate distributions such as dividends, interest, and royalties.

The BLT *can* be reduced by the amount of income actually reinvested in U.S. operations. However, accumulation of income beyond the reasonable fixed-asset or cash-flow needs of the business (and into nonbusiness assets, such as passive investments) will, in effect, be subject to the tax. In any case, the amount taxable under the BLT is limited to current earnings and earnings accumulated after 1986. Further, there is no BLT on the disposal of plant and equipment when a branch is liquidated.

The BLT for interest represented Congress' attempt to equalize taxation of branch interest with that of the interest of a U.S. subsidiary. Thus, any interest paid by a branch of a foreign corporation engaged in a trade or business in the United States will be treated as if it were paid by a U.S. corporation. Also, if the amount of interest allowable as a tax deduction in computing the effectively connected (see below) taxable income of a foreign firm exceeds the interest actually paid by a branch, the excess will be treated as interest paid by the branch to its foreign parent on the last day of the foreign firm's taxable year. The rate of tax on branch-level interest stands at 30 percent, provided that there is no reduction of the tax rate by a treaty.

The key impact on foreign-based MNCs is that many will now convert their U.S. operations from branch to U.S. subsidiary status to avoid the BLT. But in spite of the added complication, a number of foreign firms, namely banks, cannot easily convert to the status of a subsidiary. U.S. regulations, including the Glass-Steagall Act, would have negative effects on the core businesses of these banks if they were to shift to that status.

● **Tightening of the secondary dividend withholding tax threshold.** Under the old law, the U.S. government was empowered to levy a 30 percent withholding tax whenever a dividend paid by any foreign corporation was determined to have come from trade or business activities conducted within the United States. Before exercising this right, U.S. authorities were required to show that 50 percent or more of that corporation's total income had been rightfully earned through a business conducted within the United States (termed "effectively connected income"). This tax was often referred to as the "secondary withholding tax."

The new secondary withholding tax brings a punitive development. The new threshold starts when 25 percent or more of a foreign corporation's gross income is found to be effectively connected to a business conducted within the United States. It should be noted, however, that the secondary withholding tax applies only when a treaty obligation of the United States precludes assessing the BLT but permits secondary withholding.

When secondary withholding is specified as the means of withholding by a particular tax treaty, withholding tax will be exacted out of any dividends paid by the foreign corporation, according to the following formula: For dividends, the withholding is the amount of the dividend times the ratio of (1) the foreign corporation's U.S. effectively connected gross income for a three-year base period (the three years before the year of the dividend payment) to (2) worldwide gross income for the same base period.

● **Elimination of the secondary withholding tax for interest.** One piece of good news is that the secondary withholding tax for interest has been eliminated. The rules (and threshold) for this tax had been essentially the same as for the secondary withholding tax on dividends.

● **Elimination of dual-resident companies (DRCs).** DRCs were tax vehicles that enabled users to gain simultaneous interest deductions in two countries, thus substantially lowering the cost of funds. The loss of such vehicles especially affects companies making investments from the United Kingdom, Australia, and New Zealand.

TRA86 does not specifically eliminate DRCs. Instead, the law provides that the losses of a U.S. corporation cannot offset the income of another U.S. corporation if the losses also reduce the foreign taxes of a related foreign firm (i.e.,

if the DRC is subject to the income tax of a foreign country on its domestic or foreign-sourced income or is subject to such a tax on a residence basis). This amendment to the current tax code effectively destroys the DRC technique for all foreign MNCs.

● **Establishment of new transfer-price ceilings.** TRA86 also limits foreign firms in the charges they may bill their U.S. operations for imports. Specifically, the transfer prices for these goods must be consistent and cannot exceed customs valuation (although they can be less).

This new rule is an attempt to make taxpayers act consistently. In the past, firms could make dual valuation using a high value or a low value, depending on where it would be beneficial. For example, firms would list a high transfer price for goods from abroad (to shift profits home and into what could be a lower-tax environment). However, a low value would be listed at customs valuation, resulting in lower duties.

Practically speaking, there are a number of items, such as freight and sales commissions, that quite properly may cause customs and tax values to differ. But in response to TRA86, foreign MNCs should be careful to consider such costs before establishing the ultimate transfer price.

● **Tighter rules for transportation income.** The new code provides for a 4 percent return collected tax on the *gross* income from all shipping/transportation activities that begin or end in the United States. In determining gross income, the U.S. authorities will assume that 50 percent of all transport income so described is eligible for the tax.

Foreign firms will be exempt from the tax if the home country maintains reciprocal tax exemption with the United States. But a foreign firm organized in a foreign country that grants a reciprocal exemption may not claim a U.S. exemption if 50 percent or more of its beneficial shareholders are not residents of the country of organization or another foreign country that grants a similar exemption to U.S. shippers.

The gross-income method is also superseded if the transport income is taxed on a net basis under the effectively connected rules. These rules prevail if (1) the MNC maintains a U.S. fixed place of business through which transportation income is earned and (2) substantially all the income comes from regularly scheduled transportation.

● **The "book-income" adjustment on the alternative minimum tax (AMT).** The AMT, applicable to U.S. and foreign MNCs, ensures that corporations with substantial economic profit will pay federal income tax in an amount somewhat commensurate with that income, despite (1) tax-free and partially tax-free income and (2) qualification for tax preferences that otherwise would substantially reduce or eliminate taxable income.

The AMT is calculated as 20 percent of AMT income, which is defined as regular taxable income adjusted (generally increased) to negate various preference items and exclusions.

The most unique adjustment the AMT imposes, particularly from the standpoint of a foreign MNC, is the "book-income" adjustment, also called the "business-untaxed-reported-profits (BURP) adjustment." This is 50 percent of the excess of the adjusted net book income over AMT income (before making the book adjustment). It is perhaps one of the few adjustments that can be different for the U.S. branch of a foreign firm or for a U.S. subsidiary of a foreign MNC than for a similarly situated U.S.-controlled corporation.

This distinction occurs because a major U.S. company will surely have financial statements prepared according to U.S. GAAP, while the branch of a foreign firm or the U.S. subsidiary of a foreign MNC might not. There are two reasons why a foreign branch may not use U.S. GAAP financials: (1) it is not publicly traded in the United States or (2) it will not need GAAP or certified audited financials if it does not borrow locally or report to shareholders for any other substantial purpose not related to taxes.

For foreign firms operating as branches, this may present a temporary opportunity to reduce the AMT. U.S. GAAP financials must be used if available. However, in their absence, less sophisticated financial statements can be substituted in a prescribed order. Thus, a foreign-controlled entity may well manage to use a book-income figure for AMT purposes that is far lower than the figure that is computed using U.S. GAAP.

In any case, this window is only temporary; the book-income adjustment was replaced by an earnings and profits (E&P) adjustment for tax years beginning on or after January 1, 1989. This replacement ended the differing treatment for foreign MNCs (and any major planning opportunities that arose as a result).

● **Transfer pricing.** In addition to increasing direct foreign investment in the United States, TRA66's lower corporate rates will encourage foreign-based MNCs to price intragroup sales of goods and services so that as much income as possible will be allocated to U.S. operations and as little as possible to operations in countries with higher tax rates. With the United States already the largest market of consumer goods and capital in the world, TRA86 offers foreign MNCs an ideal opportunity to profit from a low-tax jurisdiction.

But caution is needed. Tax authorities in other industrial countries will undoubtedly scrutinize the pricing of transactions between their taxpayers and the U.S. affiliates of their taxpayers with new vigor.

Chapter 10
Minimizing Banking Costs and Risks

Managing the costs and risks associated with banking services has always been one of the key tasks of the corporate treasury function. But over the past several years, as the financial services sector has gone from bust to boom to bust again, it has become increasingly difficult for treasury managers to determine which strategies yield optimal results. Should MNCs continue to pursue, as they have in the recent past, an aggressive approach aimed at reducing the overall cost of using banking services by seeking the lowest bid for each transaction? Or does the new, more cautious postcrash environment also dictate a return to a more traditional strategy based on strong relationships with only a few top banks (and ones with still-strong balance sheets)? Does it still make sense to deal only with banks from the parent country? Or does the expertise of local banks in local markets more than offset the advantages that a longstanding relationship in the home country seem to provide—especially as the latter banks now seem more and more likely to withdraw from difficult markets?

This chapter deals with these and other key questions facing the corporate financial manager regarding the practical aspects of banking relationships. The checklists are divided into three main sections. The first section deals with key aspects of the overall corporate-bank relationship. The second one discusses what corporations need to consider when approaching banks for services in key market segments. The last one reviews some of the questions corporate managers need to ask themselves when picking an appropriate bank to handle local financial affairs.

76. Organizing for Banking Relations

Without effective coordination and clear banking policies, firms cannot hope to achieve the quantitative and qualitative benefits of efficient bank account and relationship management. But all too often, companies take a fragmented approach to banking relations, dividing the function between headquarters and local staff, and even among different departments at both the parent and subsidiary levels.

To get a handle on your firm's situation, and to avoid the administrative complexities and unnecessary costs of mismanaged bank relations, the following questions should be answered:

(1) What are your objectives in managing bank relations?

(2) Who is responsible for banking relations at the parent, regional, and subsidiary levels?

(3) What role does the parent or regional headquarters play in monitoring or managing local bank relations?

(4) How do you coordinate the banking needs of various departments within your company—e.g., treasury, export sales, and so on?

(5) Who has the authority to establish new relations or sever existing ones?

(6) Do you have a complete listing of all accounts with all banks held by the corporation as a whole? Do you have access to account balances and activity reports for each of these accounts?

(7) Have firm guidelines or policies been set on such matters as the number of banking relations, the use of foreign vs. local banks, and bank selection and evaluation criteria? What are they?

(8) What steps have been taken to measure, control, and reduce bank risk?

77. Tracking Banking Costs and Evaluating Services

Once a treasury manager is sure of how his banking relations are organized, it's time to find out if those responsible are getting the best combination of cost and service. Specifically, firms should identify and rigorously monitor all banking charges, including both direct (e.g., fees, commissions, and interest rates) and indirect (e.g., value-dating and compensating business) costs. They should also set up a system for evaluating the overall performance of their banks. The following questions can be used to evaluate performance problems:

(1) Do you regularly review and evaluate banking costs and services? What method do you use?

(2) Do your banks furnish regular accounts analyses that break down transactions and fees? How regularly are these verified?

(3) Do local cash managers systematically calculate the value of your business to a bank, including FX transactions, letters of credit, float, and so on?

(4) Do you regularly negotiate costs—such as for reduced check-clearing times or lower compensating balances—with your banks?

(5) Do your banks consistently quote competitive rates on money market investments, short-term borrowings, and FX transactions?

(6) Are they willing to tailor their services, or do they offer systems only "off track?"

(7) Do they transfer funds efficiently and provide other services to accelerate domestic and export collections?

(8) Do they offer advanced services, such as electronic banking, concentration and zero- or target-balance accounts?

(9) Are bank officers responsive?

78. How to Control Banking Costs

MNCs are entering an era of higher banking costs. Buffeted by Third World loan losses and a lackluster equity market, the banking sector is now in the midst of a major restructuring. Most leading institutions are now ensuring that all pricing adequately reflects both the level of risk involved in any particular transaction and a realistic profit margin. As one banker recently told BI, "The days are gone when we will underprice just to maintain our position in the league tables. Profitability is the key now."

For corporations, the trend necessarily means higher costs for banking services in the years ahead. Some financial managers are greeting the new environment with equanimity, claiming it just reflects the delayed cost of the great deals they got on banking services during the preceding several years. Others are feeling less sanguine and are still looking for ways to control banking costs.

Rather than be fatalistic about banking charges, treasury managers should follow these guidelines to improve their rates:

(1) **Negotiate fees aggressively.** There are essentially three strategy points here. First, companies can often achieve dramatic savings when they review existing terms

and conditions with their banks on a service-by-service basis. The review often turns up pricing anomalies that give the company the upper hand.

In addition, many firms are no longer shy about insisting upon a set fee for services, making the costs of banking services fully transparent and thus easier to evaluate. Long-standing problems with regard to monitoring and controlling value dates have increased the appeal of this negotiating tactic.

Once the review is completed, however, companies should not hesitate to try to negotiate a package deal based upon the total volume of business. For example, a firm can arrange to bring a certain amount of business to a bank for a set fee that will include a number of services.

(2) Monitor banking charges carefully. Once it has reviewed and reestablished the terms of the relationship, a company must be prepared to track banking costs closely.

If the value-dating problem was not solved in the first review, it deserves special follow-up attention, as banks will often ignore the agreed-upon date. To tackle this problem, many firms advocate keeping tabs on all transactions and making claims as soon as any deal is stalled.

(3) Create a computerized system to evaluate the bank's performance. With the advent of personal computers, it is virtually inexcusable for MNCs not to create automated systems for monitoring banking costs. All terms and conditions negotiated with banks—including value dating, fees, and interest rates—should be part of the system, allowing the company to compare contracted costs with those shown on the actual bank statements.

(4) Insist on a formal agreement from the bank. No matter what method of compensation a company uses or how close the banking relationship is, always ask for a written agreement on terms and conditions.

---

79. Twenty-Two Questions to Use in Evaluating Your Bank's Cash Management Services

All banks promise their corporate clients first-rate cash management services—and often they mean it. The pitfall for corporate cash managers lies in dealing with a bank that fails to deliver on its promises. A poorly designed system can mean lost interest revenues, lost work hours, and, worst of all, a system that does not really fit the needs of your company.

To avoid such losses, companies must monitor their banks' cash management services. BI recommends that firms carry out a review at least once a year and focus questioning on the key areas that follow.

Responsiveness

(1) Is there an account officer assigned to handle your cash management inquiries?

(2) Is it necessary to initiate second and third follow-ups before your original inquiry is properly addressed?

(3) Is the bank's response timely?

(4) Is there a backup when your account officer is out of the office?

Services

(5) Do you hear from your bank at times other than when it wants to raise prices or when a problem exists?

(6) Does your bank approach you about new ideas for improved servicing of your account?

(7) Does your bank understand the complexities of your business and those of your competitors?

(8) Does your bank offer a full range of cash management services, such as cash collection, concentration accounts, zero/target balance accounts, electronic information reporting, courier services/cash letters, lockboxes, FX, and consulting services?

Customized Services

(9) Is your bank amenable to providing customized cash management services to meet the specific needs of your company?

(10) Does the bank absorb, in whole or in part, the costs incurred in the development of these customized services? In the latter case, what proportion of the costs do you pay, and are they itemized in the invoice you receive from the bank?

Pricing

(11) Is the pricing of your bank's cash management services consistent with industry standards?

(12) Are you offered a variety of pricing formats, such as fee-based, compensating balances, CD purchases, and value dating?

(13) Does your bank provide—via account analyses—information on how much it is charging you and for which specific cash management services?

Credit

(14) Are short-term/overnight lines-of-credit needs consistently met by your bank?

(15) Does your bank provide long-term loans at preferential interest rates?

Funds Transfer/Check Clearing

(16) Are your incoming and outgoing funds transfers handled accurately?

(17) Are the outgoing funds transfers timed appropriately to give you maximum use of the funds?

(18) Does your bank's operational staff assist you in locating funds transfers that have gone astray?

(19) Are deposited checks and drafts cleared on a next-day basis or at an equally acceptable time?

Errors and Compensation

(20) Does your bank make frequent or repetitive errors in processing wire transfers or checks and drafts, handling documentation, or balance-information reporting?

(21) Are your bank's errors resulting in lost interest compensated to your account with full back value?

Technology

(22) Does your bank have a high level of computerization?

---

80. Evaluating Capital Market Services: Six Ways to Narrow the Field

It should not be forgotten that capital market services are part of a total relationship. With fierce competition in capital markets still in evidence, this is one area in which companies can afford to play hardball with their bankers.

Moving beyond both relationship and transaction-oriented banking, more and more treasurers are rigorously scrutinizing their banks' services. Some firms have computerized their bank evaluation process, relying on a data base to compare prices and other factors. Others utilize equally rigorous but less automated techniques. "Companies are clear about what they want from banks," quips one banker. "They want everything done 100 percent better and 100 percent cheaper." Whatever evaluation approach is used, there are at least six characteristics of a bank's capital market services that should be evaluated. They include the following:

(1) **Pricing.** When it comes to capital market services, more corporations are awarding deals on a competitive-bid basis than ever before. "Of course our clients shop," says the general manager of a major European bank. "They are approached by a lot of banks, and they look for the cheapest deal."

Price evaluations can sometimes be tricky, however. Hidden costs and subtle differences between bank proposals can result in a comparison between apples and oranges. "We read through all the proposals and try to eliminate the extras that just give the impression of being innovative," says the corporate treasurer for a European manufacturer. "The most important thing is to bring the proposals to your desk on a comparable basis."

(2) **Quality of service.** The main question here is, once a service is purchased, will the bank follow through, or will it just pocket the fee and forget about you? "We want to make sure that every time we come to market, our deals trade," says the vice president and treasurer of a U.S. beverage maker. "We ask the banks to come in and ask them how they will support the deal, who they will sell it to, and why people are going to buy it at the levels they indicate. We need to have a strong view of how they propose to do it."

(3) **Expertise of bankers.** As the trend toward niche banking gathers steam, certain banks will earn a market reputation for particular kinds of services. "Companies are

willing to go to Bank A for whatever services its expertise lies in," says one New York banker, "and they go to Bank B for whatever it does." Adds the treasurer of an Asian transportation firm: "We know who the major players are and who is good at what. We know their strengths, and we consider these when they come up with a proposal."

(4) **Creativity of the bankers.** Companies always want first shot at a new idea, because when an instrument is fresh, it usually yields the greatest savings. What's more, that process usually snowballs. By giving preference to banks in the vanguard, a firm puts itself in line for the next novel idea the bank may develop. "The bank that approaches us with the most innovative idea almost always comes first," says the European treasurer.

Keeping track of capital market innovation, however, is a demanding task. Treasury staffs have to be competent and sophisticated enough to distinguish between a cost-saving new twist and mere glitz. "Our staffing policy is to go for absolutely top quality," says the CFO at a U.K. firm. "Unless we can respond quickly to a bank's propositions, we won't get the good ideas coming to us. And we want to be the first to hear of a new idea, not the 501st."

(5) **Credit risk of the bank.** As margins fall and costs rise, banks have been forced to take on increased risk to generate profits and meet competition. As a result, many large companies are now grappling with an unprecedented issue: How can firms assess the risk of their banks, rather than the reverse? "I don't think it's sunk in that many companies are really in a better credit position than some banks," says the assistant treasurer of a U.S. pharmaceuticals firm. "Now that a lot of the banks are single A's, we are buying more advisory services like Keefe Bruyette's and Moody's to track the banking community."

At one large British MNC, the answer is to apply the same tight prudent standards that banks use when evaluating the credit risk of companies. The firm will use only banks that can back up their transactions. The company has also installed automated systems that record and monitor all financial exposures with banks to ensure that limits on money market and FX dealings are not exceeded.

However, with the growth of off-balance-sheet transactions like interest rate swaps, it has become much more difficult to assess a bank's credit worthiness. Therefore, when a regional telecommunications firm recently put together a long-term swap transaction, it asked for and got "cross-default language on the bank that was equivalent to what the bank received from us," says the treasurer. "Every paragraph they wrote for themselves, they wrote for us. Some banks wouldn't play, but from my standpoint there's the same risk for me as for them, and I want the same coverage."

(6) Strength of the relationship. Contrary to banks' repeated accusations, companies have not totally abandoned relationships. While old bonds may have weakened, new ones have developed based on quality, pricing, and service. In other words, firms want relationships with the best banks. "No company in its right mind turns down a good deal because it doesn't have a relationship," says the director of corporate finance at a U.K. brewery. "However, I think that relationships in banking are very important." Past performance has thus become a key element in a company's evaluation of its banks. Says the treasurer at the telecommunications firm: "We just did a deal where the bank that did the documentation was absolutely brilliant. If we do another deal like that and the bids are roughly competitive, those bankers will get the deal. A basis point or two does not make such a difference. They will simplify things, saving us time and legal fees." Some bankers agree that, when all other factors in competing proposals are equal, the overall relationship can be the deciding factor. "If we're competitively priced and the product's good," says one bank vice president, "the relationship still makes a difference."

81. How to Protect Your Funds Against Bank Risk

The Third World debt crisis, depression in the energy and agriculture sectors, and intense competition within the banking industry have adversely affected the book value of many leading banks. These trends, combined with the explosion of off-balance-sheet transactions, have made it increasingly critical for corporations to assess the creditworthiness and the potential longevity of their top banks. Whatever the outlook for their key banks may be, financial managers need to keep in mind the following seven key points to guard against banking risks.

(1) Look at the complete relationship. Firms are exposed to banks in more than one area. Managers should view their exposure to a bank in terms of all activity: FX, borrowing, investing, export financing, and capital markets.

(2) View credit ratings carefully. To ensure security—and also to exploit market inefficiencies in yields—companies should obtain accurate, independent knowledge on the creditworthiness of the banks where they invest excess cash. This process, undeniably time-consuming and expensive, involves visiting banks' CFOs, accountants, internal auditors, and the heads of major departments to gain a detailed understanding.

A key problem for companies doing their own ratings is that published financial information is often incomplete or faulty. States one corporate treasurer: "You can't judge a bank by the numbers. There are about three countries in the world where there is enough published information—the United States, the United Kingdom, and Canada. But when you get to the continental European banks and Japanese banks, published information tends to be very incomplete and could even be misleading if one is not a well-trained accountant familiar with the country's reporting requirements."

To skirt this problem and reduce the costs of gathering accurate information, many corporate treasuries rely, at least in part, on rating agencies that cover the banking sector.

(3) Develop internal expertise. Despite the arguments in favor of using outside consultants, it is still preferable to have an analyst on your side of the court. Companies must develop internal expertise in order to analyze the ratings and recommendations of outside consultants in light of their own needs.

(4) Be aware of repudiation risks. It is important to know not only the credit risk of the bank but also the political or sovereign risk of the country where the bank is domiciled. For instance, a number of years ago the Philippine government extended its control over the FX markets. Citibank Philippines reacted by freezing its interbank deposits. Many of the bank's depositors complained, and one sued. The Citibank episode makes it clear that depositors must consider sovereign risk as well as credit risk.

(5) Establish a cutoff risk point . . . Once a firm knows who its banks are, it must develop clear policies on tolerable risk. Since many relationships are global, and since on-line, interactive risk-tracking systems are prohibitively expensive, a firm's tolerance for each bank must be translated into precise dealing limits.

(6) . . . but remain flexible. A company's dealing limits must be designed to keep the banking relationship at an acceptable risk level. However, it is improbable that a firm will reach the established ceiling in all categories at the same time. So to prepare for the instance when an attractive opportunity conflicts with the preset limit, firms should have a clearly defined and rapid approval process in place.

(7) Be vigilant. Monitoring bank risk is a never-ending task for corporate treasury. Reviews of principal relationships should be conducted at least annually, and more often when circumstances demand.

82. Investing Short-Term Funds: A Checklist for Safety

As investment opportunities assume global dimensions, corporate money managers must deal with the very simple yet extremely important question of how to protect the integrity of corporate cash investments. Naturally, this should be done while preserving, if not improving, liquidity and maintaining optimal yield. After an intensive review of potential protective measures with corporate investment bankers and other specialists in the financial community, the following checklist was compiled.

(1) **Establish formal investment guidelines.** These should be reviewed and revised to reflect new risks and opportunities in financial markets. Remember that there are legal differences in international securities. A Eurodollar CD is only a moral obligation, for example, while a domestic CD is a legal one.

(2) **Know your sources of information.** Several rating agencies evaluate the strength and creditworthiness of short-term issuers. In the United States, the major securities rating services are Moody's Investors Services; Standard and Poor's; Fitch; Duff & Phelps; and Robinson and Humphrey's.

Several services focus on the evaluation of commercial banks. In the United States, such services include Keefe, Bruyette & Woods; Cates Consulting Analysts; and A. G. Becker. Financial Spread (done by Manufacturers Hanover Trust) offers credit information on non-U.S. banks, and Bankroll (put out by Chase Manhattan Bank) covers only U.S. banks. In the United Kingdom, a comparable service is offered by International Bank Credit Analyses (IBCA), which covers major banks in Western Europe, Japan, and Latin America; and Bank Spread (offered by Libra Financial Services) covers mostly Latin American banks.

(3) **Augment with in-house analysis.** If your investment portfolio is large enough, you should do your homework more thoroughly and augment external credit ratings with in-house assessment of issuers. If you are considering a bank's CDs, you should be able to gather a good deal of information from a variety of sources, including correspondent banks that keep tabs on one another for the soundness of interbank placements. (Such banks may be willing to share data if your corporation is a major customer.)

(4) **Look at the ratios.** For both bank and nonbank issuers, consider a battery of both qualitative and quantitative factors. These include the position of the bank/corporation within the industry (market share and competition); capital requirements and expenditures; earnings and profits (return on investment and return on capital); debt leverage and assets protection liquidity; availability of discretionary cash flow; and management quality (business philosophy, track record, operating efficiency, strategic planning, overall performance, etc.). In computerized quantitative analysis, numbers may have to be adjusted for inflation.

(5) **Review limits on investment vehicles.** Limits can clearly be broken down into maturity, industry, rating, issuers, and, of course, type of investment. Such predetermined ceilings will protect against, for example, the irrational predispositions of a particular investment officer.

(6) **Recognize and review country risk exposure.** Spreading sovereign risks is a principle of diversification, but setting limits should also include assessing the credit standards of sovereign issuers and the companies in each country. Some business information organizations (including BI) provide country assessment services for a broad range of purposes. Various countries' export credit/investment protection agencies (including some private insurers) will assume all or part of some investment risks (including securities investments)—at a price.

(7) **Seek backing.** If collateral is not available, as in the case of overnight repos or Eurodollar deposits, there should at least be careful book entries.

(8) **Keep checking your trader.** Top-grade securities in your company's portfolio could be worthless if the dealer defaults or mishandles the paper.

(9) **Be a skeptic on mergers, acquisitions, and divestitures.** Carefully note the underlying debt and assets in corporate mergers and acquisitions, and pay close attention to the financing of the deal. A bigger company is not always a stronger company. Similarly, evaluate the assets and liabilities of the offshoots of corporate divestitures and antitrust-motivated breakups.

Be skeptical of corporate "defeasance" (early extinguishment of debt via trustee accounts) and analyze the real advantages of debt-equity swaps. Scrutinize the balance sheets of leveraged buyouts.

(10) **Hedge with forwards and futures.** When a foreign obligation falls within your credit and country risk criteria, FX exposure remains. It may be worthwhile to hedge fully (or partly) against U.S. dollars or against your company's balance-sheet currency with a forward exchange contract. In some cases, hedging can actually increase yields (though decreasing the possibility of an FX gain). It may help to hedge a second time, against fluctuations in interest rates via financial futures contracts.

83. Choosing and Managing a Third World Banking Relation

Choosing banks for their global cash management and capital market capabilities is fine in most instances. But when dealing in the Third World, firms would be well advised to at least consider a different perspective.

Third World banks have more to offer firms dealing in exotic currencies than treasurers might think. The U.S.-based Foster Parents, a charity that operates in 22 Third World countries from Bolivia to Zimbabwe, recommends turning away from the big banks when doing business in Third World countries for three reasons. First, local banks are more familiar with the customs, traditions, and financial tools available in individual countries. Second, a small company often gets lost in the shuffle at big banks. Local banks aim to please. Finally, big banks pull out of unprofitable regional markets when such action meshes with banks' global business strategies. Local banks are there to stay.

When looking at banks, Foster Parents evaluates the method of transferring dollars to the country and the conversion rate into local currency. The finance manager at the company also advises that firms keep the following points in mind when looking into banking in exotic countries:

(1) Realize that Third World bankers are sophisticated. The manager asserts that MNCs underrate Third World banks. "I have been advised that Third World banks don't have the sophistication of the banks in the United States. This is a misconception," he says. "If anything, many of them have equal sophistication, and maybe some methods are even more efficient."

(2) Consider nonlocal Third World banks. The manager of Foster Parents stresses that even though the company does not work with a U.S. bank, that does not mean it works only with local banks. For instance, some Third World quill pen-type bank operations have been shaken by modern and intensely competitive Arab Emirate bankers. "In some West African countries, we find we get more efficiency from a Middle East bank that is based thousands of miles away— because it appears to understand local banking problems."

(3) Use Third World banks with U.S. branches. Foster Parents especially prefers local banks with U.S.-based branch offices. It needs U.S. banks to make transfers to the Third World. Arab banks, for instance, have branches in both the United States and many Third World nations.

(4) Make a firsthand evaluation. As in most MNCs, the company's managers at the local level may not be profes-sionally qualified in cash management. Therefore, the firm periodically sends in trained financial staff from its headquarters to scout banks, services, and procedures in each country.

(5) Don't be afraid to switch banks. "We have switched banks within the same country to obtain better conditions and promises of better conditions," says the manager. The firm follows up by reviewing reports from local managers to ascertain that the new bankers are keeping their promises.

(6) Train local staff. While a visit from headquarters staff can help attain promises of the best services and pricing, it is up to local staff to ensure that pledges are kept. Also, well-trained local staff can come up with improved procedures.

Foster Parents typically seeks natives for its local finance staff. While these employees are well versed in local laws and bookkeeping, they have not been trained to deal with banks and other suppliers. To that end, the company recently began to train its local financial staff. The seminars include discussions on banking relations and cash management run by the assistant international controller from headquarters and the finance director. "We're guiding them in how we think they should think," explains the manager. "We, in turn, are learning more about local situations."

(7) Ensure that local managers test bank efficiency. To determine whether or not a Third World bank is giving the best FX quotes, a firm must rely on personal communication with colleagues. However, other areas, such as value dating, can be objectively tested. "We do a lot of experimentation," says the director. "I just spoke with a field director in a West African country who said he is going to open an account with [a second bank]. He's asked us to break down our next $50,000 remittance and send $25,000 to one and $25,000 to the other." This way, the firm can compare rates, charges, and efficiency.

(8) Be flexible. The manager explains that optimal cash management in the Third World is a constantly moving target. "When you find a solution, several months later the laws have changed, the philosophies have changed, and techniques have changed." When this happens, the finance director explains, "You have no alternative but to go back in and update."

Chapter 11
Investing and Operating Profitably in Volatile Environments

Active treasury managers should be willing to do more than simply setting the right hurdle rate for investments in less developed countries (LDCs). They should get involved in the project-development process. The most successful international firms make a standard operating procedure of negotiating the best local conditions for their investments. Treasury managers should make it their business to ensure that the best possible incentives—like access to FX, protective tariffs, and tax holidays—have been obtained up front. Then and only then should an NPV analysis, using an appropriate hurdle rate, be conducted.

The following checklists will be useful to treasury managers interested in helping their project-development teams find the most lucrative Third World investments. They deal with topics ranging from determining an appropriate hurdle rate, to negotiating with local authorities, to structuring the most beneficial ownership arrangements. Finally, the chapter presents two checklists on how to continue operating profitably through a local-pricing strategy.

84. Doing a Self-Audit on Country-Risk Assessment Procedures

Whether a firm is considering a new investment or merely needs to stay current on existing ventures, some form of risk assessment must be in place. This first checklist will help firms determine if its country-risk procedures are accomplishing the right task for the right audience:

(1) Decide what tasks you want the risk assessment system to accomplish. Do you want it to examine a broad range of potential risks—economic and financial, as well as political? Do you want it to provide a ready comparison of potential investment sites or export markets? Will it be used to monitor underlying changes in investment conditions? Will the emphasis be on spotting developments that might affect the firm's ability to operate profitably in the future? Will it take into account opportunity, as well as risk factors?

(2) Determine which levels of your company are already carrying out some form of country-risk assessment. If such evaluation is not being done on a coordinated basis, this would be the time to assign to a department or executive the responsibility for harmonizing and conducting it. The reorganization also presents a chance to improve the assumptions and methods used in evaluation.

(3) Determine what kinds of executive decisions take risk assessment results into account. These decisions might involve the following areas: investing in, expanding operations in, or pulling out of a country; setting the level of export effort; determining maximum investment exposure; adjusting expected rates of return; establishing the pricing of dividend remittance policies or components; providing guarantees for foreign-affiliate borrowing; or choosing the form of corporate structure.

(4) Based on this analysis, decide what form of assessment best suits your company's needs. Among the possibilities are a purely qualitative, judgmental analysis; a structured analysis that considers specific factors for each country and assigns a qualitative weighted checklist; and a quantitative econometric analysis.

(5) Determine who should receive the assessment results and who will be the ultimate users. In most MNCs, these will be the CEO and/or executive committee, the financial staff, and, occasionally, the board of directors. Others might also be designated as recipients.

(6) Decide how often the assessment should be carried out for each country. The key determinant should be the purpose of the system (ranging from examining the feasibility of an investment site on a one-shot basis to alerting recipients to changes in investment conditions).

(7) Draw up a list of risk variables that you feel adequately span your firm's investment or export concerns. Nonpolitical risk factors (e.g., macroeconomic, financial, and business variables) should be included in the assessment. The more sophisticated computerized country-risk systems enable firms to readily incorporate industry- and company-specific variables as well.

(8) Consider using outside services or consultants. Sources like the *Business Environment Risk Index* (BERI) and *Frost & Sullivan* can supplement a firm's own risk assessment activities or help provide a better design. In-house models based solely on internal inputs can lack objectivity. On the other hand, a company may hesitate to rely extensively on outside services (particularly when the output is largely quantitative) that fail to take their specific needs into account. A good alternative may be a hybrid system that bases assessment on an outside model (thus providing independent country evaluations) but allows user firms to vary the weights and assessment variables and add industry- and company-specific factors.

(9) Test the accuracy of your past assessments of country-risk exposure. This will help the company determine whether any adjustments—whether to the criteria used, the system's sensitivity to relevant variables, or the adequacy and validity of the company's information sources—are necessary.

85. Fine-Tuning Quantitative Country-Risk Analysis

One of the most critical tasks for MNC treasury managers is the process of evaluating risky investments. Apply too high a risk premium, and attractive opportunities will be left for the competition. Set yields too low, and the firm accepts a bad return for the commensurate risk.

Most MNCs define a discount rate for expected returns from overseas investments as the required U.S. hurdle rate plus a risk premium. However, firms that use this strategy would do well to ensure that they are not missing out on solid opportunities by oversimplifying the process. The following is a checklist of five recurring weaknesses of quantitative risk assessment and how to avoid them:

(1) Risk assessment indices are not always specific to the investment . . . When building a country-risk component for their NPV calculations, inexperienced analysts are apt to focus on general operating conditions. Often they rely on risk assessment services that can boil a country's situation down to a single number. However, these are often too broadly based to use in evaluating a specific situation. As one senior executive contacted by BI explains, "We feel that risk assessment should be tailored to our company's own situation and that it should be product or investment specific." The manager uses published services but would never rely on them as the sole source of analysis.

The point is that the kind of product or service to be provided by the investing company makes a tremendous difference in assessing the risk of a proposed investment. For example, a proposal to build a non-labor-intensive product for local consumption might get a cold reception from an LDC's government or local labor unions. However, if the plans were to create a labor-intensive export manufacturing operation in a country with a high unemployment rate, enthusiasm within the local environment would be considerable. The latter project's political risk would be far less. Says the executive, "The standard political-risk indices won't help you here."

(2) . . . and they may even prove inaccurate. Another manager says that his firm compared the discount factors of several assessment services with the historical performance figures of the investments. "We reviewed empirical evidence, including several indicators from various services, and found that the models rarely agreed with our own assessments for individual investments. In fact, in our written evaluations we usually found a definitive and well-placed argument that would negate the indices."

(3) Discount factors in isolation prohibit objective comparison. When firms use a risk factor to discount returns from a prospective investment, it is critical that a rationale for the factor be presented in any analysis. Otherwise, an internal investment committee looking at the final numbers can't see the assumptions that formed the discount factor. "We want to have full verbal disclosure of the risks and all the factors that are involved in it," says one MNC's manager. "We just don't hide it in one number. For us, risk management is not a numeric exercise. At best it's very subjective, because it's our perception of the future and the issues that are involved."

One manager explains how his company overlays a subjective risk assessment on the undiscounted internal rate-of-return (IRR) numbers. "We use a finger-in-the-wind approach," he says. "For example, say we calculate an IRR of 28 percent for a project in Korea and are considering a similar project in Kansas City. We know that the 28 percent is nowhere near as good as the 24 percent we have for the Kansas City investment."

He also points out that discounting expected returns may not help the corporation weigh risk against opportunity. He says, "Very often, where risk is higher, opportunity is higher. It's never a clear-cut decision. And it's certainly not clear-cut in terms of standard risk indices."

(4) A quantitative system may push analysis too far down. Firms contacted by BI frequently use a quantitative NPV system to filter the projects being analyzed. Says one MNC manager, "We don't have time to look at each and every proposal." To streamline the number of projects, the firm uses a headquarters analyst to conduct a simple analysis. "That way, we see only promising projects," he says.

However, the danger in such a system is that the process may be pushed down to too junior an executive. A junior analyst, or perhaps an inexperienced analyst newly appointed to a senior analyst's position, may not be sufficiently familiar with the relevant variables. (A situation that can be just as bad is to have senior staff perform the analysis, but with discount factors generated by junior staff.) In general, firms should take steps to ensure that project analysis is conducted under the close scrutiny of a senior-level manager.

(5) The NPV analysis must take all cash flows into account. Firms must be certain to incorporate all marginal cash flows resulting from the investment in the NPV analysis. For example, a new overseas plant may be constructing cars for the domestic market. In addition to that subsidiary's profits, any royalties or licensing fees to the parent (a cost to the local operation) should be included as part of the benefit from the new investment. In addition, the parent's profits must be included—for example, on the sale of partially completed chassis kits.

---

86. One Firm's Three-Step Approach to Investing Profitably in LDCs

Fears of a new international debt crisis have made most MNCs leery of pouring new investment into debt-burdened Third World nations. However, investors' perception of high risks and the willingness of governments to compete aggressively for foreign capital may also result in investment bargains.

In any case, managers proposing any Third World investment will see a better chance of having the deal accepted if they first attempt to reduce the risk by any available means. The financial manager at one major U.S. company recently employed a three-step risk-reduction strategy when he prepared for a new foreign investment.

(1) Identify and thoroughly research the risks;
(2) Negotiate investment terms and guarantees with the

local company and the government (a desperate need for foreign capital ensures that the government will be a motivated seller); and
(3) Share the risks with other investors—especially investors whom the government won't dare offend.

Researching the Risks

To evaluate the feasibility of the investment, the manager planned a trip to the country in which the investment would be made. He highlighted four areas of interest: the risk of political disruption; the risk of devaluation, exchange controls, or a shortage of hard currency; the economics of the local company and the industry; and current and future government policies that could affect the local company.

During the trip, the manager met with representatives from the following organizations:

- the company in which the investment would be made;
- the relevant industry ministry;
- the finance ministry;
- the central bank;
- local pension funds;
- local commercial and investment banks;
- the local offices of foreign equipment suppliers;
- the ruling and opposition parties;
- the U.S. commercial attaché; and
- the local office of a U.S. accounting firm.

At the end of this series of meetings, the manager had discovered several facts about his risks. First, the risk of a catastrophic political disruption over the next five years was low. Representatives of the opposition party assured the manager that any investment terms or guarantees negotiated by the current government would be honored by subsequent rulers.

Second, although the risk of currency devaluation was significant, the central bank and the finance ministry were open to various means of alleviating this risk. The country's International Monetary Fund (IMF) compliance record was better than average. Also, while debt-service obligations ate up much of the country's export earnings, both private and foreign-government lenders had indicated some flexibility on rescheduling.

Third, after interviews with local management about business risk, the manager determined that the local company was satisfying only about 50 percent of local demand. Two of the company's problems represented opportunities for foreign investors: a need for new funds and a need for updated technology. A third problem was more serious. The company had large FX losses due to local-currency revenues and a high level of dollar debt.

Finally, the risk of unfavorable government policies was probably his biggest problem. In the past, government-imposed price controls and heavy taxation had depressed earnings and robbed the company of funds needed for expansion.

An Investor's Wish List

The government invited the manager to prepare a list of conditions under which his company would be willing to invest. In response, the manager prepared a "wish list": a series of conditions that, if met, would minimize the risks of the investment. The manager's list included the following conditions:

- **Dollar-linked pricing.** The local company would be allowed to link prices to the dollar/local-currency exchange rate. Prices would rise in line with the proportion of dollars on the right-hand side of the balance sheet. Thus, an increase in costs due to local-currency devaluation could be passed through to customers.
- **A tax holiday.** In the past, the company's profits had

been virtually expropriated. Under this condition, profits reinvested in the company would be subject to a very low level of taxation. Dividend payments to foreign investors would face a slightly higher rate.

- **A restructuring of the local firm's balance sheet.** Much of the local company's dollar debt would be converted to long-term local-currency debt. The local company would get the go-ahead to borrow local currency, sell it for dollars, and use the dollars to pay off a portion of its dollar liabilities.
- **A guarantee on the availability of hard currency.** The central bank would guarantee the availability of FX for dividends or the repatriation of the original investment. In addition, the investor would attempt to negotiate some form of exchange rate guarantee.
- **Permission to invest through debt swaps.** Under this plan, the investor would purchase from U.S. banks a portion of the country's existing dollar debt. The debt could be bought at a discount of up to 30 percent of its face value and then sold back to the country at full or close to its face value. The result would be a price of $0.70–0.75 for each dollar of equity invested. Dividends would be calculated based on the face value of the equity rather than on the dollar amount invested.
- **Permission to invest in the form of equipment.** The U.S. investor would contribute needed equipment to the local company. The investment would be valued at the price the local company would otherwise have had to pay for the equipment. However, thanks to established supplier relationships and volume discounts, the U.S. company would probably be able to get a better price. This would allow the U.S. company to invest at a discount off the face value of its equity.
- **The creation of a special class of preferred stock.** The local company would create a special class of preferred stock and sell shares to foreign investors. The stock would pay fixed dividends whether the local company was profitable or not. In a good year, dividends might be less than those on common stock, but the risk would be substantially lower.
- **A government-guaranteed "put option" on the investment.** The purchaser of a put option receives the right to buy the optioned item at a given price, regardless of the market price of the item. Under this catch-all agreement, the government would sell to the U.S. investor a put option on the investment. The option would obligate the government to buy out the investor at a specified price if certain conditions were not met. Essentially an investment guarantee, the agreement would reiterate the above conditions on price flexibility, taxation, hard-currency availability, and so on.

Selling the Deal to Other Investors

The third step of the manager's plan is now to sell the deal to other investors. This serves two purposes. First, it spreads the risk. Second, it brings into the deal a much broader "investor constituency" and reduces the chance that the government will renege on the agreement.

Potential investors include local banks, foreign export-credit agencies, and foreign suppliers. (The last two groups would enter the deal in return for agreements by the local company to purchase equipment.) However, the two investors most crucial to the consummation of the deal are local pension funds (at least one of them) and the World Bank. Any government move that jeopardizes the investments of

a local pension fund would be politically unpopular. Likewise, the government would be unlikely to interfere with any investment in which the World Bank was involved.

At this point, the deal is far from done. The government may not grant the wish list. Even if the conditions are granted, the deal may still not be attractive enough to entice foreign investors. If the investment has potential, however, the manager is convinced that this three-part strategy—evaluating the risks, stipulating conditions, and finding other investors—is the way to go.

87. How to Prevent JV Headaches

Joint ventures (JVs) are the preferred entry into new and risky markets. "It's a good way of getting to know a country," says one treasurer. "Where there's country risk or it's too costly to introduce a product on our own, we go in with someone who knows the market and will share the initial risk."

However, despite their strategic business benefits, JVs often give financial executives nightmares. While each JV is unique, there are four general reasons why JVs can increase financial headaches:

First, partners in a JV seek to maximize their own interests. Conflicts, which tend to be resolved in the controlling partner's favor, are inevitable. Second, financing arrangements and FX questions often cause problems for JVs. Third, partners from different business cultures can disagree on the basic substance of financial management—accounting practices, budgeting, and reporting operating results. Finally, and perhaps most important for U.S. MNCs, U.S. tax reform has changed the rules drastically for 10–50 percent owned companies. Each 10–50 percent owned subsidiary will be subject to its own separate foreign tax credit limitation.

On the other hand, financial managers agree that the problems are not insurmountable. Below is a collection of commonsense pointers for firms considering a JV.

(1) Anticipate every possible problem. The best way to reduce friction in JVs is to account for most contingencies at the beginning. Financial people must make their concerns known and get them on the negotiating table. "If it is just unmanageable, we expect finance to say so," says the VP of planning at a chemicals firm. "But if it is manageable and just causes a lot of problems, we expect finance to work with us to achieve our goals. We try to anticipate the major issues that we are going to come up against—capital needs, dividend policy, how leveraged the business should be."

In one case, the firm discovered during negotiations that its prospective partner had a policy of paying 3 percent of pretax earnings to an endowment in support of local education. "If that had come up after the JV was up and running, it would have caused problems," says the VP. "It would have looked like he was taking 3 percent off the top for his

own purposes. As it happened, we were able to work it out in negotiations. And we found it a good point to give in on."

(2) You have to give to get . . . In spite of the problems caused by power sharing between partners, firms must keep in mind that the venture is a partnership. A win/win attitude, where neither side is overly defensive of its position, normally yields more fruitful negotiations. "Each side must recognize what the other side is putting into it and respect that demarcation," cautions one consultant.

(3) . . . but get all you can. During the negotiations, opportunities can open up to a company's advantage. For instance, if the JV needs a certain input that the firm makes but its partner does not, and if the product is high in quality and price competitive, a lucrative arrangement of sole supplier to the JV might be negotiated.

Similarly, firms should push for strict valuation of all their assets. Good negotiating can reduce the amount of capital needed to meet your obligation. "Get your partner to accept that your technology, trademarks, copyrights, and know-how all have a market value," says one executive. "Give your soft inputs as much value as you do your hard inputs."

(4) Leave a way out. With many financial executives pessimistic about the long-term chances of cooperation between JV partners, many advocate working an exit window into the agreement. One Swedish firm, for example, will not enter into a JV unless the contract contains buyout provisions and clauses for ending the agreement.

That approach may not be the best in all cases, however. Negotiations with foreign partners can be touchy, and a negative attitude could ruin the deal. "Laying out provisions for the breakup would not play well with most foreign cultures," says Du Pont's spokesman.

Nevertheless, some managers insist that not accounting for an eventual parting of the ways is bad business. One executive feels that if an explicit agreement is out of the question, an implicit exit provision may solve the problem.

One such strategy is to set up the payment schedules from your licensing arrangements with the JV so that they hinge on meeting certain profit and sales conditions. If the managing partner fails to meet the conditions down the road, a decision point is reached and the two parties must return to the negotiating table to review the JV's status. "You're trying to get the best revenue schedule you can," says the treasurer. "But you're also setting a quiet little time bomb he may not even be aware of."

(5) Don't be afraid to say no. While negotiations require give-and-take, a set of firm priorities is imperative. If you cannot get management control, says Du Pont's spokesman, "you've got to decide what are the 'musts' you insist on controlling. If you hit an irreconcilable point, you've got to be prepared to back away from the negotiations." It's much easier to say no at the outset than after the deal has been consummated.

(6) Remember that the foreign country is involved, too.

Nailing down the specifics with the JV partner is the most crucial part of the negotiations. However, don't forget about the operating environment and the local government. Many developing countries offer JVs attractive financial incentives. China, for instance, allocates foreign exchange to companies in preferred sectors. Debt-equity swaps in Latin America can help a company reduce its capital input. "You can bring $1 million into Mexico in dollars, but through a debt-equity swap you can gross it up to the equivalent of $1.4 million in pesos," says Du Pont's spokesman. "It shows $1 million in cash, but your equity in the Mexican JV is $1.4 million." Firms attuned to incentives can help turn JVs from financial nightmares into successful operations.

88. Expanding in the Third World? Why Debt-Equity Swaps May Not Be a Bad Idea

Next to moratoriums and reschedulings, debt-equity swaps are the hottest issue in Third World debt today. For international banks, swaps offer a profitable opportunity to channel money to the private sector. For debt-ridden countries, they provide a mechanism for reducing external debt. And for MNCs, debt-equity swaps promise cheap financing windows for expanding plant and retiring debt.

Why swap debt for equity in the Third World? Read on.

Under a debt-equity swap program, a firm buys a country's hard-currency debt on the secondary markets at a discount and swaps it into local equity. Only five countries—Chile, Costa Rica, Ecuador, Mexico, and the Philippines—have ongoing programs. However, international bankers expect—and would like to see—more programs in the future.

Most MNC managers run highly leveraged operations in developing countries, not only because debt is cheaper than equity but also because it offers more flexibility. Debt can be paid down, and the foreign and local-currency components of debt portfolios can be adjusted to manage devaluation risks. Local-currency debt is particularly attractive as a natural translation hedge.

So why swap debt for equity? The simple reason is price. Debt-equity swaps often provide the cheapest source of funding available. While corporate plans must consider numerous variables, debt-equity swaps can change the equation when companies want to expand their investment or strengthen their debt-equity structure:

(1) Debt-equity swaps can modernize or expand existing plant and equipment. Firms with a long-term commitment to a market can use swaps to expand operations at a low cost. PepsiCo, for example, used a swap to fund its operations in the Philippines. The firm's strategic plan for the Philippine market meant that equity would eventually be needed, and the swap provided an avenue to bring it in cheaply.

Similarly, to fund its new plant in Mexico, an automotive MNC opted for a swap into pesos over a straight equity injection because, in the words of the firm's international finance director, "we basically got a preferential exchange rate." Agrees the assistant treasurer of Chrysler, which also swapped in Mexico: "We decided to increase our level of output in Mexico. The swap program enabled us to provide long-term, cost-effective funding for a long-term investment."

(2) Debt-equity swaps can "lower" high hurdle rates. Firms often find it hard to justify new equity because of the high hurdle rates for investing in difficult countries. Debt-equity swaps' bargain funding rates can make existing hurdle rates easier to achieve. Chrysler considered a number of production sites for a new line of luxury sports cars before it decided to expand its Mexican operations to produce the vehicle. "The swap program was instrumental in the decision to source the vehicle in Mexico," says the assistant treasurer. "Had it not been available, we would certainly have chosen a different location for the new line."

(3) Debt-equity swaps can restructure the balance sheet by allowing the firm to pay down debt. For highly leveraged firms, the low-cost equity financing available through swaps can make it attractive to pay down local-currency debt. Chile, Costa Rica, and the Philippines permit swap funds to be used for this purpose. "I don't like to increase equity and decrease debt in those countries because I lose some flexibility," admits the assistant treasurer at one U.S. firm that has done swaps in Chile and Mexico. "But at these prices, I close my eyes to that."

Moreover, the manager argues that he is not really increasing the company's exposure with the swap. Once the firm makes a long-term commitment to operations in a country, it takes on a certain base risk composed of equity risk, guaranteed bank debt, and intracompany debt. "If we need $50–60 million to operate in Mexico, we are going to get it and not worry about it," says the manager. "Debt or equity has nothing to do with it. The swap may change the mix between the two, but the risk remains the same."

In Chile, firms can arbitrage the difference between the discounts available on the secondary market and the price at which the government redeems the debt. Because exchange controls are looser, companies can round-trip funds acquired through swaps to pay down offshore dollar-denominated debt. The key to the arbitrage is keeping subsidiaries undercapitalized, according to the finance director of a U.S. high-tech firm that round-tripped funds out of Chile. "If you have been smart enough to be undercapitalized, then you can play this game," says the manager. "But as soon as you're adequately capitalized, the door is closed to anything but true expansion."

89. Twenty-Seven Windows to Capital for Investment Abroad

The last checklist in this chapter can help firms identify financing alternatives for the Third World—and the developed world as well.

Dollar Sources

(1) The Export-Import Bank (Eximbank) of Washington, D.C., is one of the world's best sources for long-term loans for productive projects in developing countries; loans to private borrowers require host-government guarantee. Eximbank's medium-term export credits can finance U.S.-made machinery for a new plant abroad.

(2) The Agency for International Development (AID), through its Office of Development Finance (the successor to the Development Loan Fund), can lend up to $2.5 million for up to 15 years to private and public investors in less developed areas.

(3) The World Bank makes the bulk of its loans to governments, but has occasionally lent to private enterprises for basic industrial projects (several have included U.S. participation). Host-government guarantees are required.

(4) The International Finance Corporation (IFC), a World Bank affiliate, is the only international institution exclusively devoted to financing private investors. Each deal is custom-made and often involves convertible notes, stock options, and profit sharing over and above interest payments. IFC concentrates on underdeveloped areas and has granted loans to a number of wholly owned U.S. ventures.

(5) The Inter-American Development Bank (IDB), though primarily interested in basic economic and social development, has already financed a number of U.S. affiliates in Latin America. Interest rates are set at a standard rate, and repayment terms are highly flexible. No government guarantee is necessary.

(6) About 50 foreign development banks currently have hard-currency funds from the World Bank, the IDB, European banks, and AID for relending to private enterprises. Rates vary with the country's interest structure.

(7) Private investment bankers are growing more numerous and more active. Their lending generally echoes the IFC in demanding contingent profits, convertible debentures, and so on.

(8) U.S. commercial banks may lend to prime customers on a term basis (rarely over five years) for overseas use. However, laws, regulations, and commercial-banking policy limit most overseas loans to shorter periods.

(9) The U.S. parent or its foreign base company may make direct loans to operating affiliates. Such loans could be funds borrowed by the parent from a U.S. commercial bank at the prime rate. The foreign affiliate is usually requested to protect itself against currency fluctuations.

(10) Lagging payments—prolongation of payment terms on merchandise sold by the parent or foreign base company to an operating affiliate—is another source of funds.

(11) In free markets, borrowing dollars or other convertible currencies from foreign banks for use in third markets can be a useful source. Exchange risk is usually hedged through forward purchase of the face amount. Such loans are usually for a year or less but are frequently renewable.

Foreign Currency Sources

(12) Local development banks, in addition to their hard-currency loans, are also sources of local funds on easier terms. They often tie in with foreign government incentives in offering loans to new or expanding firms.

(13) Foreign commercial banks, with or without parent guarantee, ordinarily lend on a one-year overdraft basis, almost always renewable; the proceeds may be treated as long-term funds.

(14) Export credit on machinery purchased from third countries (mainly European) can cover a major part of the initial capital requirements of a new venture or an expansion.

(15) Swap transactions are deals in which the parent or foreign base company opens a dollar account in a foreign bank in return for a local-currency loan to an affiliate. At maturity, the affiliate repays the bank and the bank repays the dollars.

(16) Sale of nonequity securities, such as bonds and debentures, is possible in many markets but usually impossible in inflation-ridden countries. Underwriting costs are frequently very high.

(17) Sale of callable, nonvoting preferred stock is similar to the sale of nonequity securities, mentioned above.

(18) Local insurance companies and pension funds, against mortgage collateral, are also sources; placing the insurance business with the lender is a normal quid pro quo.

(19) Self-financing pension and other benefit reserves

offer opportunities, where local law does not forbid this form of funding.

(20) Local wealthy families, trusts, universities, and churches have been used by a number of U.S. firms.

(21) Blocked currencies form a pool of local funds in many countries; often an affiliate of one U.S. firm lends to the affiliate of another.

(22) Government or regional investment incentives are in reality a capital source—either as grants or as loans at subsidized rates. These are offered in some parts of Europe, as well as in LDCs.

(23) Finance companies in LDCs will finance installment sales of machinery and equipment and discount notes at going market rates. Financing of accounts receivable is also increasing abroad.

(24) Leasing, whereby a plant is built to order and leased to a manufacturer, often with an option to credit rental payments as purchase payments, is a helpful arrangement. Lease-back is another route, under which the firm builds its own plant, sells it to a leasing firm, and leases it back. Leasing of equipment is another alternative that is rapidly gaining in popularity.

(25) Delayed payment terms from local suppliers can sometimes be arranged.

(26) Tax reserves may be used where tax payments are annual. They become, in effect, a short-term but revolving non-interest-bearing loan from the local government.

(27) Discounting, or using as collateral, foreign government contracts is also a form of financing.

Chapter 12
Managing Currency Exposures in the Third World

The LDCs of Latin America, Asia, and Africa offer special challenges to the treasury manager. Since they are often rocked by high inflation, depreciating currencies, and high government debt, operations in these countries must navigate the most volatile financial waters—without the aid of developed or cost-effective risk-transfer markets.

To help managers reduce, control, and in some cases even profit from Third World risk, this chapter reviews the nuts and bolts of financial management south of the equator, beginning with the basics of LDC cash and currency management. The chapter also highlights opportunities for arbitrage profits and shows how firms can find hedges when, in the traditional sense, none exist. Finally, a list of nonrecourse financing sources is provided for the simplest and safest means of doing business in the Third World.

90. Fine-Tuning Cash Management Systems

The best way to minimize the risks of Third World operations is to establish efficient cash management policies and to follow up with strict control. Effective cash management can both reduce exposure in inflation-ridden economies and cut financing costs in countries with sky-high interest rates. The following list of points should be checked when developing your firm's cash management policies in the Third World.

● **Are the most efficient transfer instruments being utilized?** Cable transfers should be used for all types of trade terms (open account, letter of credit, etc.) whenever the average payment is sizable. From the bank side, investigate carefully the availability of wire transfers. Just because a bank has the capability to make such a transfer does not mean that it will publicize such a service.

● **Is your firm using the best available banks?** Banking relations should be carefully screened to ensure that they provide the most efficient service available. In addition, it is important to find banks with correspondent relationships with your firm's concentration banks.

● **Are the payment channels as simple as possible?** Whenever possible, cross-border transfers should be made within the branch network of one bank. Routine payment delays of three or more days are not uncommon when more than one bank becomes involved.

● **Are credit terms optimal?** MNC subsidiaries in LDCs should be told to keep credit terms as short as possible. While the trade-off is lost sales and goodwill, firms should often err on the side of tighter terms.

● **Are leading and lagging permitted?** Where possible, firms should attempt to lead payments from and delay payments to LDC operations.

● **Are remittances of sufficient value to warrant couriers?** For dollar payments, companies should consider using courier systems to deliver checks to convenient locations in the United States (such as Miami, New York, and Houston for Latin America) for accelerated deposit into the Federal Reserve System.

● **Are foreign-currency hold accounts permitted?** Exchange controls permitting, foreign-currency-denominated hold accounts should be established to reduce currency exposure and FX costs.

● **Is netting permitted?** Global netting systems should be expanded to include eligible Latin American countries. Even if the flow of funds from these countries is small, netting may be useful to achieve increased discipline and control and standardization of intercompany activities.

● **Could reinvoicing provide cash benefits?** Reinvoicing companies should be considered when multiple manufacturing entities are used to source products in a single region or country. A number of companies have found this technique useful for both tax and currency management purposes.

● **If funds are blocked, have all avenues been explored?** Firms stuck with blocked funds should investigate ways to free funds, including loans between related companies, capitalization of blocked funds, sponsorship of local conventions, transfer pricing, investment in land and buildings, technical fees, and parallel loans (see Chapter 13 for more on blocked funds techniques).

91. How to Cut Third World Exposure

Sound cash management procedures can help keep currency risks to a minimum. But the remaining exposures in risky currencies still need to be hedged.

In the Third World, unfortunately, hedges are either expensive or unavailable. Nevertheless, treasurers who care about their consolidated income never give up the search for ways to protect their LDC subsidiaries from the triple threat of high inflation, maxidevaluation, and Financial Accounting Standards Board (FASB) No. 52's cruel rules for hyperinflationary countries.

The following checklist, compiled from interviews with major U.S. MNCs, was developed to help treasury executives evaluate their options for managing Latin American exposures. However, most of these strategies (with minor adjustments) are readily applied to other developing regions and countries.

● **Improve local cash management.** It is worth repeating: the most important concern for MNCs should be sound cash management practices at the local level. Here firms should strive to operate with minimum cash assets, including accounts receivable.

● **Diversify your hedges.** In Latin America, no single hedging technique is foolproof. The best approach is to diversify hedging instruments.

● **Close the books early.** One way to accelerate outbound dividends is to get a head start. The Brazilian subsidiary of a major U.S. electronics MNC reaped the benefits of getting a jump by remitting its 1982 dividends just days before a February 1983 maxi. The subsidiary accomplished the feat by closing its books on November 30—a month ahead of the pack. While the firm had to pay auditors overtime to finish statements by mid-January, it was able to tender its audited statements and dividend application to the Brazilian Central Bank far ahead of other companies. Says a spokesman from the company's treasury group, "It was a classic case of leading ahead of devaluation."

● **Export.** To reduce its Brazilian exposure, a capital goods manufacturer is converting one of its Brazilian subsidiaries from a domestic-oriented operation into an export-oriented operation. In this way the company hopes to gain hard-currency receivables and soft-currency costs. Attractive interest and tax incentives and postexport financing provided by the Brazilian government also led the company to adopt this strategy.

● **Reorganize ownership.** One manufacturing firm has changed its strategy by accepting minority control and seeking licenses. The company is looking for a U.S. or European company to inject equity financing into its Brazilian subsidiary. The capital injection means that the parent doesn't have to provide additional financing for its Brazilian company and that it will allow the partner company to "expatriate" money via currently dormant intracompany loans.

Similarly, one technology conglomerate is looking to reduce the tax liability of its profitable subsidiary by merging it with others that operate in the red. The unprofitable subsidiaries could not take advantage of the tax benefits of their interest expense, which was high because of heavy reliance on local financing.

● **Convert debt or blocked funds to equity.** Companies are taking a more liberal view of reclassifying intracompany or bank loans as equity because they don't see dollars coming out of Latin America anytime soon. This is especially true if the subsidiary's bank debt is backed by parent guarantees. Companies convert blocked funds into equity in the hope that when hard currency is available in the future, they will be able to remit more dividends.

● **Restructure intracompany loans.** Financing decisions remain mind-boggling for companies in Latin America. Although local financing helps reduce a company's exposure to currency devaluations, "It's tough to earn a nickel when you incur that kind of financing cost," said one official.

Companies that consider giving dollar financing to their subsidiaries may want to adopt some new strategies. For example, one food company believes that because Latin American governments have more leverage over multinational banks than corporations, the authorities will allow freer payment on intracompany debt than on bank debt. Based on this view, the firm is taking a hard look—especially in Argentina and Brazil—at moving from "fronted" or "participation" vehicles (essentially parent-subsidiary loans that use banks as intermediaries) to intracompany loans.

92. Exploiting Arbitrage Opportunities in LDC Markets

Often a firm's response to financial management in the smaller, more exotic countries of the world is to ignore careful analysis and simply transact at market. These countries, characterized by shallow markets and tight regulatory climates, are in some managers' minds not worth the effort it takes to probe financial investments.

For MNCs willing to take the time to monitor local conditions, however, these same markets are ripe with arbitrage opportunities. For example, one firm can often swap into offshore Malaysian ringgit deposits, and earn 50 basis points over deposits in Kuala Lumpur, while another company remains oblivious to the opportunity. In this type of situation, regional treasury staffs serve as the eyes and ears of corporate headquarters. They are in the field and should be called upon to spot these opportunities.

Spotting and capitalizing on arbitrage opportunities is not easy. It requires a corporate mind set that encourages financial vigilance and an internal structure that allows the managers of the deal to respond quickly to market situations. Below is a list of policy steps that corporate treasuries can implement so that local managers can take full advantage of inefficient Third World markets.

● **Recognize that opportunities exist.** One of the most important rules companies have discovered about Asian and Latin American markets is that they are not perfect. Because they are thin, frequent arbitrage opportunities exist. Headquarters and regional treasury staffs must realize these exist before they can find and take advantage of them. "In New York, it all washes: Do I go forward, do I swap, do I spot and invest?" says one firm's Asian regional treasurer. In Asia, however, "that is not necessarily so."

● **Create an aggressive corporate attitude.** This means putting the successful exploitation of market opportunities in job descriptions and training programs. "We want our people to be aware of the opportunities, understand them, and look for them," says one executive about his company's regional and local treasury staffs.

The criteria used to evaluate local performance should be reviewed to see if they encourage local treasury staffs to seize opportunities. The evaluation system should take into account the number added to the bottom line through innovative treasury management.

● **Spread the word about successes.** Successfully seizing arbitrage opportunities is a creative task and requires a cross-pollination of ideas over geographic boundaries. The headquarters treasury unit must serve as the conduit for communication. Staffers who visit or at least communicate with the various regional and local treasury staffs should offer ideas and examples that have worked in other regions and other countries.

● **Hire local treasury staffs that are attuned to innovation.** Many local financial markets are in a state of flux, pressured by the increased internationalization of finance. Money, FX, and capital markets are growing increasingly complex with the introduction of new hedging, financing, and investment instruments and the reduction of regulatory restraint. Companies must have treasury/finance staffs in local markets that understand and can use these changes in the company's interests. "You need a good set of eyes out in the field," states one regional executive. "Where market and business circumstances called for a simple accounting function five years ago, a more sophisticated treasury manager may now be needed."

In Korea, for example, where regulatory changes and a fluctuating FX market are posing new threats and opportunities for treasury managers, more than one company indicated that it is waiting to see if the existing financial group can handle the new responsibilities. If the existing staff is unable to adjust, the companies plan to make personnel changes.

● **Stay on top of the market.** A company must have a regular presence in the local market to spot and take advantage of windows of opportunity. This often means having a good treasury/finance person as close to the market as possible. One company BI contacted split its Asian treasury staff between Hong Kong and Singapore, dividing responsibilities between North Asia and Southeast Asia—allowing the respective staffs to be as close to their markets as possible.

● **Maintain good banking contacts.** Bankers and other financial intermediaries can make the difference in moving profitably on arbitrage opportunities. Local, regional, and headquarters finance personnel should make it their business to know local bank staffs and their capabilities.

Moreover, bank officials will take the time and effort to keep a corporation informed of market windows only when they know there is a chance that a deal will go through. A company must spread the word that it is ready and able to take advantage of the right opportunities when they come along. Then it must follow up with deeds and act on banks' advice.

● **Judge banks by their local capabilities.** Local, regional, and headquarters finance personnel should not rely too much on the international reputation of a bank, but rather on its local name. While the New York office of a bank may not be known for its interest rate arbitrage, a sharp trading manager in its Bangkok branch could put the bank on top of the local market.

● **Keep it profitable for the bank.** Although it is still a buyers' market as far as general banking services go, there aren't always as many arbitrage deals available as there are takers. And the more deals that pour into a window, the narrower the opening becomes. Banks will relay the good deals to sweeten beneficial corporate relationships. All things being equal, therefore, keep a potential arbitrage relationship profitable for the bank with a flow of FX, payroll, letter of credit, and other types of business. "You have to give the banks volume business," states one treasury manager.

● **Streamline the approval process.** While strict controls are necessary throughout the corporate trading function, local staffs must be able to move freely within those parameters. "If you have to wait for approval from headquarters every time you leave your desk, you'll never hit a market window while it's open," comments one regional treasury staffer.

When authorization is required, companies should make sure that all concerned know the lines of communication and the chain of approval—and that time is crucial. One area treasury manager complained of an interest rate arbitrage profit that dwindled fourfold in the time it took to get an okay from headquarters. One option is to assign a headquarters staffer the specific responsibility to approve or reject such plans.

93. Devaluation Checklist: How to Spot Currencies in Distress

Corporate treasurers who know the signs of an imminent devaluation may be able to minimize financial risks in foreign markets or even avoid losses. As clearly stated in the previous checklist, thin markets can translate into significant opportunities for profit. But sudden devaluations in these markets can burn through a firm's profits. A list of vital signs that warn of devaluation follows.

● **Balance-of-trade trends.** A decline in exports—or a halt in exports compounded by a burgeoning of imports—often leads to devaluation. This is done to bolster a country's exports and to shrink its imports automatically, thereby adjusting the country's balance sheet.

● **Money in circulation.** This should be monitored, for it naturally accompanies the rate of inflation. When the growth of the nominal money supply exceeds the level of real GNP growth, inflation ensues. The resulting higher prices, exchange rate pressures, and ultimate loss of investor confidence are not-so-subtle hints that the value of the currency is about to be adjusted.

● **Bank credit.** A tightening of bank credit points to new resolutions in the fight against inflation and devaluation. Official moves to curtail credit may be a way of limiting currency erosion.

● **Budget deficit.** Continuous deficit financing stokes inflationary fires and imposes devaluation pressures. This type of financing is a chronic cause of devaluation in Argentina, Brazil, and Mexico.

● **Inflation relative to export subsidies and currency depreciation.** In Latin America, this situation is particularly complicated. Mexico, Brazil, and Argentina have all institutionalized periodic downward currency adjustments to compensate for, or at least partially offset, runaway inflation. Brazil and Venezuela both make use of cash subsidies to spur exports. Thus, when evaluating the possibilities of a major devaluation in Latin America, currency watchers must compare inflation with both currency depreciation and export subsidies.

● **Premiums on dollar-linked money market instruments**

such as National Treasury Bonds (OTNs), bonex, and petrobonds. Brazil, Mexico, Argentina, and Venezuela, for example, have offered these government-guaranteed, dollar-denominated investment tools to attract hard currency. When fears of devaluation loom, premiums on these items rise sharply.

● **Real estate/stock prices.** In an economy that is otherwise not rapidly expanding, booming real estate and/or stock markets often reflect debasement of the currency. For instance, prior to one peso devaluation, stocks of Mexican companies with little dollar-denominated debt were bid up as firms sought a hedge against further depreciation.

● **Gold and dollar reserves.** Try to read between the lines. For example, a rise in reserves reported by Venezuela in September 1982 was achieved by revaluing gold holdings from $35 to $300 per ounce. Authorities used this technique to disguise erosion of reserves caused by outflows of short-term capital.

● **Capital flight** is a vote of no confidence in an economy and its currency. For example, the capital drain out of Hong Kong caused by uncertainties surrounding the colony's political future was a harbinger of the reeling Hong Kong dollar.

● **Negotiations with international lending institutions** such as the IMF and the U.S. Treasury often result in a barter-type accord: We'll bail you out with our loans if you devalue your currency. The IMF is notorious for driving a hard bargain in these types of situations, especially in Latin America.

● **Import restrictions.** Restricting imports is merely the flip side of the balance-of-trade coin—the other side being, of course, boosting exports. Cutting back on imports can delay, but not eliminate, the economic need for devaluation. Again, beware of blossoming trade deficits.

● **Currencies of major trading partners.** No country can maintain a currency that is overvalued relative to the currencies of its major trading partners (or competitors) for long. The overvaluation of the cruzeiro relative to European currencies helped fuel the February 1983 cruzeiro maxi. And the 15.5 percent Greek drachma dive in January 1983 came on the heels of devaluations in Spain, France, and Sweden. The cheaper French and Swedish units particularly threatened tourist-dependent Greece.

● **Forward foreign exchange quotations.** For currencies that can be hedged on the forward market (e.g., offshore bolivares), rising dollar premiums indicate diminishing confidence in the local currency.

● **Gap between black market and official rates.** The emergence of a significant black market is another sign of waning confidence and oncoming devaluation. When Brazilian officials could not compete with the soaring black market rate in February 1983, they admitted defeat and devalued the cruzeiro.

● **Political developments.** Upcoming elections, party platforms, and the upsurge of new political movements can all affect currency risks. Elections especially have proved to be faithful indicators of devaluation: France, Indonesia, and Australia all devalued their units almost immediately after the polls closed. Devaluation prior to an election is politically undesirable. Political stability is also a key factor. Hong Kong and the Philippines are examples of how the political climate can ultimately change the economic situation. The aftermath of the assassination of Filipino opposition leader Benigno Aquino was marked by capital flight and a deterioration in economic conditions. Faced with a no-win dilemma, the government devalued.

● **Prices of primary export items** are also linked to devaluation. As with the rupiah, Mexican peso, and bolivar devaluations, a drop in oil prices took a bite out of national revenues and trade accounts and spurred devaluations. Watch the economic soothsayers of oil prices and crop reports.

● **Dollar-linked currencies,** whether weighted in a basket or one-on-one, are often victims of devaluation when the greenback soars to new heights. Most recently, the Saudi riyal and the Greek drachma fell prey to a strong dollar. To counteract this development, the Greeks decided to detach the drachma from the dollar and peg it instead to a basket of European currencies.

94. Ten Ways to Dress for Devaluation

When there are warning signs of an impending devaluation, firms need to take steps to strengthen their hard-currency position. While there are few surefire approaches, firms should take as many of the following actions as possible.

(1) **Move to hard-currency accounts.** Believe it or not, as obvious as this first step appears, many firms often overlook the simplest defense. Firms should look for all means of converting local currency funds into dollar or other hard-currency accounts.

(2) **Keep local cash balances low.** Where future commitments require local-currency payment, purchase the funds only when needed. Where possible, accelerate all means of withdrawing excess funds.

(3) **Remit profits and dividends promptly.** Reinvestment of net income increases exposure. If funds are needed locally, they may be returnable as a dollar loan. Remit royalties and fees.

(4) **Use the forward markets.** Third World forward markets are expensive—frequently far more expensive than prudent for routine hedging. In the face of an imminent devaluation, however, the forward premium should be reexamined.

(5) **Borrow locally for working capital.** Local funding is

often the best and most convenient hedge. As always, however, the local cost of funds must be balanced against the cost of other alternatives.

(6) Accelerate collections. Reduce local receivables through accelerated collection and discounting of customers' drafts. Reduce credit terms if this can be done without becoming uncompetitive and endangering market share.

(7) Delay payments. If possible, firms should try to obtain longer credit terms for local purchases. First, look for interest-free supplier credit. If it is unavailable (or if payment delays will cause significant damage to local suppliers), negotiate for supplier credit at rates below the percentage of expected devaluation.

(8) Invoice exports in hard currency. When exporting from a soft-currency country to hard-currency countries, invoice in the buyer's currency (e.g., to Germany, in deutsche marks). If this is not possible, cut payment terms as far as the competitive position permits.

(9) Invoice imports in a soft currency. When importing into the soft-currency country, buy in local currency on terms as extended as possible. If imports are invoiced in dollars, cover your commitment on the forward market. Build up your inventory of those imported materials and components whose price is likely to rise after devaluation.

(10) Take advantage of local financing opportunities. If a firm is planning new investments in the soft-currency country, they should be financed locally as much as possible. If a parent company guarantee is required, restrict it to a local-currency guarantee. Using local assets or stock as collateral may make it easier to obtain a loan. In rare cases, a stock swap may be used to pay for an acquisition.

95. How to Hedge in Brazil

While no two Third World nations are alike, managers' experiences in any country can often translate into worthwhile ideas for other regions. The following checklist shows what MNC managers have been able to accomplish in the Brazilian market. While it is not intended to be exhaustive, it does catalog the most common forms of hedging undertaken by firms in Brazil, and it can generate ideas for managers in other LDCs.

(1) OTNs. The preferred hedging instrument of many corporations is the OTN. The security pays 8 percent per year plus devaluation. Unfortunately, the government issued a fixed amount of these bonds in the early 1980s and the last series matured in April 1988.

The bond's price fluctuated wildly depending on the market's view of the chances of a maxidevaluation. To hedge the risk of a volatile bond premium, some companies arranged sale-and-repurchase agreements with banks. The bank agreed to repurchase the OTNs at a determined point in the future at a preset price.

(2) Central Bank dollar accounts. In October 1986, Central Bank dollar accounts were authorized for companies. These accounts pay monthly interest at LIBOR rates, and the deposits can be left at the Central Bank indefinitely. Foreign MNCs can deposit unremitted profits and registered foreign capital awaiting disbursement. Exporters may deposit dollars earned abroad. The interest paid on the deposits is considered export revenue and is deductible from taxable income.

Importers can deposit foreign-sourced trade financing that may be withdrawn at any time, but only to make import payments. One U.S.-based beverage maker with a strong cash flow hedges by contracting import financing, depositing the amount in the Central Bank, and then paying for the import out of cash flow—leaving the sum of the loan perfectly hedged for the term of the borrowing.

(3) Intercompany loans. Companies can also hedge their excess cash by lending cruzados to another company. Via a *contrato de mutuo,* a cruzado-rich company can lend to a cruzado-poor company that wants to borrow on a dollar basis to avoid high local-currency interest rates. A bank usually serves as intermediary, bringing the companies together and guaranteeing the operation.

Brazilian law prohibits contracts quoted in any currency but cruzados. Therefore, the loan rate may be explicitly stated in the contract as a basic cruzado rate, with a side letter exchanged that delineates the dollar terms to which the counterparty agrees to adhere. If the transaction takes place between two MNC subsidiaries, a letter of comfort or stand-by letter of credit is sometimes offered by the parent of the cruzado-poor company as an additional guarantee.

(4) Intercompany OTN transactions. Brazilian legislation is vague on intercompany loans, forbidding "systematic" lending by an institution without an official banking charter. This legal gray area can be avoided by disguising an intercompany loan as a rental of securities. The cruzado-rich company that had OTNs loaned its securities to the cruzado-poor company. The cruzado-poor company sold the securities to a bank, which simultaneously sold them to the cruzado-rich company. The twin sale of the securities transferred cruzados from the cruzado-rich company to the cruzado-poor company, which was actually a loan that paid devaluation plus a spread. At maturity, the entire transaction was reversed.

(5) Bank hedging contracts. A few international banks maintain hedging books and will agree to pay a firm official monetary correction plus any exceeding exchange rate variation on its deposits. An up-front fee of 15–16 percent is charged by the bank, so this strategy would pay off only when the spread between monetary correction and devaluation is larger, that is, when a maxidevaluation of greater magnitude is anticipated.

(6) FX futures contracts. A small futures market for cruzado equivalents of foreign currencies functions on the major commodities exchanges. The largest number of contracts is traded on the São Paulo Commodities Exchange (BMSP), which pioneered the contract. In June 1987, the average daily trading volume was only 349, according to BMSP figures. While cruzado equivalents of the U.S. dollar, the deutsche mark, and the yen are available, only the U.S. dollar contract is currently trading. Contracts are marked to market each day.

Only a few MNCs have ventured into the futures market. First, the small size of the market limits its effectiveness. For instance, the BMSP stipulates that no more than 40 contracts can be offered simultaneously, which restricts the amount of exposure that a company can cover. Second, many companies do not find the premiums attractive, particularly when a devaluation is widely expected. Finally, the government's reputation for intervening in the stock and commodities markets deters many firms.

The companies that have dabbled in the market report that it works well, despite the liquidity problem. "We're very interested in these markets," says the finance director of one MNC that has long played the Brazilian commodities markets. "There's a huge potential here if more companies get involved."

(7) Third-party exports. A company can hedge its excess cruzados by buying another firm's exports—a tactic known as "meia trading." The original exporter has generally lined up customers for the goods, and the hedging firm merely obtains a temporary offshore position for its excess cash.

(8) Gold. The appreciation of gold over the past 10 years has consistently outstripped inflation, and many companies maintain a portion of their excess cash in gold. This entails a twin risk, however. Gold is quoted in Brazil at the international commodity market rate, which is translated at the black market dollar rate. "You bring inside the company the risk of how the parallel rate will move versus the official rate and the risk of how the price of gold will move," says the planning manager at one Brazilian subsidiary.

To minimize the risk, MNC executives recommend gold as a hedging mechanism when it is on an upswing in the international markets and when the gap between the parallel and official rates is relatively small. Then the parallel rate has few ways to go but up.

(9) Other commodities. Some companies hedge by building up inventories of world-priced goods such as coffee and soybeans. A drawback to this ploy is cited by the finance director of a commodities firm: "If you don't know from one day to the next whether the government will put an export tax on those products, your hedging strategies are very limited." Such a tax could effectively remove all gains from a potential maxidevaluation. Historically, the government has levied such taxes immediately following major devaluations.

96. How to Hedge When No Hedge Exists: Take the Korean Won

Major U.S. MNCs contacted by BI are in nearly total agreement: There is nothing available to hedge the won. Even balancing local-currency assets and liabilities can be difficult. "We are looking for won financing for some of our JVs in Korea," reports the FX manager at a major U.S. chemical producer. "It's hard enough to borrow won, much less to hedge any kind of exposure."

Nevertheless, a small minority report success. Another prominent U.S. chemicals concern claims that it has been able to hedge the won through an occasional structure brought by its line banks. The firm has told its banks that it is interested in hearing about any structures that can accomplish the hedge. As a result, the firm is regularly presented with possible deals.

In general, most of the structures presented to the firm are quasi-legal at best. However, the chemical company has found that sometimes a deal will surface that is either clearly legal or is at least of sufficiently tolerable "interpretational" risk to warrant acceptance.

In any case, pursuing such structures is not an amateur's business. In building won-hedging deals, or similar hedges of any restrictive currency, firms should abide by the following principles:

● **Tell your line banks you are interested.** Putting together deals that hedge the won is part of the "squeaky wheel" section of a bank's business. While there are a significant number of possible structures, they are shown only to parties who have expressed an interest. A spokesman for the second chemical manufacturer says firms have to make it clearly known that these deals are desired.

● **Insist that the bank act as a counterparty.** This not only reduces counterparty risk but also guarantees access to the bank's corps of professionals, who possess extensive experience in the Korean market.

● **Know the regulation.** Bank of Korea exchange control regulations are tight and place corporate treasury staffs in a virtual straitjacket. In certain circumstances, however, companies can hedge. Further, regulations—and their interpretation—do change.

In addition, firms should try to differentiate between the spirit and the letter of the law. While one treasurer may be pulling hair out in frustration over restrictive regulations, another may be doing exactly what the hair-pulling treasurer wanted to do.

Finally, MNCs should not rely exclusively on local staffs or, for that matter, on a single banker for local rule interpretations. Local staffs can be overly conservative or simply lack the expertise to interpret these regs.

● **Be prepared to commit resources.** While this exercise is initially rather expensive, it normally pays increasing returns. The structures that arise are typically combinations of a finite number of components. As a firm encounters each of these components for the first time, it will make evaluations of their legality and risk. Eventually, the acceptable and unacceptable components will become instantly recognizable, making a relatively rapid evaluation possible.

● **Use your JV partner as a sounding board.** One way to improve evaluation of possible structures is to involve your local partner. According to the chemical firm's spokesman, locals' working knowledge of Korean corporate practice makes them an excellent resource for this purpose. For example, local managers are closer to the local government and so are good in determining how the authorities are likely to view a transaction.

● **Be discreet.** This is a sensitive area. In all cases, it is important to discuss any such dealings with as few outside parties as possible. A good rule of thumb is to keep it to one or two line banks and perhaps a legal or consulting firm well versed in Korean law.

● **But be warned.** Even though the chemical firm has been able to structure won transactions that it considers to be of acceptable risk, each firm will have to abide by its own risk criteria. In evidence, the FX manager at a major U.S. industrial firm reveals that his company, working with its bankers, prepared a list of seven won-hedging transactions. Says the manager, "There were pros and cons to each approach. Some didn't fit what we were trying to do, others were illegal, others were quasi-legal." The bottom line? "We have yet to find an optimal solution."

Chapter 13
Managing Blocked Funds

In dozens of countries, rigid exchange controls and desperate hard-currency shortages prevent MNCs from bringing their foreign earnings home. To help treasury managers increase remittances from these difficult countries, this chapter offers five checklists on blocked-funds management.

The first suggests ways to prevent blocked funds. The second is a comprehensive checklist of 25 management techniques that BI has learned about over the years directly from corporate managers. This is supplemented by one manager's own checklist for making sure he does not overlook solutions to his company's blocked-funds problems. Next, the chapter focuses on one key blocked currency of ever-growing concern for corporate managers—the Chinese renminbi. Finally, a seasoned manager's experiences with countertrade are revealed.

97. Preventive Medicine: How to Avoid Blockage of Funds

Managing blocked funds usually entails complex schemes to get money out of a country. But there is another side to this critical treasury task: avoiding the problem from the outset. The following checklist offers eight pointers on how to prevent funds from becoming blocked in the first place.

● **Research the risks thoroughly.** Companies should take a close look at a country's present and historical exchange control environments before putting funds at risk. For instance, a European shipping line found it had a good chance of increasing its business if it allowed importers in Latin America to pay freight charges incurred for shipments from the Far East when the goods arrived in the Latin American ports. Generally, the exporter in the Far East prepaid the charges, but a number of exporters had been trying to shift the burden of payment to their customers.

Before shifting the responsibility for freight costs, shipping line executives sent a detailed telex to their agents in the Latin American ports involved. They asked agents to detail applicable local controls on the remittance of freight payments to regional headquarters. Were remittances subject to withholding taxes or income taxes, and at what rate? Were remittances restricted above a certain level? Did they require central bank approval? How long were typical approval delays? If remittances were restricted, could they be offset against locally incurred expenses?

The executives also asked whether any such controls had ever been in force, when, and for how long. "This is just a preliminary step," says the regional controller at the firm. "But from our initial findings, things look pretty good, and we'll probably go ahead and accept local payment."

● **Keep talking.** Maintaining open lines of communication to the government should help reduce blocked-funds problems. "Because we're one of the biggest companies in a lot of these countries, our local managers usually have a lot of prestige," says the finance manager of a large oil company. "They are enough in tune with the government that they can stay out of the crowd of companies clamoring for attention. We get our case heard separately."

Of course, MNCs that provide priority merchandise or that dominate a particular sector are in the best position to pressure the government for access to hard currency.

● **Stay current.** Governments often have short memories. It is important in negotiations, therefore, to focus on current or even future transactions. "If you talk about transactions that happened last year," says one manager, "you've lost your leverage, and it's easier for them to sweep you under the rug."

Concurs the oil company manager, "We focus on never falling behind. We don't want to have to come up with innovative ways to get money out of these countries."

● **Decipher government priorities.** All blocked funds are not the same. Some governments tend to restrict dividend payments, while others take a dimmer view of interest remittances. By examining government priorities, companies can often take the path of least resistance.

When one firm expected trouble in Chile, for example, it ordered its subsidiary to maximize dividends while headquarters financed the operation through intracompany loans. "We saw a window of free dividend remittability that we weren't sure would last," explains the firm's regional treasurer. "So we wanted to substitute loan repayment rights for dividend payment rights."

Adds the treasurer of a chemicals firm, "We keep most of our exposure in trade payables, because countries generally have a high respect for them."

● **Don't ship the goods until the money is in hand.** Import credit delays are a common problem in countries that are trying to keep trade accounts healthy. Equipment imports by subsidiaries can sometimes lock up funds for months as the subsidiary waits for central bank authorization to obtain hard currency to pay for the import.

One company faced import financing delays in Guatemala. "Generally, we won't ship a truck to Guatemala unless the subsidiary can come up with the dollars," says a financial executive at the firm. "We'll hold up the shipment until they show us they have the hard currency."

● **Take it out when you can.** Anticipating government policies is never an easy task. But when companies expect stricter exchange controls, the best strategy is to get as much money out as possible before the door closes. "We were expecting a maxidevaluation in Venezuela, and we thought tighter exchange controls would come with it," says the treasury manager of a household goods manufacturer. "We maximized dividends from our subsidiary, told our customers we would give them a nice discount if they paid early, and put all new orders on letter of credit."

● **Stay clear of restructuring agreements.** Government debt restructurings can lock up funds for years. Debt enrolled in Mexico's Ficorca scheme, for example, was recently restructured on a 20-year repayment schedule. "We try to avoid government papers. We never went into Ficorca," says the manager of a chemicals firm. "Venezuela also had a program in which you enrolled for seven years and received payment at the preferential rate. We collected at the free rate; we wanted our money up front."

● **Take the hit now.** In many cases, less money now is better than a promise of more money in the future. Rather than wait for hard currency at a preferential exchange rate, for instance, companies can take a shortcut through the free market. "We don't want to get bogged down in negotiations," says one manager. "I tell my subsidiaries to keep it moving, clean it up, keep their cash flow current. Take the hit if necessary."

98. Unblocking Blocked Funds: 25 Ways to Get Your Money

To help treasury managers increase remittances from difficult countries, the following comprehensive checklist of blocked-funds techniques was developed. A quick review of the list will reveal techniques that might remain untried when a new blocked-funds problem crops up. (Some of the techniques are not permitted in some countries, and their listing here does not imply that BI approves of their use in those countries.)

(1) Improve internal controls. Establish company guidelines to outline the objectives, options, and preferred procedures for freeing blocked funds. Set up a task force to monitor currency conditions abroad and to implement the blocked-funds management guidelines. To improve internal blocked funds, controls may require the creation of new staff positions or in-house departments, but the potential long-run savings may outweigh the costs.

(2) Explore local investment opportunities. Investments in local government paper—e.g., Brazilian OTNs, Argentine dollar-denominated bonex bonds, Republic of Venezuela paper (also dollar denominated)—and real estate will shield blocked funds against the ravages of currency erosion and hyperinflation. And when these economic storms eventually blow over, or at least subside, the investment will more than likely have appreciated in value.

(3) Capitalize. Instead of letting your profits take you to the cleaners—due to heavy local taxes on dividends—let them take you to the bank. Countries short of hard currency usually slap a hefty tax on dividends remitted above a set percentage of registered capital. Most anxious blocked-funds managers end up paying the heavy penalty, and not enough of them consider using the blocked funds for new investment or expansion, which eventually relieves such a tax burden by raising the registered capital base.

(4) Extend loans to subsidiaries. Where a remittance ceiling seems to be the major culprit in blocked-funds schemes, some companies have found it useful to "move" the funds out of the country in the form of interest payments rather than as dividends. To do so, the parent converts outstanding intercompany receivables into medium- to long-term loans. This simple tactic will release liquidity for the subsidiary while it offers the parent company a viable method of freeing blocked funds.

(5) Formulate royalty agreements. The key to the successful application of this blocked-funds technique is strategy. For instance, local governments would, understandably, be surprised if, after 20 years or so of manufacturing, your subsidiary suddenly had to pay royalties. However, less abrupt approaches can be used to implant a system of royalty payments that will placate government officials at the same time.

The "new-products royalty" is one such tactic. A royalty agreement can be established with every new product and, while the local officials may not be overjoyed at the prospect of cash leaving the country, they will be pacified by the local income generated by the new product. Similarly, when drafting new-product agreements in different countries, royalty-improvement programs should be instituted from the start. This will allow the firm to reclassify products over time and adjust the royalty fees accordingly. For example, if a particular product's content or manufacturing process can be altered ever so slightly, that item will then be entitled to new-product status, and the royalty payment can be increased.

(6) Decapitalize. It may not be the most direct technique for releasing funds, but a subsidiary can borrow capital from its parent and use the money to repurchase shares of its own stock. This is advantageous because interest payments on the intercompany debt usually receive higher priority on the government's list of dollar payments than do dividend remittances. Depending upon LIBOR and current regulations in each country, remitting via interest payments will free more blocked funds than remitting dividends.

For instance, if the subsidiary pays interest on the loan at LIBOR plus 5 percent—with LIBOR at around 10 percent—and there is a 10 percent ceiling on remittances, then the parent procures 5 percent more cash with interest payments. Companies should consider transferring funds between two subsidiaries in the same country, especially if one is cash-rich and the other cash-poor. The cash-rich subsidiary can invest in the stock of the cash-poor one, which, as a result of the capital injection, will be able to remit dividends to the parent. Another option is to merge the two subsidiaries, creating a larger capital base from which the subsidiary can remit a greater amount of dividends.

(7) Push for expansion of existing avenues. Existing avenues for remittances—such as dividends, royalties, technical assistance fees, and interest on intercompany loans—may offer the simplest and cleanest way to boost remittances. Are remittances through any existing channel below the legal limit? Are limits negotiable? Can you prepay or pay more frequently? Can you redirect flows to channels with lower withholding rates? Can you charge higher interest on intercompany receivables?

If the answer to any of these questions is yes—and it often is—focus on exploiting these existing avenues to the utmost before turning to the more exotic blocked-funds techniques.

(8) Bill for everything. Business and production technologies are constantly evolving, and technical, financial, operations, marketing, manufacturing, design, and computer assistance services may all be billable. Do changing orders offer an opportunity to justify an increase? Can new trademarks be sold?

(9) Be prepared to justify higher remittances. The expiration of a contract marks a time of opportunity and danger. If local officials want to cut back your remittances, justify your need for an increase. Make thorough preparations for arguments to increase fees and for defenses against cutbacks. Prepare aggressive arguments to counter any validity challenges.

(10) Remit more and pay the penalty. A government imposing exchange controls may specify a penalty for firms violating the rules. Find out if any type of remittance—dividend, royalty, technical assistance fee—can be increased with a penalty payment. Is it worth it?

(11) Investigate local currency payments to the parent. After a subsidiary pays local currency into the parent's hold account (some payments may be tax deductible for the subsidiary), the parent can use the funds to pay local expenses or to invest in dollar-linked assets.

For instance, one U.S. company held a training seminar and convention in Greece for 600 European managers to use blocked drachmas. Locally held funds can also be used to initiate the various indirect remittances below.

(12) Manage local debt-equity ratios to maximize remittance potential. Many countries limit dividends to a percentage of registered capital. Once the dividend limit has been reached, it may make sense to capitalize leftover profits in order to remit more later.

When an aggressive dividend policy threatens to push a company's local debt-equity ratio above the level permitted by local regulations, managers can still reap the benefits of a leveraged balance sheet by turning to off-balance-sheet financing methods.

(13) Negotiate a raw material commission or surcharge. Subsidiaries that import raw materials from the parent often pay a standard surcharge for pricing, procurement, quality control, and on-time delivery. Companies should explore the possibility of collecting the same surcharge when the subsidiary imports raw materials from third-party suppliers.

For example, one U.S. manufacturer received a standard surcharge for procurement services of 7 percent from its subsidiary in a Latin American country. However, when the subsidiary imported raw materials from third-party suppliers, the parent did not receive surcharges for these sales, even though it was providing the same procurement services. The parent asked the government for a 7 percent surcharge on shipments from third-party suppliers and was able to increase remittances by $900,000 per year.

(14) Charge an export commission. If a subsidiary exports to a third party and the transaction yields hard currency for the central bank, the parent may be able to charge a commission to the subsidiary for arranging the transaction.

(15) Use countertrade. Despite government restrictions hampering countertrade deals—particularly those that involve trading products rather than cash—countertrade is a useful technique for moving funds across borders. Scout out an export market for your subsidiary and arrange for the customer to remit hard money directly to you. The accrued funds can then be credited to the subsidiary's intercompany account.

(16) Make a straight charitable contribution. If devaluation, low interest rates, high taxes, or a combination of these factors make attrition of local cash very high, a straight donation may make sense. Under this scenario, the subsidiary pays a dividend to the parent in local currency. The parent donates the locally banked proceeds to a local charity, consolidates at the official exchange rate, and takes a tax deduction in its home country.

(17) Swap with a charity. The subsidiary donates local currency to the local branch of a U.S.-based nonprofit organization. From the charity's point of view, the donation replaces a dollar infusion it would otherwise have made. Therefore, the parent charity reimburses the parent corporation in dollars for a portion of the local-currency donation. The parent company gets dollars at an acceptable discount; the parent charity gets local currency at a better than official exchange rate; and the local subsidiary gets a tax deduction.

The transaction does not violate the letter of local exchange control laws because the parent's offshore transaction falls outside the jurisdiction of local authorities. (This logic would not justify a straight currency swap with a profit-making organization as a partner because the subsidiary would be unable to account for a local-currency payment with no value received in return.) However, this technique may be difficult to implement. As a rule, charitable organizations will shy away from swaps to avoid angering local government authorities.

(18) Sell remittances to third parties. Governments may be more likely to approve new remittances to a nonaffiliated company than to a parent. To take advantage of this, the parent can sell a patent or trademark to a third party at a discount for hard currency. The third party would then license the patent or trademark to the subsidiary and take the remittance risk.

(19) Shift expenses. Any one-to-one substitution of local-currency expenses for dollar expenses has the same effect as increasing remittances. For example, if an increase in local taxes results in a lowering of U.S. taxes, companies should increase their local taxable income via slower depreciation schedules or use of the FIFO rather than the LIFO method for valuing inventory. Blocked funds will have been paid in local taxes in exchange for savings of hard currency in the parent's home country.

(20) Swap stock with another MNC. Central to the success of this technique is that no cash is exchanged across borders—only "goods," in this case stock certificates. Stock swaps require two MNCs with local subsidiaries, one with a local currency surplus (Subsidiary A) and one with a local currency deficit (Subsidiary B).

It works as follow. Step 1: Subsidiary A declares a local currency dividend to Parent A's local account. Step 2: Parent A uses the local currency to buy stock in Subsidiary B. Step 3: Parent B buys the stock of Parent A for hard currency. Now Subsidiary B has the local currency it needs and Parent A has the hard currency it needs. However, the two companies are also holding each other's stock. Step 4: To wrap up the transaction, Parent A exchanges the stock of Subsidiary B for Parent B's holdings in the stock of Parent A.

(21) Engage in JVs. Many governments are favorably disposed toward JVs, making vertical integration investments an attractive possibility for firms seeking to occupy their blocked funds productively. Companies can merge two subsidiaries and increase remittance potential as a result.

(22) Swap with a JV partner. The JV partner obtains import licenses for the foreign parent's products. The parent receives excess dollars through transfer pricing, then reimburses the local partner by drawing down local currency balances and paying some of the partner's local expenses. Transfer pricing, of course, risks punitive actions by both home and local country authorities and is not recommended.

(23) Grant a liberation loan. This technique can be used to free payables blocked due to a hard-currency shortage. A foreign bank makes a loan to a cash-poor country equal to the amount of a local subsidiary's payable. The major portion of the loan goes directly to an offshore account of the parent. The remainder goes back to the bank that made the loan. The local subsidiary then pays the local currency equivalent of the payable to the central bank.

The country benefits because it has rescheduled debt from the short term to the medium or long term. The MNC benefits because it has freed funds at an acceptable discount. The bank benefits because it has received fee income and the prepayment of a portion of the loan.

(24) Grant a liberation loan with recourse. Bankers are often reluctant to increase their country exposure. However, they may take on extra risk if ultimate recourse rests with the parent. Companies can take advantage of this to get earnings today in return for an off-balance-sheet loan guarantee.

The parent can limit its risk by negotiating a "best-efforts" clause—a list of steps the bank must take before turning over the loan. For instance, the bank must pool the loan with the rest of the bank's country exposure, or it must roll over the loan indefinitely, provided that interest payments are maintained.

This variation of the liberation loan again benefits all parties. The MNC gets hard currency and replaces its blocked receivable with cash and a contingent loan. It also obtains the support of its bank, in league with other banks, in negotiating repayment. The bank gets fee income and an enhanced relationship, and the country reschedules its debt.

(25) If it works anywhere, try it everywhere. Remember that a given approach may look like a onetime solution, but with a few changes it might work somewhere else.

99. How One Aggressive Manager Unblocks His Funds

Bringing foreign earnings home can be difficult, particularly from a developing country, since government officials there are especially concerned about their currency's value. The blocked-funds troubleshooter for a large U.S. MNC offers the following advice.

● **Talk to everybody.** Consultants and auditors in troublesome countries accumulate a pool of knowledge about what is possible in various blocked-funds situations. "It's amazing the amount of information that resides in consultants and auditors," says the executive. "There are many opportunities that aren't known to your local people because they aren't in the business of concentrating on this issue alone." In his experience, lawyers in host countries can also be helpful.

Generally, this manager finds that local bankers are least likely to come up with good blocked-funds ideas. "I think it's two things. One is the fact that they're staffed by nationals, and their natural orientation is the preservation of the currency, so they would not like to see any additional outflows. The other is that, because local banks are doing business within the country only, they aren't experts on currency alternatives. The local branch of an international bank isn't going to be a good source either. The more aggressive second-tier banks are usually the ones anxious to pursue this."

● **Keep asking questions.** "Never stop asking 'How?'" says the treasury manager. "Even if the answer is negative, never stop trying to establish how it can be done, or how it might possibly be done, even though everyone thinks it's not possible. Usually people who say it can't be done have not gone through the process of questioning." The logic behind this approach is that the worst that can happen is that the blocked-funds manager may have to abandon his method. In the process of researching it, however, he may uncover some other techniques.

● **Define important terms.** Currency swaps between companies are not a legal blocked-funds technique in many countries. For example, a cash-rich subsidiary can transfer local currency to a subsidiary of another MNC and have its parent receive the hard-currency equivalent from the parent of the other subsidiary in a location outside the country.

But what is legal really depends on how the terms are defined. "A lot of things that you would think are not legally possible may be possible in some modified form," says the executive. "They [local officials] will tell you that it's absolutely illegal for you to receive funds from an affiliated party in the United States or some other country. But you can receive 'goods.' And if you keep on asking questions, you'll find out that shares of stocks are 'goods.' That's a very useful definition to know." In other words, in some countries, straight cash swaps may not be legal, but stock swaps are legal.

● **Start simple.** According to the blocked-funds specialist, " 'Simple' means I just want the foreign subsidiary to give me some money. No complexities, just send the money over here." "Simple" also means less work and quicker approval, both internally and by local government officials. Complex deals are more likely to run into snags. Says the treasury manager: "Take a countertrade arrangement involving rice. You've got to be an expert on rice. You've got to know what grain content is acceptable. You've got to know you might miss the true content in a routine inspection. You've got to know the pricing and the price fluctuations. You have to be able to find a buyer. Do you know how hard it is to find a buyer for Guyanese rice? I do."

● **Don't be afraid to retry old ideas.** In many countries, the law is not interpreted by the courts, but by individual government officials. Different officials may have different responses. Moreover, the attitudes of regulators may change over time or with new governments. For instance, according to the blocked-funds specialist, "It's amazing, the number of countries where one can find a major company that doesn't have a royalty agreement. The world changes to such an extent that a country where such a thing wasn't viable five years ago would entertain that idea today."

● **Try drawing up a matrix of possibilities.** "I began by making up a very large matrix of all the different types of possibilities and all the countries. It had countries across the top and generic ideas down the side, and I simply outlined the areas where there was a possibility and where something had already been done," the manager says.

● **Set your priorities.** This particular MNC ranks blocked-funds priorities according to currency, tax, and interest rate considerations. "Obviously you can have countries where there's a low tax rate, a high interest rate, and a high probability of devaluation—and just the fact that it's a high-devaluation country doesn't necessarily mean that the funds should be flowing out," explains the executive. "It's got to be weighted by the other two factors. The best way to visualize it is to say there's an uphill and a downhill pipeline. If it's an uphill pipeline from that country to the United States, then the funds really are doing better by remaining in the country." Country rankings can be surprising. For instance, the MNC found that after taking tax, interest rate, and devaluation factors into consideration, the pipeline from the El Salvadoran subsidiary to the U.S. headquarters ran uphill—i.e., the company was better off leaving the funds in El Salvador.

● **Don't be afraid of the government.** "There is very little risk in taking things to the government. If you take something to the government, the worst that will happen is that they will say no and you will have an effective delay in the time until something else can be implemented."

● **Be open about your goal to increase remittances.** "Government officials understand that we're in business in that country for business reasons and that we have to expect a reasonable return," the executive says. "In the least developed countries that I have been in, I have always been very much impressed by the intellectual capacity and the expertise of the central bankers. There is no sense trying to put something over on them, since they are much smarter than some people give them credit for being."

● **Involve local management.** One blocked-funds proposal might require a year to clear both internal and central bank obstacles; another might be approved in only six weeks. What's the difference between the two?

Says the treasury specialist: "It has to do with the complexity of the proposal, but it also has to do with the amount of enthusiasm which one is able to generate. There's a very basic, commonsense management principle involved. If you can generate enthusiasm on the part of local management, you can get ideas approved a lot faster. Needless to say, the only way to run this or any other activity is to make sure everyone gets the full credit, and that means everyone who is even marginally involved should get credit in his area."

Moreover, it's important to involve local managers because these are the people most likely to be adversely affected when blocked funds are remitted. For example, managers at the subsidiary level want to maintain as much liquidity as possible—meaning they would like to remit as little as possible. On the other hand, headquarters managers want to see as much profit remitted as possible—or as little liquidity at the subsidiary level as possible. How to deal with this inevitable conflict of interests? Says the blocked-funds specialist, "You have to set up good people-to-people communications, especially with the subsidiary managers."

● **Pull increasing numbers of key people into the decision-making process.** "A practical, even-handed approach is to do enough homework, come up with three or four viable possibilities, and then present them all. Then you follow up very conscientiously, especially in your biggest problem countries, the ones with the largest amounts of cash. Then, as the decision process matures, you have discussions with wider and wider circles of people—including the head of your tax area, your legal area, and government officials."

The executive stresses that "it's very important to get the people and you to cosign the proposal. It has to have some piece of paper with signatures on it and the other names next to blank lines, so that everyone knows he's expected to do something about this, either reject it or pass it on."

100. Where to Find FX in the People's Republic of China (PRC)

China's FX shortage shows no signs of easing. Hence, for the foreseeable future, foreign investments in the PRC will have to obtain foreign currency in a variety of different ways. The general rule governing JVs in China is that they must balance their FX inflows and outflows. Foreign ventures in the PRC are beginning to show a profit in renminbi. But unless the investment is structured with a means to earn needed FX in mind, the venture is likely to remain in the red in parent currency terms. The following list spells out the possible sources of FX and the difficulties involved in each one.

(1) Sell JV goods domestically for FX. JV products can be sold for FX to Chinese end users with access to FX, or to domestic customers who would otherwise import the product. However, selling for FX in China is not simply a matter of finding a buyer with hard currency. It may be necessary to obtain the permission of the Ministry of Foreign Economic Relations and Trade (MOFERT) and the State Administration for Exchange Control (SAEC) for such transactions, and a deal may have to be put through the appropriate foreign trade corporation, such as Machimpex or Sinochem.

However, the right to sell JV products for FX is fairly recent, put forward by the Chinese in 1984. With the proliferation of import-export companies not directly under MOFERT, outlets for moving products domestically should expand.

A natural market for the JVs' output is other JVs or foreign companies in China. Parker-Hannifin, for example, plans to sell its seals to Hughes Tool's drill-bit manufacturing operation in China. The Schindler JV sells its elevators to construction projects of Sino-foreign JVs, as well as to PRC-owned entities in Shenzhen and Guangzhou, for hard currency. JVs set up to service foreign petroleum contractors charge for their services in hard currency.

Another source of hard currency is JV goods sold to taxi companies or the tourist industry—e.g., hotels or Friendship stores—for eventual sale in FX certificates.

(2) Export JV goods for FX. Some JVs produce goods that are in such demand in China that they would have trouble meeting even a small export target. One company has so far diverted enough of its output for export to cover its FX needs, but as domestic demand for its product increases, it worries about maintaining enough exports to cover its growing foreign currency needs.

(3) Make auxiliary products for the parent. Anticipating export problems, several foreign investors have arranged for the JV to manufacture materials or products the foreign parent can use in its own operations, and for which China is—or could become—a competitive sourcing point. A pharmaceutical JV, for example, will produce not only finished pharmaceuticals, but also certain chemicals to be bought by the foreign parent for its own use or for resale to third parties.

Volkswagen's arrangement is a variation on this theme: In addition to assembling cars for sale in China, the Shanghai JV will produce engines, with the German partner purchasing 80 percent of the output for integration into VW's automobile operations throughout the world. Another company had its JV take on the manufacture of toys to generate more FX for exports, thus using the JV's machinery for a secondary, but exportable, product.

(4) Market parent company goods in the PRC and earn a royalty. Several foreign investors have designated their Chinese partner—or the JV itself—as a sales and service representative in China for its own products manufactured abroad; thus, they build up FX through commissions. Examples include Bishop Graphics' JV, Winton Design Products Ltd., which is the company's exclusive sales representative in China.

Hewlett-Packard several years ago set up a sales and service organization (wholly owned by the Chinese), to which it pays commissions in hard currency for sales of its products and servicing in China. HP's own JV has absorbed that office, which will continue to receive hard-currency commissions on sales of HP products in the PRC. In addition, HP will procure locally made electronic components and subassemblies through its JV and sell them abroad.

The marketing arm of Foxboro's JV sells not only JV products but also Foxboro products not manufactured by the JV. The latter are sold in China only for FX. The hard-currency commission accrues to the JV to help balance its FX outflows, and the JV then pays the service operation in renminbi.

(5) Export other goods for FX. Since the Chinese have yielded little on the question of converting renminbi earnings, investors try to negotiate the right to use their accumulation of local funds to buy products on the domestic market, then ship the goods out of China for sale to their own company or to third parties overseas. Though frowned on before, new provisions, which took effect January 20, 1987, provide for the ability of foreign firms to purchase and export local goods to balance FX accounts. However, approval must be secured from MOFERT, the suppliers, and their supervisory organizations. In addition, China doesn't allow JVs to export products under export license control—i.e., basically anything worth exporting.

Foreign firms with international trading subsidiaries are making efforts to put JVs' renminbi earnings to use by purchasing PRC-made products that are marketable internationally, then disposing of them via their trading arms. The problem with this option is that the Chinese entity from which the purchases are made may be unwilling to forego the hard currency it could earn by exporting directly.

(6) Source for the parent within the PRC. Companies may be able to find suitable inputs that can be sold to parent companies for FX. One company was negotiating such an arrangement as part of its upcoming JV. Its Chinese partner makes relatively sophisticated optical products that would be marketable abroad or useful in the foreign parent's own operations. The investor is convinced that the JV can obtain FX credits via such an arrangement, though the project has yet to get the final go-ahead. The stumbling block of getting the Chinese entity to relinquish the right to the hard currency exists here as well.

(7) Take FX from a related JV. Companies that have more than one JV in China can use the surplus FX of one to make up a deficit in another. This has appeal only to firms that can operate an industrial venture alongside, say, a tourism venture that earns FX.

Reinvest renminbi earnings in a JV that generates FX. Ventures that are heavy in renminbi can invest in such JVs, earning dividends in FX.

(8) Find a JV partner with FX. In theory, the PRC partner may use its own FX to meet the JV's hard-currency requirements, but in practice this method may be difficult to implement, as higher authorities are apparently reluctant to approve such transactions.

One firm negotiated a JV contract with the understanding that its PRC partner (an enterprise that generates FX exchange through exports) would make its hard currency available for the JV's raw material imports from the foreign partner. But later, before the contract was approved, the Chinese partner balked at that provision—probably, the foreign firm suspects, because higher authorities objected to it when they reviewed the contract.

The PRC partner, obviously fearing official rejection, is now even unwilling to submit the contract for approval until this FX matter is clarified. As a consequence, the foreign company has to consider alternatives, such as buying products from the Chinese partner for resale abroad—but it is unclear whether any of the PRC partner's own FX funds will be available for the JV.

(9) Apply to an FX adjustment center. At least seven FX trading centers were established in 1986–87. The centers are meant to allow the relatively free exchange of FX between FX-rich and FX-poor entities. Centers exist in Shenzhen, Shanghai, Guangzhou, Dalian, Zhuhai, Tianjin, and Beijing. Trading in the centers is shallow. There are more buyers than sellers. Hence, FX costs are higher when buying at the centers. However, these centers can relieve severe FX problems and offer a more efficient and relaxed environment in the future. The first two centers are described in more detail below.

Shenzhen: Open all week; open to both local and foreign entities; limited to legitimately earned FX; limited to entities registered in Shenzhen; no ceiling rate; sellers are normally hotels; buyers are manufacturers; charges fee of 1 percent.

Shanghai: Open only Thursdays; open only to foreign entities; limited to legitimately earned FX; limited to regional entities; rate ceiling of Rmb1 over official rate; sellers are normally hotels; buyers are manufacturers; charges fee of 1 percent.

(10) Purchase FX from a third party. This is basically the black market. But companies with good relations with entities rich in FX can buy small amounts of it for working capital needs. Going direct to the FX holders avoids the adjustment center fee, but it is illegal.

(11) Purchase FX from the Bank of China (BOC). Article 78 of the JV regulations provides for this: "A joint venture can apply to the Bank of China for foreign loans and renminbi loans according to business needs and following the Provisional Regulations for Providing Loans to Joint Ventures Using Chinese and Foreign Investment by the Bank of China."

A new set of regulations instituted in April 1987 gives JVs greater leeway in negotiating interest rates with the BOC. However, the regulations tighten the criteria for the loan, insisting that the JV pays its registered capital in full and giving priority to technology and exporting ventures. Foreign banks are reluctant but sometimes can be persuaded to make FX loans on the basis of a BOC guarantee or a guarantee from another source on a specified list of possible guarantors.

(12) Get a cash injection from the parent company. In a few cases, foreign parents have committed themselves in advance to make up for any FX shortfalls via periodic capital injections. A European investor contractually agreed to neutralize any FX deficits that might develop through additional remittances. Another European firm also promised to put FX at the disposal of its JV, if needed, to cover hard-currency costs.

Another early investor, unable to export because of the JV's unexpectedly high cost structure, has put in more FX in the form of equity. To keep the relative equity shares constant, the PRC partner matched these funds with renminbi injections.

(13) Beware of convertibility negotiated under Article 75. This is not a solution. China's FX shortage can void almost any prior agreements. According to Article 75 of the JV law implementing regulations, FX imbalances may be resolved by using government reserve funds or by including the JV's needs in the overall national plan. To stand a chance of getting Article 75 treatment, however, the JV must have written its plans for domestic sales into the feasibility study and the JV contract.

Even if domestic sales written into a JV contract have already been okayed, Chinese authorities are unlikely to approve convertibility of the proceeds unless the deal involves heavy capital contributions, the foreign firm is a heavyweight in its industry, or the technology involved is badly wanted and needed. In brief, a guarantee of convertibility under Article 75 is very difficult to get; even if it is secured, it may be vague and leave much room for argument when the moment to convert arrives.

Companies should not only negotiate this matter in minute detail with the Chinese partner and the respective supervisory organization(s) but also plot out on paper with the BOC exactly how this guarantee will work. As part of the formal JV contract, a supplementary agreement should be concluded and signed by the BOC. If the bank is unwilling to sign, it is a clear warning: It may not allow the conversion of future renminbi earnings into hard currency.

101. How to Excel at Countertrade: One Firm's Experience

When all else fails, don't give up. Firms always have one last recourse when dealing with blocked funds: trying countertrade. To give managers a feel for the complexities of countertrade, the final checklist provides one manager's advice about the best way to proceed.

(1) **Ensure legality.** Before getting involved in a countertrade or offset arrangement, make sure the foreign government's demand is not viewed negatively by the Department of Justice as a reciprocal agreement amounting to a restraint of trade.

(2) **Ensure proper product selection.** It's critical that only sellable (i.e., exportable) products are used in countertrade arrangements. Don't take on goods that you don't know about or don't need.

(3) **Negotiate with the foreign government.** Countertrade is an adversarial process and, as your adversary, the foreign government will always try to obtain a commitment for the highest percentage of sales possible. Demonstrate that there is an ongoing benefit when a new export market is opened for a country's product, and that the percentage of the company's obligation should therefore be less.

(4) **Calculate the real commitment.** What's the true cost of countertrade to a company? Is a 100 percent countertrade requirement really 100 percent? The cost depends on the time lag negotiated with the foreign government for fulfillment of the countertrade obligation. Therefore, companies should calculate the NPV of a countertrade transaction by factoring in the time allowed to fulfill the deal. For example, a countertrade requirement of 100 percent is significantly less than 100 percent in real terms if the company has 15 years to fulfill a contract but receives payment for its export in 4 years. Only by taking into consideration the NPV of a countertrade commitment can a company estimate the real cost of the deal.

(5) **Assess the risk.** Country and commercial risk analyses must be undertaken for every specialized form of trade financing. Check the quality of the product, and determine how extensively it can be marketed and sold and to which of the world's export markets. Sophisticated firms use a computer model and key in such variables as the country's stage of industrial development, the variety of products available, the duration of the commitment, and the contract risk.

Business International's Financial Advisory Services

Weekly Report

Business International Money Report (BIMR). Written expressly for international financial managers, this weekly report alerts you to current and upcoming developments that may affect your firm's worldwide profitability—including changes in exchange controls, borrowing costs, currency conditions, sources of credit, tax and accounting regulations, and banking services. It describes innovative strategies and the latest instruments used by leading firms to raise and invest funds worldwide at the best rates, optimize global cash flows, hedge currency exposures, and free blocked funds. *BIMR* also features comparative tables on leading, lagging, and netting regulations; worldwide borrowing and exchange rates; consensus currency forecasts; monthly updates on market conditions for currency options; and much more.

Reference Services

Investing, Licensing and Trading Conditions Abroad (ILT). Valued by international executives and attorneys for more than 20 years, this continuously updated reference service puts all the details on how to license, organize, locate, and invest in 53 countries at your fingertips. And it shows you how laws are actually interpreted in a country, not just how they appear on paper. *ILT* answers questions on corporate tax rules, exchange and price controls, trade and licensing restrictions, labor conditions, and much more.

Also available in regional editions:

ILT—Europe/Middle East/Africa

ILT—Latin America

ILT—Asia/Pacific

Financing Foreign Operations (FFO). This continuously updated reference service on financial conditions in 38 countries has a proven track record for helping executives manage international finance more successfully. *FFO* provides full details on local financial environments, including exchange controls, sources of funding, financial markets, cash management, and trade credit facilities, as well as international financial techniques and cross-border sources of financing, such as swap and export financing and state-of-the-art cash management techniques. And with *FFO* you also get actual corporate case examples that map out the innovative financial strategies and techniques used by some of the world's leading MNCs.

Also available in regional editions:

FFO—Europe/Middle East/Africa

FFO—Latin America

FFO—Asia/Pacific

Worldwide Financial Regulations. The most comprehensive guide available to current regulations regarding tax, exchange controls, and trade in the countries that international executives follow most closely, this quarterly service covers regulatory information on more than 40 key countries, interprets local laws from a corporate perspective, and suggests strategies to help you deal with them. The service includes:

(1) **An Executive Briefing** highlighting all the latest and most critical regulatory changes around the world.

(2) **An in-depth reference section** covering regulatory changes in 18 major countries.

(3) **A comparative table of worldwide exchange controls for 41 countries.**

(4) **Special Reports** to alert you to major overhauls in trade, tax, or exchange controls between issues.

Currency Advisory Service

Cross-Rates. A unique monthly currency management service for treasurers, planners, and active currency managers. It includes consensus forecasts from over 40 companies on 22 major and exotic currencies, as well as technical and judgmental forecasts for better FX planning. And you get consensus interest rate forecasts covering 20 key rates in 13 countries. *Cross-Rates* also analyzes factors behind the forecast assumptions and offers practical advice—with corporate case examples—on how to adjust hedging, financing, pricing, and investing strategies and on how to use the new currency and interest rate instruments.

On-Line Service

Global Report. Now you can have the answers to today's most important business and financial questions at your fingertips. This unique on-line service combines news and analysis from Business International and 13 other leading independent news services—including Citibank, AP-Dow Jones, Comtex, DAFSA, Financial Times Business Information, Global Analysis Systems, Knight-Ridder, Money Market Services, Quotron, and Standard & Poor's—to bring you all the up-to-the-minute business and financial information that is so critical in today's highly volatile environment.

With *Global Report* you will get news and commentary on financial, economic, political, and corporate events in 140 countries, real-time FX and financial-market rates and commentary, and daily information on companies and stock prices to help you evaluate your customers *and* competitors. You also get Business International's in-depth analysis of financial conditions—including changes in exchange controls, financial regulations, tax rates and practices, currency markets, trade controls, financing instruments, currency and interest rate consensus forecasts, overviews of national economies, and more—with practical advice on how your firm can respond.

In-Depth Reports

Meeting the Challenge of Global Tax Reform. Sweeping changes imposed by the U.S. Tax Reform Act of 1986 and major tax overhauls in other countries are forcing companies everywhere to rethink their entire global tax strategies. Designed for managers of both U.S. and foreign-based MNCs, this report covers all your key concerns, such as organizing staff for maximum tax effectiveness; financial and legal restructuring; managing taxes locally and in other countries; making tax-advantageous FX decisions; revisiting tax and treasury vehicles; resolving compliance issues; managing excess foreign tax credits; and using creative financing techniques. In addition, the report includes practical, insightful case examples drawn from in-depth interviews with more than 40 companies that explain exactly how and why they are implementing their new corporate strategies.

Managing Risks and Costs Through Financial Innovation. To help you reap the benefits of financial innovation without exposing your firm to added danger, this report examines the new instruments now available on the world's money, capital, and currency markets. A practical handbook of actual corporate strategies and practices, *Managing Risks and Costs Through Financial Innovation* explains all the latest instruments, tells you when and how to use them,

and shows you unique new ways to apply them to help you gain a competitive edge. The report also supplies up-to-date information on trends, regulations, and available instruments on global financial markets and examines critical behind-the-scenes issues such as the impact of financial innovation on corporate policies, organization, and performance evaluation.

Boosting the Bottom Line Through Global Cash Management. Today's erratic financial environment presents constant demands for new and innovative strategies to protect corporate profits and optimize global cash flows. Written as a "do-it-yourself" guide, this unique report will provide your company with a complete action plan for fine-tuning all aspects of your global cash management system by showing you the cost-saving systems that are recommended by top cash management consultants and that have proven successful for major MNCs. You will learn how to improve cash management systems in specific countries, as well as how to set up a successful cross-border cash management system. And by applying just a few of the cost-cutting measures explained in the report, you will save many times its price.

Coping with Global Financial Turmoil: An Action Guide for Solving Today's Critical Financial Problems. One of the best sources on the latest, most sophisticated strategies for succeeding in this era of revolutionary change, this report compiles some of the most important articles to appear recently in *Business International Money Report.* Among the important topics covered are refining financial organization and control, automating international treasury systems, hedging worldwide currency risks, improving intracountry and cross-border cash management systems, freeing blocked funds, applying innovative financial techniques, reducing trade financing risks and costs, upgrading banking relations, and taking advantage of tax and accounting opportunities.

How to Order

To order any of these services, or to receive further information along with sample copies, please write to the order fulfillment department at your nearest Business International office, listed on the back cover of this book.

Index

126

Swaps, 27–36; broker costs, 29; collateral, 29–30; currency swaps, 29; debt, Third World country investments, 100; debt-equity, 102–103; documentation, 28, 30; exposure management, 30, 37; flexibility and, 28; futures used to emulate, 34–35; interest rate swaps, 29; marketplace and, 28; objectives, 28; portfolio risk, 29; price maneuvering, 30; pricing, 32–34; protective clauses in contract, 30; reversing of swap, 36; risks, 29; strategy, 29–30; taxation, 30; Tax Reform Act of 1986, effect of, 86; Third World countries, investment in, 102–103; timing, 28; unwinding, how to, 36; value of, 29. *See also* Forward swaps; Futures

Taxation: automation and tax analysis, 16; cash management, 53; cross-border cash management system, 59, 60, 62–63; decision-support systems, 72; factoring vs. reinvoicing, 60; global tax management, involvement of managers, 3; options and, 19; reinvoicing vs. factoring, 60; swaps, 30; Third World country investments, 100, 104; treaties, 62–63. *See also* Tax Reform Act of 1986; Withholding tax
Tax Reform Act of 1986, effect of, 71–88; arm's length transactions, 81; audit, 81–82; book income adjustments on alternative minimum tax, 87–88; branch tax, 86–87; business-untaxed-reported profits adjustment, 88; dual resident companies, elimination of, 87; foreign-based multinational corporations, 86–88; foreign-controlled corporations, 88;

foreign tax credit, 73–80; forward contracts plus loans, 85; functional analysis, 82–83; funding equation, 84–85; GAAP (generally accepted accounting procedures), 88; hedging transactions, 86; intangible charges, 77–78; loans, 85, 86; management, 72–73; overview, 71–88; parent and subsidiaries, 78–80; simulation model, building of, 72; straddles, 85; subsidiaries, 78–80; swaps plus loans, 86; transfer pricing, 80–82, 87, 88; transportation income, 87; U.S. branches of foreign banks or firms, 88; withholding tax, 87
T-bills: capital markets and, 39
Technology, transfer of: foreign tax credit, 79
Third-party exports: currency exposures, Third World countries, 111
Third World: banking relations, 95; debt crisis, 93. *See also* Currency exposures in Third World countries; Third World country investments
Third World country investments, 97–104; arbitrage, 103; currency, 100; debt-equity swaps, 102–103; debt swaps, 100; discount factors, 99; dollar sources of financing, 103; equipment, investments, 100; export finance, 103; financing alternatives, 103–104; foreign currency sources, 103–104; internal rate-of-return numbers, 99; joint ventures, 101–102; leasing, 104; pension and benefit reserves, 103–104; preferred stock, 100, 103; profitability, 99–101; put options, 100; risk assessment, 98–99; self-audit on risk assessment, 98–99; swaps, 103; tax consequences, 100; tax reserves, 104
Tokyo Stock Exchange, 42–43
TRA '86. *See* Tax Reform Act of 1986, effect of

Trading: companies, export collections and, 70; defensive surveillance and, 6
Transfer of funds: banks and banking, 91–92; credit and, 52; overseas affiliates, 76
Transfer pricing: audit, 81–82; documentation, 81; factoring vs. reinvoicing, 59; foreign tax credit, 76; Tax Reform Act of 1986, effect of, 80–82, 87, 88
Transportation income: Tax Reform Act of 1986, effect of, 87
Treaties, tax. *See* Taxation

Uniform percentage discount, 80
Union Carbide, 4
U.S. branches of foreign banks or firms: export finance, 66; Tax Reform Act of 1986, effect of, 88

Vacations, 5
Volatility of market: investments in volatile environments, 97–104; losses and, 2; options and, 18, 22
Volkswagen, 5, 119

Warrant couriers: currency exposures, Third World countries, 106
Warrants, 40
Withholding tax: foreign tax credit, 74; Tax Reform Act of 1986, effect of, 87
Work stations, automation, 9–10; account activity reports, examples, 13; automated cash management, 11–14; banking management, 11; financial information reporting system, examples, 12–13; internal management, 11–14; selection of, 10–11; service features, 10–11; software features, 10; support features, 10–11
World Bank, 66, 103

Zero-coupon bonds, 40